THE HIGH
PERFORMANCE
ENTERPRISE

THE HIGH PERFORMANCE ENTERPRISE

Reinventing the People Side of Your Business

Donna R. Neusch

Alan F. Siebenaler

THE OLIVER WIGHT COMPANIES

Oliver Wight

Oliver Wight Publications, Inc.
5 Oliver Wight Drive
Essex Junction, Vermont 05452-9985

To "leadership" wherever it exists in your company, and to the "reinventors"! To those courageous people in companies everywhere, dedicated to the hard work and unrelenting persistence required to create the High Performance Enterprise.

Contents

Establish a Habit of Continuous Improvement
    and Renewal   83

5 A New Work Covenant   85

The Traditional Operating Environment   86
The New Work Covenant   91

Section II
REINVENTING THE PEOPLE SIDE OF YOUR BUSINESS

Overview   101
The Process Is the Same—the Results Differ   103
Getting Started   107
Readiness Assessment   107
Formal Project Management   108
Education   121
Communicating the Case for Change   122

7 Consuming the 500-Pound Enchilada   127

Preliminary Work   130
The Profiling Process   131
Migration Strategy Elements   142
Wrap-up   146

8 Value-added Movement   147

Characteristics of Inflexibility   148
Traits of a Flexible Work Environment   150
Flexibility Is the Name of the Game   151
Defining Flexibility Mapping and Boundaries   154
How Flexible Can We Be?   159
Wrap-up   165

9 New Work   166

Advantages of Work Redesign   171
Changing Work Content Through Job Redesign   172
Defining Teams   182

Introduction

IT'S A SNOWY DAY in late November here in the Rockies. There are 30 or 40 elk spread out down the sloping hill behind the office. Mostly cows and juvenile bulls, and a few youngsters. They've been here for a couple of hours. Eating. The grass in the big field down by the creek in the valley is covered by a thick layer of snow, and the highland meadow to the southeast is more deeply covered. They can't get at the grass, so they are working their way through the evergreen forest eating shrubs, tall grasses, and bark from the aspen trees we planted earlier in the spring.

It is an idyllic scene. We call it an "elk hazard"—an event that interrupts the writing of books, the doing of chores, and the preparation for the seminar coming up in a few weeks. It reminds us that while we're holed up here in the office doing our human-type business stuff, the cold winter world of the animals outside our windows goes on much as it has for aeons.

It also reminds us why we are writing the book. The good, sweet grasses of the field and meadow are not available to the elk. Mother Nature has temporarily placed them off limits. And they can't get at the haystack the size of a small house that the farmer down below has surrounded with a double-high barbed wire fence (he's reserving that for his cattle). The elk are staying alive by eating the tougher, hard-to-get-at, and less tasty twigs on the low bushes and tussocks of tall, dried grass. They are getting by on what's available, what's left.

We are writing this book because too many companies are being forced to get by on what's available, what's left. Just like Mother Nature did with the elk, Mother Business has placed the sweet market shares and tasty profit margins off limits to these companies.

They have been forced to become "opportunistic feeders," existing on the leftovers ignored by the stronger companies.

There is a difference, however, between the elk and these companies. There isn't much the elk can do except keep on "existing," and wait for easier times. Their options are limited—in a sense, they are powerless. A company should not have to just "exist"—and for many, waiting for easier times may not be realistic, or even possible. More importantly, *every* company has options available to it to improve its opportunities, to improve its performance.

We wrote this book because we deeply believe that opportunities for improved performance have been placed off limits for many companies. Not because they are powerless, like the elk, but because they *don't really know how to go about improving performance.*

This book is about *performance*. Not the buzzword "performance," but legitimate, exceptional performance. Not the performance of just "doing," but the performance of carrying out what has been planned with perseverance and in spite of obstacles along the way. *On-purpose* performance clearly superior, clearly above the average.

It's also about performance promised but not delivered. It is about the promise of the High Performance Enterprise, a promise made in the '80s but still unavailable to most companies here in the '90s.

The purpose of this book is fourfold. First, to provide the reader with useful knowledge about the concepts and principles underpinning the promise of the High Performance Enterprise. Then, each chapter was written to provide the reader with insight into an important management issue or specific people systems issue. Third, the book establishes a benchmark for performance that moves beyond the hype and fluff of what most companies mean when they use the words "high performance." But, most importantly, our purpose is to provide the reader with *processes for improving performance.* Not pie-in-the-sky, have-you-tried-this?–type processes, but processes proven to produce the improved performance necessary to become a High Performance Enterprise.

Companies are far from powerless. What's missing is the "how to," and that is exactly what this book is all about: "How-to" become a

High Performance Enterprise with its high performance operating environment; and "how-to" reinvent the people side of your company to make that operating environment a reality. The processes presented are the result of our 18 years' accumulated hands-on experience at designing, developing, implementing and continuously improving world-class initiatives and people systems, and the shared experiences of world-class High Performance Enterprises around the world.

In the '70s, '80s, and '90s, we worked with good people inside and outside our companies, in the United States, Canada, Mexico, Latin America, and Europe. We benefited from their insights and experiences. We had many opportunities to try new things; enjoyed the freedom of learning from our mistakes. And most importantly we were successful. Now, in the '90s, we continue to learn from our experiences, and receive reinforcement through the efforts and successes of our clients.

During this time, one broad nagging issue has regularly and consistently bothered us. Why is it the "bits and pieces" of the High Performance Enterprise are seen, and so seldom a "whole"? Why is it that when we seek validation of a "success story," we too frequently find that it exists off in a corner somewhere, or ". . . well, we were doing that last year, but it kind of went away 'cause no one really stuck with it." Why is it that significant, sustained performance improvement continues to elude most companies in the Western world?

We observe a polarization of companies around the factor of performance. A *few* companies, the High Performance Enterprises, have clearly staked out the sweet grass of the meadow. Most companies, however, seem to be relegated to the chewy twigs and dried-out leaves of the hillside bushes. Based on their dedication to continuous improvement, the High Performance Enterprises, once ahead, stay ahead.

It is not that companies haven't tried to make changes. For the past 15 years across the Western world, we have witnessed unprecedented changes in the ways companies do business. Companies have embraced new concepts, undertaken new initiatives for improvement, and in the process changed the fundamental way work is performed. They have done JIT and TQC . . . Kaizen'd and QFD's

. . . activity-base costed and sociotechnologized . . . practiced flattening and rightsizing . . . moved from low to second gear in speed-to-market, and focused mightily on total customer satisfaction.

Companies have asked their employees to abandon a lifelong individual orientation, and to work in teams . . . and, along the way, to become involved, empowered, committed, and productive. But today most companies still pay for an employee's whole day on the job, but fail to get the *whole* employee for the day. They still lose the employee's creativity, dedication, and initiative because changes to the people side of the business have been ineffective and even counterproductive.

All this change makes it difficult to be a successful manager today, because change produces its fair share of problems and failures. The environments in which managers work present them with ironic, paradoxical, and seemingly impossible challenges—make significant improvement by changing every fundamental process in the operation, but without fail meet the budgeted bottom line every month; exhibit strong leadership, but turn the office, laboratory, and factory floor over to self-directed work teams. The fact is, as the wise man said, people and companies are like the turtle—they never make progress unless they stick their necks out.

But sticking one's neck out is risky, and the traditional operating environment of most companies does not make risk taking attractive. How can managers reduce the risk? Is there a proven approach to success, one that guarantees improvement? Our bookshelves are full of books giving us insight, knowledge, and even how-tos on each of the major components of the process for becoming a High Performance Enterprise. There are books on leadership and vision; others on the high performance work environment; and many more on JIT, work cells, TQM, and the other initiatives companies implement in their pursuit of world-class status. However, there are few books that pull the entire process together in a manner that makes sense; even fewer that reduce the complexity of the process down to a make-sense plan that is at once doable and continuously improvable.

And up 'til now, there are no books that simultaneously provide (1) a process for creating the High Performance Enterprise with its high performance operating environment; and (2) a process for linking the people side of the company to that operating environment. It is our goal to do exactly all of that, and to provide a model for tying both processes together to achieve the promise of the High Performance Enterprise. These processes have held up well. But because we are committed to continuous growth and renewal, future change to these processes is likely and welcomed.

We worked hard throughout the book to balance an honest exposition of the detail and difficulty of the process for becoming a High Performance Enterprise with the danger of overwhelming the reader with that difficulty. The fact is, it is difficult, and we have made no attempt to romanticize the effort and dedication required. However, the processes outlined here provide a framework for systematically and effectively making the High Performance Enterprise a reality.

We also struggled to balance the specificity of the processes with the accessibility of the book—to balance the needs of the implementer with the quick-hit skimming of the interested executive. However, because this is a book for action takers, there is plenty of detailed information and suggestions. But for the executive skimmer or the company not undergoing significant change, the first six chapters and the synopsis of the remaining nine chapters provide a solid read, and a good overview of the processes.

It is our desire that you learn from this book. That you learn that there is more to the people side of the business than a few policies and procedures. That you learn about the "how-to" of leadership, and the Strategic Process for becoming a High Performance Enterprise. And that you learn how to reinvent the people side of your company to create the high performance operating environment required to be a world-class competitor.

It is our desire that your company share in a process to get away from the chewy twigs and tussocks on the mountainside, and down to the sweet grass in the valley below.

DONNA R. NEUSCH
ALAN F. SIEBENALER
Evergreen, Colorado, 1992

Section I

THE PROMISE OF THE '80S . . . PROCESSES FOR THE '90S

The first chapter establishes that in the 1980s a promise was made to companies—a promise that has remained largely unfulfilled. Chapter 2 first outlines a strategic level process for moving your company toward that promise—toward becoming a High Performance Enterprise. Then it provides a brief overview of a tactical level process called the High P·e·r·f·o·r·m·a·n·c·e·s People Systems Process, which is covered in detail in section II of the book.

Chapters 3 to 5 treat concepts, principles, and action steps underpinning the Strategic Process. The accent, however, is on "how to"! The focus is on the craft of leadership and a strategic process for applying that craft and the creation of a high performance operating environment with its *new work covenant*.

CHAPTER 1

The Promise of the '80s— Unfulfilled

IN THE '80s, you were promised if your company listened to the voice of the customer; implemented JIT, work cells, or TQM; and empowered its people, it would achieve the "world-class" business equivalent of eternal happiness and life everlasting. In essence, it would become the High Performance Enterprise, an enterprise completely in touch with its customers, delivering high-quality products and services exactly on time, bringing new offerings to market in half the time, and, best of all, an enterprise whose outstanding *performance* would guarantee an endless flood of money plummeting to the bottom line. Here it is, almost the mid-'90s, and where are most companies? Where is your company? After an incredible expenditure of time, money, and personal effort, what is the *reality* of that promise of the '80s? What happened to the High Performance Enterprise?

If body language meant anything, the meeting was a disaster. Some team members slumped in their chairs, others sat with their eyes down and their arms folded tightly across their chests. A few leaned back in their seats with their eyes closed . . . and slept. The supervisor's arms-akimbo stance and her withering stare clearly indicated her current disgust with the group. At that moment, the 3:30 P.M. buzzer sounded. The team, without acknowledging they had been in a meeting, began to disintegrate in a blur as folks grabbed for purses, lunch boxes, assorted carrying bags, and beat it out the door.

Now with the room empty, Mary Masters just stood there. She'd been the supervisor of this motley crew for almost two years and team leader for the last three months. Sometimes she wanted to scream. They were *so* exasperating! It wasn't that she didn't like these people—before the Total Customer Satisfaction program began six months back, they had been the easiest group in the plant with which to work. They came on time every morning, knew their jobs, worked hard, and they did exactly what she said. And they respected her.

Now things were different. The meeting on cross-training and problem solving had been a bust—they'd spent the 30 minutes beating her up. Everyone had his or her own ideas about what cross-training meant. It sounded like a lot more work for everyone. No one was completely happy with the concept. Mary, too, was unhappy, but with an Operations Team meeting in 15 minutes, she just sighed deeply, and said to herself, "Okay, get it in gear. This is what you get the big bucks for! . . . Sure?!"

A few minutes later, as she wound her way through the back offices along her shortcut to the conference room, she spotted Bart Williams, one of the senior assemblers on her team. He was reading the bulletin board in the hallway down from the conference room, and turned as she came down the hall.

Oh, no!, she thought. Mary knew an ambush when she saw one, and Bart was looking at her with a look that said, "I've-got-something-important-to-say." Although he could be a pain at times, Bart was a good employee. He liked the role of spokesman, so when he talked, it was often the group speaking.

"Mary! You got a minute?"

"Sure, Bart, but only a minute. I can't be late for the meeting."

"Yeah, Mary. I know." Bart drew in a deep breath. I'm not looking forward to this, he thought. Mary's gonna be awfully defensive. Aw, what the heck! She and the other supervisors are going to have to face the facts, sooner or later.

"There are a couple of things you need to know before you go into your meeting, Mary. I didn't say anything in our meeting, but you can tell that no one really likes this team stuff. It's just another program of doing-more-with-less. The company wants us to do more things, be on teams, work different jobs . . . and what do we get out of it? A lousy 3 percent increase! Who's kidding who?"

"Now, hold on, Bart . . . !"

"No! You hold on for a minute! This is crazy, Mary, and you know it is. One program after another, and every one of 'em went down the toilet when the shine wore off, and no real change took place. Five years ago, it was quality circles, and that died when the production schedule came back strong. Then it was setup reduction and smaller batches, and that folded when you supervisors got pounded by Finance because you weren't putting enough finished goods into stock. And now it's teams. Why are we *really* doing teams? What's behind it?"

Mary could feel her neck and face begin to turn red. If he wasn't so close to the truth about what was going on, she wouldn't feel so angry. But he was right and she knew it. And she really couldn't say what she wanted to say. Not only was this teams thing just more management mania, it was scary. She'd weathered all the other programs okay. Just wait long enough around here, she thought, and almost every program faded away. But this one was different—it was dangerous. If things kept going, this program was going to cost her her job. You could see it coming. Turn everything over to the teams, they become empowered and self-managed, and, then, *adios* Mary.

"Now, listen, Bart. Teams are an integral part of the Total Customer Satisfaction program. Teams are essential for problem solving and satisfying our customers. And we're going to do them no matter what. It's important." But her own words didn't ring true to her. Worse yet, the employees' name for TCS popped into her mind: Total Company Stupidity . . . yeah . . . that was TCS all right. She really didn't believe everything she said, and as she thought about it, there was no reason why she should make a fool of herself in front of Bart.

Consciously, or unconsciously, at this point Mary began to distance herself from a program in which she did not believe. "Bart, I'm only telling you what they tell me. When I get into the meeting, I'll bring up the teams' concerns. I know we've had a lot of different programs. That's just the way business is. You have to be doing the new things. But I understand what you mean. We've had just too darned many programs the past few years. It's downright confusing. And I know it's confusing to you guys. But that's the way it is. Maybe we need to slow down a little, or back up until we get our act together. Tell you what. I'll get to Charlie in the meeting, and see if we can get some answers."

"I know you're trying, Mary, and I don't mean to be a pain in the neck, but it's getting hard to work around here. There's too much goin' on, and I don't see what's in it for me. Somehow we have to make sense of it if we're to pull it off."

The Operations meeting had already begun. Larry Milson, the HR manager, was already at work explaining how efficiently the 3 percent annual increase would be handled this year. It was impossible for Mary to slip in quietly—the only empty chair was front and center. "Sorry I'm late," she mumbled, putting her stuff down on the table and turning around to the screen. There in all its glory was projected the Annual Appraisal Form. Lord, no, she thought, what a farce—everybody's gonna get the same thing when it's all over. But here we go again. She glanced around the room and saw that all her fellow supervisors looked as she felt. Boy! How they hated the appraisal process.

Eddie MacMillan, a second-shift supervisor, raised his hand. "Larry, how is that thing going to work this year? We're doing teams, and there doesn't seem to be a place for teamwork and all the issues we face in teams."

Larry frowned at the form for a minute and mused out loud: "Well, the categories we have are: Quantity of Work, Quality of Work, Attendance, Cooperation, and Safety. Ah . . . how about 'Cooperation.' Yeah. Cooperation—that'll cover the team stuff."

That's it, Mary thought. Maybe losing my supervisor's job isn't so bad after all.

THE UNFULFILLED PROMISE OF THE '80s

Every day, teams fail. Employee involvement leads to mistrust and employee disenchantment. Empowerment becomes a two-edged sword that cuts the wrong way because it is used incorrectly. Compensation systems fail to reinforce behaviors that lead to becoming a High Performance Enterprise, and instead support doing things the same old way. The promise of the '80s remains little more than a promise.

In none of these cases, much less in Mary and Bart's, is failure or disappointment necessary. But it is preordained. The inability to fulfill the promise of the '80s is determined in advance by a wide-spread, traditional management approach characterized by four failures:

1. A fragmented treatment of business strategy.

2. A flawed view of performance.

3. A soft-issues mind-set toward people programs.

4. No viable, defined processes to remedy the other three failures.

1. A *fragmented treatment of business strategy*. Change came bursting in on the industrial scene in the '80s with such force that many companies just plain did not know what to do first, much less what to do next. Manufacturing in the Western world was all of a sudden presented with a myriad of new tools—quality circles . . . JIT . . . TQC . . . Kaizen . . . work cells . . . self-directed teams. Companies reacted like rabbits in a field of wildflowers: "Maybe a nibble on this beauty here . . . Oh, I think I'll try that one over there . . . Wow, the dark green one *really* looks good!" The talk in company cafeterias moved from soup-of-the-day to "program-of-the-month." Management teams fell victim to the two age-old problems of having too much on their plates, and not having selected a balanced diet to start with.

2. A *flawed view of performance*. It sounds so simple: leaders are responsible for the company's performance. Yet, what is performance, really? When managers say the *"performance"* of the company, they attempt to encapsulate in *one* single word what is really tens of thousands of daily $p \cdot e \cdot r \cdot f \cdot o \cdot r \cdot m \cdot a \cdot n \cdot c \cdot e \cdot s$—countless individual activities, decisions, and transactions taking place at every level and in every process across the company.

The *performance* of a company cannot be compared to a one-ton boulder—*p·e·r·f·o·r·m·a·n·c·e·s* are more like a ton of thousands of tiny pebbles mounded together in one place. Both the boulder and the mound of pebbles have the same mass, but each occupies a different amount of space, responds differently to the same applied force, and requires a totally different process for effectively moving it in the desired direction.

Every day, managers at countless companies begin their management work in a traditional operating environment. They think they are using a lever and fulcrum to move the one-ton boulder of *performance*, when all they've really done is to stick the lever down in a pile of pebbles and stir things around. Companies cannot become

Figure 1

PERFORMANCE:

How we treat it...   What it really is!

Performance   P·e·r·f·o·r·m·a·n·c·e·s

High Performance Enterprises until they acknowledge the reality of p·e·r·f·o·r·m·a·n·c·e·s, and change their management approach.

3. *A soft-issues mind-set toward people programs.* There are four aspects to a soft-issues mind-set, and the first is its foundation: giving *lip service* to the importance of people, and *true service* to things and money. The "values statements" and annual reports of most companies extol the virtues of their people, and anoint them as the company's most important asset. However, few companies consistently act out their belief statements regarding the importance of people. Even in companies ostensibly practicing employee involvement and empowerment, the "importance" of people is frequently a matter of convenience—convenient until there is a conflict between people and money.

A second aspect of the soft-issues mind-set results from the complexity of dealing with the people side of the business. Managers and employees alike are hesitant in confronting people issues. More than one manager or supervisor has lamented, "Give me a machine any day. People are just too complicated."

To make matters worse, not only are people complex, they are messy—people ask questions. There appear to be no limits to the kinds of questions they can ask, or the answers they expect. And when they don't get the answers they want, or when things go wrong, there is conflict. *Avoiding conflict* is a prevalent tendency, and a common aspect of the soft-issues mind-set.

The final aspect of the soft-issues mind-set is the "squishy" factor: the feeling that dealing with people and people issues is hopelessly qualitative, indeterminate, subjective, and without definition. Dealing with people takes special qualities, and an *emotional* approach rather than one that is logical.

Combine them all—the lack of importance, a dislike for complexity, the avoidance of conflict, and the "squishy" factor—and they constitute a powerful soft-issues mind-set. It is a mind-set with deep historical roots, and one reinforced through an educational system that offers no proven alternative approach.

With such a mind-set, is it any wonder that companies treat the people side of the business differently from the "hard" technological or financial sides? With the soft-issues mind-set, people programs receive a treatment characterized by poor focus, inadequate alignment, ineffective integration, and a lack of system. As soon as a program is labeled "soft," it is deprived of the very focus, alignment, integration, and system that would guarantee its success.

How widespread is the soft-issues mind-set? Does it exist in your company? Complete the following checklist for a self-evaluation. Where does your company stand on people issues? How does your company respond when it handles people programs?

CHECKLIST FOR A SOFT-ISSUES MIND-SET

YES   NO

☐   ☐   People programs are seldom directly linked to the major thrust of the company. More than any other factor, this makes failure and disappointment inevitable. Because they do not draw strength from the envisioned direction of the company, the support given the soft issues is weak and inconsistent.

YES   NO

☐   ☐   People programs receive a lower priority in the request for scope, schedule, and resources. Companies scrimp on the effort applied to important people programs while they shift resources to hard technologies. Seldom are the best or busiest assigned to people programs. Top management delegates its responsibility to lower echelons or to the company's "people experts." And in meetings and reviews, the soft side of the company comes last, or is shunted off-line where it will not detract from the "really important" financial and technical issues.

YES   NO

☐   ☐   People programs are treated as add-ons, or fragments, rather than as programs to be integrated with mainstream operational requirements. Because they are introduced "outside-in," rather than "inside-out," they lack the network of linkages and integration to the objectives of the business to ensure compatibility and synergy with other programs.

YES   NO
☐   ☐   Soft-side issues suffer frequent and irreparable damage
                from the "bias toward action." People issues *are* generally
                complex. No less than the "hard" issues, resolving the soft
                issues requires the same discovery, analysis, and attention
                to detail. They require a significant up-front investment
                in productive, breakthrough planning. Too frequently,
                ". . . Just do it!" becomes the order of the day. Too fre-
                quently, managers rationalize "just doing something," give
                in to impatience, and exhibit an unwillingness to persevere.

YES   NO
☐   ☐   Leaders and managers put off, avoid, "delegate," defer,
                appoint, pass on, forget, and in general procrastinate in
                their having to directly confront and resolve issues on the
                soft side of the business.

If you made it through this brief checklist with zero "nos," you
work for a remarkable company, because the soft-issues mind-set is
prevalent in most organizations. Managers *choose* to label the people
issues as soft. Sometimes this is done to distinguish them from the
hard issues of industry or science. Other times, in applying the label
"soft," managers operate from the soft-issues mind-set that creates
and tolerates the poor focus, inadequate alignment, ineffective integration, and lack of system. These managers set in motion a process
that has consistently produced ineffective programs.

Actually, you don't need the checklist to determine if your company has a soft-issues mind-set. Answer this question. Does the
people side of your company support the objectives of the business,
and is your company getting a satisfactory return on its human
assets? Or look around your company for the following approaches to
the people side of the company:

EIGHT SUREFIRE WAYS TO KILL PEOPLE PROGRAMS

1. *Fear of the impact on short-term performance.* " . . . And we
will not sacrifice long-term growth and prosperity for short-term

gain." This sounds impressive in a company's vision and values statement. As a matter of practical application, how frequently is it an operational imperative? When push comes to shove, and the search is on for something for the bottom line, resources for important people initiatives are summarily withdrawn, or put on the back burner. With no apparent alternatives available, some managers feel they have no other choice—and the promise of the '80s gets pushed off farther into the future. Or worse, cut off from adequate resources, withers and dies.

2. *The quick fix, the silver bullet, and the magic potion.* Like bizarre creatures from a B-budget sci-fi movie, this trio pops up with frightening regularity. Each one is make-believe, and has never served us well. It makes one wonder why companies place so much faith in them. Surprisingly, the quick fix approach has a time-honored tradition around the world—a tradition that also includes consistent failure and disappointment.

3. *A failure to acknowledge the evolutionary, revolutionary nature of the changes required of the company seeking the promise of the '80s.* Many companies have learned this lesson the hard way. The *bad* news is that the promise of the '80s requires a virtual transformation of the company—it requires revolutionary change. The *real* bad news is that this revolutionary change takes time. It is *evolutionary*, revolutionary change: detailed, painstaking, change . . . an iterative process building and improving on itself . . . change at every level and throughout the organization. And, worse yet, a company must still function, make money, and survive while the evolutionary revolution takes place.

4. *The lack of a defined process for integrating all elements of the change process for becoming a High Performance Enterprise.* The promise of the '80s is daunting enough in its basic complexity and difficulty. Without a process to pull all aspects of the transformation together in a blueprint that makes sense, a company cannot become a High Performance Enterprise.

5. *Not walking the talk—the leadership failure.* Someone once said, "Leadership is doing right things, and management is doing things right." Leaders who launch a quest to become a High Performance Enterprise, and then only give lip service to it, fail on both

counts. They betray the trust their employees have placed in them to "do right things," and fail again because they do not follow through in "doing things right." In failing to lead and to manage, many executives create the single most serious obstacle to change—they destroy the trust of their followers.

6. Many an effort to realize the promise of the High Performance Enterprise has been derailed by the *pervasive sense of entitlement* found in many companies. Judith Bardwick describes entitlement as:

> an attitude [of those who] believe that they do not have to earn what they get. They come to believe that they get something because they are owed it, because they're *entitled* to it. They get what they want because of *who* they are, not because of what they do.[1]

And lest anyone think for a moment this is only an attitude of the blue-collar workforce, think again. It is also an attitude among managers, all the way to the top. And what a stultifying attitude it is: it kills creativity, stifles innovation, and makes risk taking out of the question.

7. Some companies run into a twin-headed monster known as "working to rules." The first head is well known. Peter Drucker says, "All available evidence indicates that work rules and job restrictions are the main cause of the 'productivity gap' of American (and European) manufacturing industry."[2]

The second head of the twin is less well known, but it has been just as damaging to productivity as its more obvious twin. The open, avowed champion of working to rules has been the old-fashioned labor union. The *closet* champion of working to rules has been none other than old-fashioned *management*. Anyone who has worked almost anywhere in Europe or the United States in the past 50 years will support the fact that employees "working to rules" has been the dominant *management* philosophy for decades. Managers in most companies want workers to keep their heads down, their mouths shut, and their shoulders to the wheel—the paradigm of the compliant worker.

The double-whammy impact of old-fashioned management and labor, unconsciously teaming up, is more sabotage than the people

---

Working to Rules

In mid-1992, shortly after the United Auto Workers returned to work at Caterpillar, it was reported that because of management refusal to come to the bargaining table, union members were told to "do exactly what the foreman tells you to do and nothing more." The approach, called "working to rules," means *following orders, but not displaying initiative.* Caterpillar responded, decrying these "actions aimed at hurting Caterpillar by adversely affecting productivity and efficiency."

Before the strike, Caterpillar had been widely publicized for its successful efforts to improve productivity and efficiency. In its fight to regain strength both at home and abroad, Caterpillar had embarked on a series of initiatives that grouped employees in teams and encouraged employee involvement in the process of increasing quality and improving productivity. Because these efforts were successful, and management knew how crucial employee involvement was in achieving the company's objectives, they were justifiably concerned about losing the benefits of employee initiative . . . losing a competitive advantage. Working to rules jeopardizes Caterpillar's bid to become a High Performance Enterprise.[3]

---

side of the business can stand. The promise of the '80s arrived stillborn in companies that failed to root out this philosophy.

8. The last and most aggravating cause of failure is a *lack of genuine commitment to the promise of the '80s.* In spite of the *surface* effort apparently dedicated to achieving the promise of the '80s, the *real* effort in many companies has been more rhetorical than soundly historical. Many companies have done bits and pieces, but lack the conviction to do the whole job. In May of 1992, *Fortune* reported:

> Says a frustrated William Buehler, senior vice president at Xerox: "You can see a high performance factory or office, but it doesn't spread. I don't know why." One reason is that nervous executives experiment where failure won't be fatal, and thereby contain the gains too. Says Jarrosiak [manager of human re-

sources for GE's Bayamon plant]: "I hate pilot programs off in a corner of a plant. You need commitment."[4]

Whether as a result of management cynicism regarding the payoff of the promise, or as a result of insecurity because they had no process to make it a reality, some companies have made little legitimate effort toward becoming a High Performance Enterprise and, because of their half-hearted efforts, have poisoned the minds of their employees to future change.

Approaching the people side of the company with a soft-issues mind-set has dulled the corporate good senses of too many companies . . . and delayed the promise of the '80s.

Here's the last of the four causes of failure to achieve the promise of the '80s.

4. *No viable, defined processes to remedy any of the other three failures.* During a recent symposium on work cells, the first speaker said, "There are no recipes." He meant, no recipes for teams, work cells, or cellular manufacturing. He was wrong. Perhaps the word "recipe" is not the right word. But whatever the word of choice—blueprint, prescription, or working plan—implementing work cells or creating the High Performance Enterprise requires a "recipe." Our experience, and that of benchmark companies around the world, indicate that to make significant change in the working environment of the company requires a proven working plan for doing so. Companies who willy-nilly begin to make changes without a proven process end up with failed programs-of-the-month, disheartened management, and disenchanted workers.

At the heart of each of the three previously mentioned "failures" is the lack of a viable, defined process to resolve or correct the issues involved: (1) "strategy," as a process, has fallen on hard times; (2) companies do not know how to link p·e·r·f·o·r·m·a·n·c·e·s to the objectives of the company; and (3) what to do with the soft, people side of the business is a mystery to far too many companies. In general, companies have looked for the "results" of strategy, *performance*, and the people side of the business, without a viable, defined "process" to produce those results.

But wait a minute! Has it all been failure? Of course not! Many companies have explored the promise of the '80s more fully. There is great richness available in the collective experiences of those companies that have attempted to achieve world-class status as High Performance Enterprise. Company after company has seen its managers reach beyond what they once considered their limits, and seen its employees gain in the willingness and confidence to participate, as management opened the opportunity for them to do so. In the process, companies have stretched their envelope of experiences to include what was once thought of as being impossible.

Many companies, perhaps yours, would not exist today, had they not taken swift action toward becoming a High Performance Enterprise. Unfortunately, these exceptional companies *are* the exception, not the rule. And most of them would admit they have not realized the full potential of the promise.

Companies have learned and attempted much in the last 10 years. Around the world, significant improvements have been made in *bits and pieces*—a *division* here in this company; *a team or two* in that company over there; and for this other company, an entire factory in which *one major product line* is built. Perhaps in a few companies, we may even find an aspect or two of the promise fully developed throughout the entire company. But there are few companies where the promise has been completely fulfilled—few companies that have achieved the status of a Toyota, Whole Foods, Inc., or Nucor Steel.

Someone said, bits and pieces are better than *nothing*. Unfortunately, in the age of global competition, not *too* much better. Too many companies have honored the principles of the High Performance Enterprise more in speech than in practice. As a result, their industries are facing a polarization of competition. At one end are the dominant players who shake the big stick, and then there are the rest, who hold on to the other end for dear life. Increasingly, companies dedicated to status as High Performance Enterprise are taking over the greater share of the market, and leaving the leftovers to the traditional companies.

If the leftovers are not enough for your company, what can you do? You have seen the "failures" that precluded most companies' fulfillment of the promise of the '80s. What is the answer? Is this a crisis? You bet it is!

In February 1990, *Business Week* reported:

Productivity in the U.S. has been in the doldrums for a long time—but now, its poor performance poses a threat to the economy. Output per hour in non-farm industry rose a paltry 1.2% annual rate in the 1980's—no improvement from the 1970's. Moreover, productivity heads into the 1990's at its slowest pace since the 1981–82 recession.

For the coming year, poor productivity growth has a number of implications for the outlook—all bad.[5]

In September 1992, *Fortune* reported:

Here's the good news: American business's campaign to improve quality is paying off so well that in many areas the Japanese no longer enjoy a clear lead. Now the bad news: While the quality gap narrows, the world's best competitors are suiting up for an even more challenging contest. It's called flexibility, and its watchwords are change fast, keep costs low, and respond quickly to customers.[6]

Yes, this is a crisis. The rising sense of urgency has seen even some of the most recalcitrant of industries—the automobile companies—begin to seek an answer to the promise of the '80s. Their answer, the only answer, is a 100 percent commitment to becoming a High Performance Enterprise: an enterprise completely in touch with its customers, delivering high-quality products and services on time, bringing new offerings to market in half the time, and, best of all, an enterprise whose outstanding *performance* produces sound bottom line profits. The answer for your company is the same: become a High Performance Enterprise. Not a bits and pieces version, but the real thing.

There are differing schools of thought regarding exactly what constitutes a High Performance Enterprise. Each offers a model that differs from others in structure, organization, philosophy, and ability to survive and prosper. But when you examine the evidence available, and reconcile the varying views, there are enough characteristics in common among them to paint a picture of the High Performance Enterprise as it should be:

THE PROMISE OF THE '80s: Characteristics of the High Performance Enterprise

· *Performance counts!* Effort matters, and learning from failure is tolerated and expected, but most of all it is performance that counts! It counts because it is a consistent and unrelenting dedication to superior performance that sets the company apart and makes it the High Performance Enterprise. It is superior performance that flows from the company's acknowledgment of and attention to p·e·r·f·o·r·m·a·n·c·e·s and the impact of the people side of the business on that level of activity.

· It practices *process-oriented management for superior results.* There is no evidence to support a sole focus on results. Results do not, cannot, and never will make anything happen—they are, after all, only . . . results! Results are generated by processes. Products and services flow from the processes that create them. The High Performance Enterprise will establish and track results, but only on a foundation of defined, controlled, and continuously improved processes to produce those results.

· The High Performance Enterprise is *customer-driven.* Quality is defined by the customer, and integrated and deployed throughout the company. The High Performance Enterprise listens to the voice of the customer, and then through its initiatives and people programs creates a direct line of sight between customer and p·e·r·f·o·r·m·a·n·c·e·s.

· The High Performance Enterprise *organizes along the flow of its processes*, and not vertically by function. Functional silos are eliminated or minimized to enhance the direct line-of-sight to the customer.

· The High Performance Enterprise is *principle-based.* It does not ignore new ideas and concepts, nor is it swayed by the latest craze or misled by the newest program-of-the-month. It concentrates on a handful of critical, renewable operating principles and maintains focus and direction in a world buffeted by change, and an increasing rate of change.

· The High Performance Enterprise is *focused*, and *smaller or modularized*. Mega- gives way to mini- as the High Performance Enterprise creates self-sustaining units, i.e., modularizes to achieve greater focus, accountability, speed-to-market, and enhanced customer responsiveness. Not the sham of the Strategic Business Units of the '80s, but a genuine *empowerment* of the operating units. While the High Performance Enterprise may be a large company, its speed, agility, and strength will flow from a mini-enterprise or focused factory approach—not so much that "small is beautiful" but that *"focused is better."*

Redundancy of resources in multiple units is offset by superior performance: a new level of performance that flows from a heightened sense of stewardship, responsibility, and ownership fostered by the sense of control inherent in a smaller operation; and from the clearer line of sight to the customer available from a tighter focus.

· The environment is *team-based*, but individually sensitive. The unit of activity is the team. The team could as well be a unit of organization. Or the team could be a locational entity, i.e., an area or process on the manufacturing floor, or a department in a laboratory or support function—a "team" to which differing numbers or mixes of people report on any given day depending on the output required or the mix of products or services planned. The High Performance Enterprise remains sensitive to the role of the individual and seeks to balance team and individual needs and reinforcement.

· The organizational structure is *flatter*. The High Performance Enterprise removes layers from the hierarchical structure in order to improve the flow of information, to strengthen accountability, and to facilitate the modularization of the company. The resulting cost savings are a welcome benefit, but *not* the primary reason for the flattening.

· It *institutionalizes empowerment to* create the high performance operating environment. Empowerment is both the foundation and the enabling force for the team-based, modularized, flatter High

Performance Enterprise. It provides energy and motivation for teams, gives ownership to the true small business unit, and fosters a sense of responsibility among all employees in a company with fewer managers.

· The High Performance Enterprise seeks advantage through *opportunistic structuring of work.* Conventional organizational structures are a response to the conventional constraints of time, space, and distance. As these constraints are removed by changes in thinking and technology, the High Performance Enterprise plans and organizes work in new ways organic to the real needs and strengths of the business. Then the only constraint is its imagination. With this final constraint removed, new opportunities are exposed and explored, and the High Performance Enterprise moves to structure work in new and exciting ways: in the concept of the "flexible worker"; in the "unbundling" or out-sourcing of routine services; in the flexibility of work-at-home; or in the distributed network and telecommuting made possible by rapidly developing digital communications.

· It fosters *a network of linkages.* "Synergy" was an important, mystical buzzword in the '70s. The High Performance Enterprise makes "synergy" a realized word in the '90s. It fosters a network of linkages among its stakeholders—the company itself, its customers, suppliers, and shareholders. It establishes linkages with other like-minded companies to encourage innovation and continuous improvement; to expand the boundaries of "team" beyond the limits of the company; and to give birth to a new generation of sharing and cross-functionality among different companies, and among units of the same company.

Becoming a High Performance Enterprise is not a trivial effort. The characteristics just outlined describe an impressive business entity. Take a moment, return to the list, scan it briefly item by item, and contrast your company with each. The immensity of the change effort most companies face can be overwhelming. Especially so if your competition is already on the move toward becoming a High Performance Enterprise.

And to make the task seem even more overwhelming, for many of the companies called High Performance Enterprises, the journey took decades, and is ongoing. Most companies today do not have the luxury of decades available for change.

Overwhelming? It can be. Some companies are so overwhelmed they no longer remember what it's like to be just "whelmed." So, what to do? It's hard to imagine companies rolling up into a little ball and just dying, but that appears to be an option selected by some. Others take the mythical ostrich-with-its-head-in-the-sand approach. Yet others have plans, or at least words, on paper outlining goals for attaining virtually every one of the characteristics. What about your company? Where are you?

If you are contemplating becoming a High Performance Enterprise and don't know where to begin, or if you are already on the way but haven't quite figured out how to bring the people side of the business in line with your company's objectives, read on! The state of being overwhelmed results from having more to do than you know how and not having enough to do it with. The Process for the High Performance Enterprise (with its two complementary subprocesses) is a tool bringing focus, alignment, integration, and system (process) to the job of becoming world-class. A tool for getting rid of that overwhelmed feeling. A tool for fulfilling the promise of the '80s.

References:

1. *Danger in the Comfort Zone*, Judith M. Bardwick (New York: American Management Association, 1991).
2. *Managing for the Future*, Peter F. Drucker (New York: Truman Talley Books/Dutton, 1992).
3. *Rocky Mountain News*, Linda Walker, July 24, 1992.
4. *Fortune*, May 18, 1992.
5. *Business Week*, February 19, 1990.
6. *Fortune*, September 21, 1992.

CHAPTER 2

Processes for the '90s

INCREDIBLE
EVERGREEN DISAPPEARING
CHOCOLATE CHIP COOKIES*

1 cup sugar
1 cup brown sugar
1 cup (2 sticks) butter
3 eggs
1 teaspoon vanilla extract
2 cups regular oats
2 cups flour

1 1/2 teaspoons cinnamon
1/2 teaspoon baking powder
1 teaspoon baking soda
1/2 teaspoon salt
12 ounces gourmet chocolate chips
6 ounces grated coconut
1 cup finely chopped pecans

Cream sugar and butter.

Add eggs and vanilla, blend well. Combine all dry ingredients, and mix well. Add dry ingredients to creamed mixture, and blend well. (This will be a challenge!) Preheat oven to 350°. Form golf-ball-sized chunks of batter on an ungreased cookie sheet. Bake 8 to 10 minutes, or longer if you like them crisp all the way through. Do not overcook. Remove from cookie sheet immediately. Will yield 5 to 6 dozen great cookies.

*Adjusted to sea level.

THIS IS OUR recipe for chocolate chip cookies. It won't make fudge. Doesn't make pork chops. But it does produce *very* good chocolate chip cookies. It was not an easy recipe to create. We have different likes and dislikes. And we had just moved to Evergreen, Colorado, to a house 8,400 feet above sea level. Things don't cook the same at 8,400 feet as they do at sea level. Water boils at less than 197 degrees instead of 212 degrees; and baking powder, sugar, and flour react together differently.

We agreed on what kind of cookie we wanted, studied a variety of cookbooks to get some ideas about high-altitude cooking and the kind of adjustments we'd have to make. Then, we began experimenting. After a few attempts, with slight variations in ingredients, and slight adjustments in temperature and cooking time, we developed a recipe that produces the kind of cookies we want—crisp on the outside, but still a little soft on the inside, and incredibly good-tasting—so good, they just seem to *disappear.*

The promise of the '80s went unfulfilled, as few companies either found or followed a proven recipe to produce the High Performance Enterprise. Some of the recipes they *did* try were so bad that instead of producing High Performance Enterprises, they produced something unpalatable, unsatisfactory, and not very enjoyable. Some companies tried to get the job done *without* a recipe, and all they ended up with was a messy kitchen.

How do you create the High Performance Enterprise and, thereby, achieve the promise of the '80s? A first glimpse of what companies must do to create the High Performance Enterprise comes from a 15-year-old book written for general managers. In the book, *No-Nonsense Management*, Richard Sloma says in one of his maxims: "Results Are Generated by Conditions—viz., The Operating Environment of the Company. Don't Expect Changes in Results if You Haven't Changed the Conditions."[1]

The operating environment of a company is composed of its *people*, facilities, products, policies, and its culture. It has a hard side composed of technology, buildings, money, things. And it has a supposedly *soft* side, composed of people. The irony is that the soft, people side is the side of the operating environment that makes things happen.

Changing the operating environment to get different results makes sense. The operating environment is the "process" that produces "results." However, neither the soft nor the hard elements of the operating environment are easily changed, nor can they be improved overnight. Changing an operating environment requires that a company do fundamental things differently; that it change fundamental processes.

Now, here is the second glimpse of what to do from an article written 15 years later by Andrall E. Pearson, former president of PepsiCo. In a 1992 *Harvard Business Review* article, he established that companies in every industry had fallen prey to "Seven Deadly Sins," seven serious problems that robbed companies of their ability to compete effectively in the global economy:

The Seven Deadly Sins

1. Inconsistent product quality;
2. Slow response to the marketplace;
3. Lack of innovative, competitive products;
4. Uncompetitive cost structure;
5. Inadequate employee involvement;
6. Unresponsive customer response, and;
7. Inefficient resource allocation.

Pearson went on to say it "is not just that they [the problems] are so pervasive but that they are all basically management induced and management directed." He acknowledged that in these same companies, management has tried program after program to correct these problems, only to have most of them fail consistently. And that management tends to get bored with old problems not fixed, and moves on to new challenging problems, leaving the old still unresolved in their wake.

The reason these programs failed to "redeem" management from the "Seven Deadly Sins" was that the programs *never* addressed the root cause of the problems, namely, the stultifying *"work environments* that flourished in the decades of easy growth but now undermine the company's competitive performance." Pearson's answer to addressing the root cause was that:

Managers have to change—or more accurately, they must *reinvent*—the *soft* [people] side of their organizations. That means reinventing the values and goals toward which people strive, the ways people approach their jobs, the pace of the work in the organization, how people work together. It's up to managers to create a work environment that stresses speed, Spartanism, innovation, and a marketplace focus. But that won't come simply from telling people to be more innovative or directing them to be more quality- or cost-conscious. Managers have to *organize* people toward these goals and *focus* them on changing. Managers have to *institutionalize* a totally new work environment.[2]

Pearson further pointed out the difference in work environments between companies that fail and those that succeed. The companies that succeed do not focus solely on the hard side. In the companies that succeed, "managers worked hard and consistently to shape the organization's soft side to produce the kind of work environment that is needed in the new marketplace."

In the traditional operating environment, the people side of the business has not served most companies well. It's time to abandon that traditional environment in favor of something more effective. But it's not enough to just change the operating environment. A company must change its operating environment, and *also* specifically change the people side of that operating environment, i.e., it must reinvent the people side of the company. The message is clear:

1. Results flow from processes.

2. If a company wants different results from its operating environment, it must *change* the operating environment.

3. And to *change* its operating environments to produce the results desired, a company must reinvent the people side of the company, or, more exactly, reinvent the people side of the operating environment.

Companies have *not* created new operating environments to facilitate becoming High Performance Enterprises. And they did not reinvent new operating environments in which the people side of the company could respond to the promise of the '80s.

Reinventing means to begin again, and invent something new. The process of invention, and reinvention, is straightforward. It begins with a *product definition*, followed by *design, development, implementation, and continuous improvement*. Our objective in the balance of this book is to present to you processes, or recipes, for creating a new operating environment for your company, and for reinventing the people side of your company—processes to ensure that your company becomes a High Performance Enterprise.

The processes for becoming a High Performance Enterprise are outlined in figure 2a under the title "Process for the High Performance Enterprise." That umbrella process is actually two related subprocesses. The first is a Strategic Process for the High Performance Enterprise—a high-level management approach for defining the new operating environment of your company. When the Strategic Process ultimately defines the high performance operating environment, you will have the "changed conditions" to give you the "changes in results" promised by Sloma's maxim. The newly defined high performance operating environment will provide the *product definition* for reinventing your company's people systems.

The second subprocess is the High P·e·r·f·o·r·m·a·n·c·e·s People Systems Process used for *reinventing the people side of your company*. Once you've defined the new operating environment, this process provides a structure to design, develop, implement, and continuously improve a new people side for your company. Together, the Strategic Process and the High P·e·r·f·o·r·m·a·n·c·e·s People Systems Process provide a recipe for creating the High Performance Enterprise.

"STRATEGY"

For some managers, "strategy" is a word with negative connotations. Part of the promise of the '80s is reflected in a collection of words with which managers became fascinated, fell in love, and eventually

Figure 2a
PROCESS FOR THE HIGH PERFORMANCE ENTERPRISE

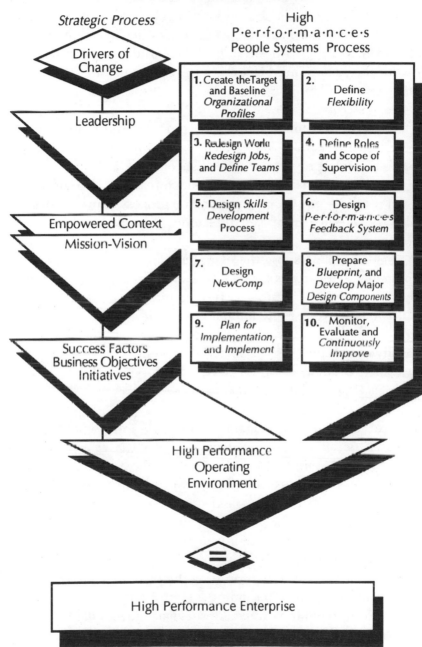

Strategic Process

High
P·e·r·f·o·r·m·a·n·c·e·s
People Systems Process

Drivers of Change

1. Create theTarget and Baseline *Organizational Profiles*

2. Define *Flexibility*

Leadership

3. Redesign Work *Redesign Jobs*, and *Define Teams*

4. Define Roles and Scope of Supervision

Empowered Context
Mission-Vision

5. Design *Skills Development* Process

6. Design *P·e·r·f·o·r·m·a·n·c·e·s Feedback System*

7. Design *NewComp*

8. Prepare *Blueprint*, and *Develop* Major *Design Components*

Success Factors
Business Objectives
Initiatives

9. *Plan for Implementation*, and *Implement*

10. Monitor, Evaluate and *Continuously Improve*

High Performance Operating Environment

High Performance Enterprise

fell out of love: strategy, synergy, and JIT, to name a few. Each word, once upon a time excited us with its promise. And now? Many managers won't use them in public. They seek alternative, new buzzwords. For example, it's no longer JIT, but "lean manufacturing" or "demand-flow manufacturing" or "cycle-time reduction."

What went wrong with "strategy"? Why did managers fall out of love with the idea? Three factors cause companies to deemphasize *formal* strategic planning:

1. In many companies, strategy becomes an end in itself, a function isolated from the realities of the world *and* the company—it becomes the sole province of specialists or the CEO.

2. In most cases, strategy fails as an exercise because of a flawed focus on results—most companies had no process to make "strategy" a reality. Results are fine as key milestones or goals, but they take the company nowhere.

3. Some companies lose the essential idea of strategy as a living, dynamic tool. They focus instead on a superficial idea of strategy as the big picture of the future—a type of published, static road map that provides an exact route to be followed. In doing so, the essence of strategy as a *process* is lost. In contrast, strategy should be an active, dynamic compass—a device that compares where the company wants to go with where it is, and provides direction and a course of action for the company.

To make "strategy" once again meaningful, a new approach must be taken. First, companies must practice strategy as an integrated, real time activity involving managers and employees, not specialists. Next, companies must use a defined, controlled process to create a strategic approach that grows and changes with the needs of the company—a process that is continuously used and improved by people at all levels (not a once-a-year spasm of the specially gifted).

Companies need strategy, but, more importantly, they need to apply the Strategic Process to running the business. Today, for companies around the world, becoming a High Performance Enterprise has become either an imperative for survival or a mandate for growth and prosperity. New world-class techniques for managing tangible and human assets, and the globalization of this new form of competition, have made it impossible for companies anywhere to compete successfully using the same old approaches to products, processes, and people. As unwelcome as it may be, the requirement to completely transform the company has been thrust upon companies with the subtlety of a slap across the face.

Around the world, efforts to become world-class have been taking place for more than a decade, with some successes, and plenty of failures. An examination of both successes and failures tells us what is required for a successful transformation. Across our own personal efforts at world-class change, those of our clients and in the press and literature reporting on world-class change, there is a consistent strategy employed by companies in their quest to become a High Performance Enterprise. It is a high-level management process. That does *not* mean that only high-level managers participate. To the contrary, top management should tap creative human resources at all levels to participate in this process. However, this process is the clear responsibility of the leadership of the company. It cannot be delegated or abrogated "down" because top management is too busy with this quarter's results. There is not a single company that has made the transformation to High Performance Enterprise in which the leaders of the company were not personally involved and viscerally committed.

The Strategic Process highlighted in figure 2b provides a "recipe," a working plan, a step-by-step process for your company to use in defining the "high performance operating environment," and in becoming a High Performance Enterprise.

A STRATEGIC PROCESS

· The *drivers of change* are not *part* of the process. They are the external and internal stimuli that *force* a company to reassess its current way of doing business. Each one is a catalyst that brings about a reaction and the creation of something new.
· It is not enough that the drivers of change be felt or forecasted. They must be deeply acknowledged, fully understood, correctly

Figure 2b

PROCESS FOR THE HIGH
PERFORMANCE ENTERPRISE

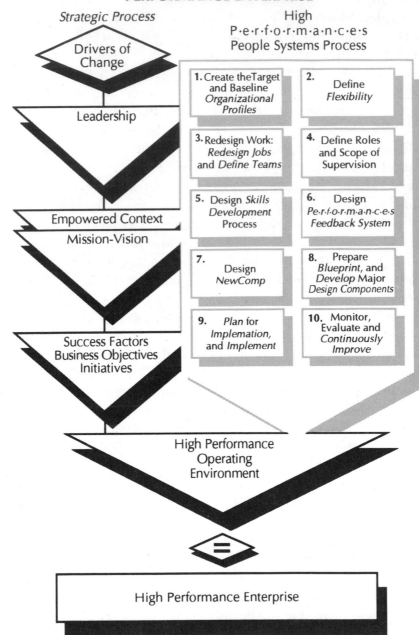

Strategic Process

High
P·e·r·f·o·r·m·a·n·c·e·s
People Systems Process

Drivers of
Change

Leadership

Empowered Context

Mission-Vision

Success Factors
Business Objectives
Initiatives

1. Create theTarget
and Baseline
*Organizational
Profiles*

2. Define
Flexibility

3. Redesign Work:
Redesign Jobs
and *Define Teams*

4. Define Roles
and Scope of
Supervision

5. Design *Skills
Development*
Process

6. Design
*Pe·r·f·o·r·m·a·n·c·e·s
Feedback System*

7. Design
NewComp

8. Prepare
Blueprint, and
Develop Major
Design Components

9. *Plan* for
Implemation,
and *Implement*

10. Monitor,
Evaluate and
*Continuously
Improve*

High Performance
Operating
Environment

High Performance Enterprise

identified, and, at some point, thoroughly communicated to all levels of the company. Leaders have the responsibility to respond to the drivers of change, to conceive of a new, transformed company built on the power of its people, processes, products, and services. The work of *leadership* begins at this point in your company. Leaders should develop the strategic direction and operational context for the company. Both challenges involve neither charisma nor a sparkling personality—they are hard work.

· To make a High Performance Enterprise possible, leaders establish an *empowered context* for their companies. Effective leaders clearly dictate the choice of this powerful corporate "attitude" or mind-set. It cannot be left up to happenstance, or a bottoms-up movement among employees. Leaders must be out in front of the change to an empowered context. Leaders who do not dictate an empowered context choose by default to continue with an ineffective traditional operating environment.

· The *mission and vision* define the company's purpose (mission) and describe the organization of the future (vision). They create a purpose-driven company, and build a foundation for shared responsibility.

· The translation of vision into action in the form of (1) strategic success factors that identify major themes for improvement; (2) operational business objectives that provide specific, measurable goals; and (3) action-oriented *initiatives* such as self-directed teams, TQM, Kaizen, JIT, and work cells that provide a framework for action. The initiatives become the focus around which the transformation process is designed.

· The *high performance operating environment* is the framework in which the transformation takes place. It's team-based, focused on p·e·r·f·o·r·m·a·n·c·e·s, and characterized by empowered managers and employees. Overall, it encourages an involvement of employees at every level that surpasses traditional levels of involvement.

This is the Strategic Process. Conceptually, the two words are one: strategicprocess. Strategy without process is *not* strategy—it's little more than wishful thinking. The strength of the Strategic Process is found in the specific steps at each stage of the process. As we develop the Strategic Process for the High Performance Enterprise, its "how-to" nature will become apparent. You will be able to use the process to define clearly your company's environment for creating a High Performance Enterprise.

Just as strategy without process is wishful thinking, strategy without *tactical* process is idle wishful thinking. The Strategic Process for the High Performance Enterprise includes several tactical level processes. Strategic market factors, for example, will require tactical marketing processes to seek out specific products or market segments in which the strengths of the company can be brought to bear. Other functional areas have similar requirements.

Our focus here, however, will be on the one particular tactical process that has the biggest impact on your company's becoming a High Performance Enterprise. It will be on the tactical process for *reinventing the people side of your company*. Remember Pearson's comments: it was not so much that the functional programs themselves failed, rather it was that the people side of the company was not up to the task.

We have highlighted the High P·e·r·f·o·r·m·a·n·c·e·s People Systems Process in figure 2c—a process designed to reinvent the people side of your company. Leading a company to accept a new vision as High Performance Enterprise, and then transforming the company to attain such status, involve strenuous effort. It is one that generally stretches and strains the systems and resources of most companies beyond their routine ability to respond. Among the systems most seriously stretched are those underpinning the people side of the business—the systems that govern how work is done, how jobs are designed, how teams are defined, how people are trained and certified, how their performance is evaluated, and how all of these are linked to the objectives of the company through how people are paid. These systems create and sustain the high performance operating environment. Essentially, they are the systems of the soft, people side of the company—the company's people systems.

Regardless of the world-class initiative attempted, it is the people of the organization that bear the brunt of the change. While most companies acknowledge people as their number-one resource, people systems are generally the last to receive world-class attention. As a result, it is not unusual to find people, people systems, and the entire people side of the company in the role of critical constraint, rather than essential supporter.

Central to a company's transformational efforts to become a High Performance Enterprise is reinventing its people side, which supports and enables the creation of the high performance work environment. Accomplishing this transformation requires a "hard," process approach characterized by focus, alignment, integration, and system.

• The process focus must be on performance, and maximizing the return on human assets at every level—managers, supervisors, and workers alike. People programs are not ends in themselves—any other focus than performance or producing a return is a poor focus.

• There must be an *alignment* of the people side of the company with the strategic thrust of the business—with the business objectives of the company. No company today has unlimited human resources, nor can it afford to have the efforts of its people wasted. Just as the focus of the people side must be on performance, alignment ensures that performance advances the specific objectives of the business.

• Because the people side of the company impacts every aspect of the business, its integration into the business does not involve a single link, but rather a network or matrix of linkages. You create this network of linkages when you ensure your people systems are *integrated* with the company's initiatives and its business objectives; *integrated* among themselves; and *reintegrated* as a responsibility for all of management, not just for Human Resources.

• Achieving focus, alignment, and integration take place only when the company's efforts are systematized in defined, controlled, and continuously improvable processes. Improved results flow from the "reinvented people side" of the company—results available to any company that applies the discipline and structure of a "hard" process to reinventing the people side of the business. The specific 10-Step Process designed to accomplish this is highlighted in figure 2c.

Figure 2c
PROCESS FOR THE HIGH
PERFORMANCE ENTERPRISE

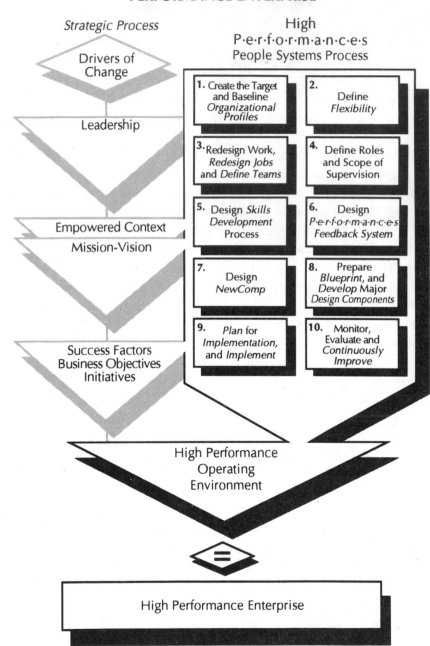

Strategic Process

High
P·e·r·f·o·r·m·a·n·c·e·s
People Systems Process

Drivers of
Change

Leadership

Empowered Context

Mission-Vision

Success Factors
Business Objectives
Initiatives

1. Create the Target
and Baseline
*Organizational
Profiles*

2. Define
Flexibility

3. Redesign Work,
Redesign Jobs
and *Define Teams*

4. Define Roles
and Scope of
Supervision

5. Design *Skills
Development*
Process

6. Design
*P·e·r·f·o·r·m·a·n·c·e·s
Feedback System*

7. Design
NewComp

8. Prepare
Blueprint, and
Develop Major
Design Components

9. *Plan* for
Implementation,
and *Implement*

10. Monitor,
Evaluate and
*Continuously
Improve*

High Performance
Operating
Environment

≡

High Performance Enterprise

THE HIGH P·E·R·F·O·R·M·A·N·C·E·S PEOPLE
SYSTEMS PROCESS

1. *Create the target and baseline organizational profiles.* The 10-Step Process begins with an analysis of the newly defined high performance operating environment and the initiatives to be undertaken. Then, through a set of devices called "targeted and baseline organizational profiles," the vision of the company is translated to a format more useful for developing specific action plans to move the company toward the high performance operating environment.

2. *Define flexibility.* Essential processes are identified and the work flow is mapped. Based on the company's requirements of flexibility, as expressed in the organizational profiles, boundaries of flexibility are drawn around areas of work. These boundaries represent areas or work processes where people can move freely to meet their performance objectives.

3. *Redesign work: redesign jobs, and define teams.* Improving the operating environment of a company means that the fundamental way work is done will change. For the High Performance Enterprise, work changes are reflected in *how jobs are designed* and *how teams are defined.* Based on flexibility boundaries, new broader JOBs are designed and evaluated. Then, teams are defined by their purpose, objectives, scope, and most importantly by boundaries such as operational restrictions, decision making, and degrees of direction and flexibility.

4. *Define roles and scope of supervision.* Because the way work is done will change, supervision must also change. New roles for supervisors are defined, and a transition plan developed for ensuring that new roles are met.

5. *Design skills development process.* The competitive advantage of flexibility possessed by the High Performance Enterprise is evident in a significant broadening of JOB scope. On the factory floor and in the white-collar and service areas, employees perform a variety of tasks up and down the work process. To guarantee quality of performance, skills are documented and flexible workers are certified in a variety of skills.

6. Design P·e·r·f·o·r·m·a·n·c·e·s Feedback System. The heart of reinforcement is a fair and effective performance management process. Critical changes to traditional annual appraisals involve: (1) the linkage of performance to specific business objectives, and (2) a major shift away from a strictly individual-contributor approach to one that balances team and individual contribution and then weights performance factors based on their impact on business objectives.

7. Design NewComp. NewComp, a "new" compensation approach: (1) links pay to business objectives; (2) reinforces the team-based environment; (3) corrects the balance of pay and reward; and (4) anchors the integration of the company's people systems by linking job design, skills development, and team and individual performance.

8. Prepare blueprint, and develop major design components. A detailed blueprint of the design is prepared for use by implementation teams, as a basis for administration, and as a benchmark for continuous improvement activities. Detailed development and documentation of JOBs, skills certification, and performance factors take place, to be folded in with other design and development documentation prior to implementation.

9. Plan for implementation, and implement. Planning and implementing require different activities, encounter different problems, and have distinct foci. In planning for implementation, the focus is on testing, gaining approval, anticipating problems, developing and presenting training, preparing the communication strategy, modifying company policies and procedures. Then, in actual implementation, the company initiates the communication strategy, and involves

management, supervision, and workers in rolling out the new programs; opinion leaders are enrolled; opportunities for feedback are
provided and prompt responses made.

10. *Monitor, evaluate, and continuously improve.* In the High
Performance Enterprise, the axiom, "It's-not-over-'til-it's-over"
means this is essentially a never-ending process. Only through a
habit of continuous improvement and renewal can a company's people systems be kept in alignment with the needs of the future. Only
through a process of continuous improvement will the full potential
of the people side of the business bring about the reality of the
promise of the '80s.

The overview just completed contained two interrelated processes
that work together to create the High Performance Enterprise:

- A Strategic Process in which the company's leadership determines the strategic direction and operating context for the company. The last element of this strategy is defining a high
  performance operating environment in which the company's
  action plans will be undertaken.

- The High P·e·r·f·o·r·m·a·n·c·e·s People Systems Process acknowledges that a company's high performance *operating environment*
  has a significant people component, i.e., the people side of the
  company. Acknowledging this, the process provides step-by-
  step guidance to reinvent the people side of the company.

Really good recipes, when placed in the hands of a variety of
creative and caring cooks, yield dishes with differing nuances of
flavor, texture, and spiciness. With any excellent recipe, there is an
underlying structure that allows the strengths and creativity of the
individual cook to shine through.

Together, both processes constitute a "recipe." This recipe, a
Process for the High Performance Enterprise, provides the underlying structure required to create High Performance Enterprises. In
the hands of a variety of caring and creative companies, this process

will produce a unique "reinvented people side," one tailored to the "tastes" of the individual company. However, the underlying structure of the process ensures that the resulting "reinvented people side" will have the essential qualities required to support the efforts of each company in becoming a High Performance Enterprise.

An extra advantage to this recipe is that the experience of the cook does not matter. The process may be used by both the newly interested in becoming a High Performance Enterprise, as well as to those companies scarred and battered from the invigorating experience of already being on the road to high performance. This is a proven process for beginning the journey, or for use as a checklist for evaluating progress already made. It may serve as a working plan to mobilize the strengths of the company; or as a compass to realign efforts that might have gone astray.

The road to high performance is long, bumpy, and often circuitous. Regardless of where your company is on this road, you will find support from the underlying structure of these two interrelated processes.

The recipe analogy is particularly appropriate and enjoyable. When you are through using a recipe properly—especially when you've put some of your own creativity into it—you get to *enjoy* the results of your labor. "Cooking up" a High Performance Enterprise is going to be a lot of hard work, but just think of how good it's going "taste" when you're through. Meanwhile, make a batch of our Incredible Evergreen Disappearing Chocolate Chip Cookies, and have one while you learn how to reinvent the people side of your company and become a High Performance Enterprise.

References:

1. *No-Nonsense Management*, Richard S. Sloma (New York: Macmillan Publishing Company, 1977).
2. "Corporate Redemption and the Seven Deadly Sins," Andrall E. Pearson, *Harvard Business Review*, May–June 1992.

CHAPTER 3

Fear, Fuzziness, and a Sense of Urgency

"TRY IT. You'll like it."

"But it *stinks* . . . bad."

"Broccoli doesn't stink, kiddo. That's just how it smells."

"Well, it stinks to me. And, I'm not gonna eat it!"

"Come on. Just take a bite. You'll like it."

"No! You never made me eat it before."

"Yeh, but this stuff's good for you, so try it."

"I don't wanna."

"I said take a bite, and I *mean* it."

"NO!"

"Listen: you either take a bite *right* now, or . . ."

"NO!"

"That does it. Now you're gonna get it. . . ."

"Okay, okay, okay. I'll try this little piece here. But it still *stinks*."

Little kids, big people, and companies don't always like to try new things—not even if it's supposed to be good for you. They generally don't like change, at least not at first—even if the change is a "better way."

The Western world prides itself as the seat of industrial and technological development. Yet, in the past decade or more, company after company, industry after industry, has been forced to acknowledge that there is a "better way" to provide quality goods and services. The better way had its roots in the West, but in the '50s, '60s, and '70s, it was grafted to new rootstock in the Far East. There it was cross-bred with new ideas, flowered, and bore new fruit. The new fruit was not a new physical entity, but rather a corporate *mind-set* represented by a dedication to exceptional performance. Today, that mind-set is manifested in a slowly growing number of High Performance Enterprises.

Most companies striving to become a High Performance Enterprise did not do so because they were bored and had nothing better to do. Each company was driven to change for compelling reasons: an impending threat to their survival, or to their continued growth and prosperity. They were not coaxed, or even cajoled, but rather they were *compelled* to change.

We call such compelling reasons to change the "drivers of change." They force change by creating energy or stimulus for change. Then, when internalized by the changing company, the drivers of change become catalysts to encourage the formation of a new company from the ingredients of the old.

And speaking of "old" ingredients, how about the black-and-white film business? That is an old segment of the film business, but one that still has the potential for profit. For years, the folks at Kodak had that business all wrapped up. It was easy low-hanging fruit . . . until fierce competition came along and what had been acceptable performance became no longer acceptable. Then, Kodak was forced to change. The employees who make black-and-white film were forced to look at how they did business—they were forced to change. When they responded to the drivers of change, the results were outstanding, with response time cut in half, on-time performance nearly tripled, and an operation running below budgeted costs.

What prompted this kind of improvement effort? According to the former leader of this organization, Zebra Steve Frangos, "We *responded to the crisis of a struggling business* by streamlining our process flow and steering all of our improvement activities by focusing on what customers told us they needed.

"The real guts of our success resulted from the achievement of an empowered partnership which emerged from an environment that encouraged everyone to contribute their discretionary efforts and to choose to make a difference.

"Our skyrocketing performance gains were fueled by tremendous bursts of spirit, creativity, energy, and even fun as my empowered partners attained unbelievably high morale and work satisfaction levels."

The Zebra Team was forced to change by the cold facts of their competitive environment. They didn't improve just for the heck of it—they were *compelled* to change.[1]

The identification of the drivers of change and their subsequent communication to the company are a frequently neglected first link in the network of linkages to be forged by aspiring High Performance Enterprises. As we shall see, it is easy for companies to be driven and whipsawed in many directions by these compelling forces. It's up to management to take firm and responsible control of the process for establishing the first critical link—to ensure the company is *driven* in the right direction.

Why, driven? Shouldn't companies *want* to seek out new, innovative techniques that promise breakthrough improvement? Shouldn't it be pretty easy to identify breakthrough technologies? And shouldn't their employees *want* to change, too? Answering these questions correctly, and understanding the implications of the answers, are the first step in creating the High Performance Enterprise. In taking this first step, we will look at the fear involved, the danger of fuzziness, and developing a sense of urgency. "It'ssss broccoli time!"

FEAR

Change is almost always forced. Especially big change. Seeking to become a High Performance Enterprise is a *very* big change. Companies don't embark on that process just for fun. In his book, *Teaching the Elephant to Dance*, James Belasco draws the analogy that companies are like the elephant—slow-moving and conditioned by constraints that tie them to the past.

Trainers shackle young elephants with heavy chains to deeply embedded stakes. In that way the elephant learns to stay in its place. Older elephants never try to leave even though they have the strength to pull the stake and move beyond. Their conditioning limits their movements with only a small metal bracelet around their foot—attached to nothing.

Do the elephants ever break this deep conditioning? " . . . When the circus tent catches on fire—and the elephant sees the flames with its own eyes and smells the smoke with its own nostrils—it forgets its old conditioning and changes." It gets out fast.[2]

For companies and people alike, there is always a perceived threat in making change, in trying new things. Is not the High Performance Enterprise clearly a "better way" to compete? Why don't more companies strive for this "better way"? Are the benefits not clear enough? Yes, they are, but that is not why companies don't change to the better way. Companies are constrained against change by conditions in their operating environments. Before the benefits of the "better way" can become a driving force, the company must against its will abandon the constraints that tie it to the past.

To begin dealing with the drivers of change, first acknowledge that in responding to forced change, the response is generally negative, fearful, and reactive. Just like the elephant, when some companies sense they are going up in flames, the reaction is to just get out of "there"—"there" being the circumstances that hold the company in peril. And just like the elephant, they respond to the smoke and fire with a wild stampede for a place, any place, where there is no smoke and fire—and Lord help anyone who gets in the way!

Most managers and employees can relate to the stampeding elephant. They've seen it. It came charging through the company just the other day. Behind it left a horrible debris: rushed, anxious task force meetings; a procession of programs-of-the-month; the search for a magic potion; and, finally, the admonition "I don't care what you do, just take care of it!" Change is a struggle. It's a struggle because our opinion is laced with negative emotion.[3]

THE DANGER OF FUZZINESS

For the elephant, smelling the smoke and seeing the fire are a pretty straightforward and compelling reason to change old conditionings inappropriate to current reality. Unfortunately for companies, the compelling reasons for change are not quite so straightforward—and even when the reasons to change seem apparent, sometimes companies become distracted by the smoke and rush headlong into the fire. Companies owe it to themselves and to their stakeholders to take a more reasoned approach than that of a stampeding elephant. They need an arm's-length perspective to provide a more wide-ranging set of alternatives than to go blindly charging out of the flaming tent.

The drivers of change come in a variety of forms and content, and impose forces of varying degrees on the companies they impact. There is no *one* way to identify the drivers of change. Some companies convene task forces and management groups and—with the help of tools such as affinity diagrams, interrelationship diagraphs, and tree analysis—struggle to uncover the competitive weapon that has them by the throat. Other companies seem to grasp the drivers with almost intuitive ease. Regardless of the approach your company takes, we offer three important cautions. All three result from the actions companies take when their analysis of the drivers of change is affected by fuzzy thinking.

SMOKE, BUT WHERE'S THE FIRE?

CAUTION!

Companies are attracted by the *form* of the smoke—the apparent drivers of change—and, consequently, fail to detect *content*, i.e., the fire—the *real* drivers of change.

A familiar example, and a classic one, of incorrectly identifying drivers of change was reported in *The Machine That Changed the World*. This book, by the MIT International Motor Vehicle Program, explored the development of the Toyota Production System, its impact on the automobile industry, and the response to it by automobile manufacturers around the world. What was the explanation for this phenomenon? What was the driver of change?

> Anything that is new is likely to be misunderstood, typically by attempts to explain the new phenomenon in terms of traditional categories and causes.
>
> One popular explanation in the 1970's of the Japanese success was simply that Japanese wages were lower. . . . A second explanation was summed up by the phrase "Japan, Inc." This theory attributed Japanese success to its government's protection of the domestic market and its financial support for Japanese car companies. . . . A third explanation was high tech, notably the widespread adoption of robots in the factory. Together, these made the emergence of Japan understandable but also sinister. . . .
>
> What these explanations could not explain was how the Japanese companies continued to advance in the 1980's despite currency shifts [which significantly raised Japanese wages] and a massive movement of [Japanese] operations offshore where MITI [the government agency] was of little help. Nor did they explain why the Japanese firms gained major benefits from automation while Western firms often seemed to spend more than they saved. Deeper explanations of these mysteries required an understanding of lean production.[4]

No, it was not low wages, nor government intervention, nor automation that powered the growth of Toyota. Those were the apparent drivers, not the real drivers of change. They were apparent drivers containing enough of a kernel of truth that the worldwide auto industry fell for the fins, frills, and chrom-elegant good looks, without ever looking under the hood to see what was producing the 10-second 0 to 60 mph acceleration. General Motors was distracted by the "smoke" from the exhaust.

What powered the growth of Toyota, what the auto industry should have identified as the real driver of change, was the development of a fundamentally different way of managing people, equipment, and material. The "fire" was called the Toyota Production System, and it consisted of the load-smoothing of production; a focus on process to produce improved results; a just-in-time material flow based on the elimination of waste, excess, and unevenness; an involved, committed workforce practicing a habit of continuous improvement; and a revolutionary process for producing in ever-smaller batches. Those were the real drivers of change.

To make matters worse for the auto manufacturers, they were lured away from the real drivers of change by a kernel of truth in each of the false apparent drivers. The MIT study points out that, yes, prior to the currency shifts in the '70s, Japanese wages were lower. And, yes, the early efforts of the Japanese government were essential for getting that national industry off the ground. And, yes, the level of automation by the early '80s was ahead of that in Western countries. Enough truth, at a given point in time, to convince a willing auto industry they were facing "sinister" drivers of change.

It is important to note that at some given point in time, each apparent driver was at least partially true. However, at that exact same point in time, underpinning and enhancing each of the apparent drivers of change were the fundamental changes in utilizing people, parts, and equipment that constituted the *real* driver of change.

SMOKE, AND OTHER "SMOKE"

CAUTION!

Sometimes the *real* drivers of change cannot be seen because of a smoke screen of distortion caused by circumstances in a company's operating environment.

If it were not bad enough that the drivers of change, in and of themselves, are sometimes confusing, a company may become further "confused" by its own internal situation. As the company analyzes the drivers of change, certain conditions in its operating environment cloud or prejudice the analysis. A company suffering horrible relations with its workforce might not "see" the essential underlying real driver of an involved and empowered workforce. Yet another company, with great technological expertise in automation, might "see" the driver of change as new and better robots, and again miss the underlying *different* way in which the equipment was being utilized.

In response to the surface driver of automation, General Motors spent $40 billion but failed to acknowledge the fundamentally different way Toyota managed people, equipment, and materials in their automation approach. As a result, GM wasted money, lost precious response time, and became even less competitive with Toyota.

TOO MUCH SMOKE

C A U T I O N !

Sometimes there is too much "smoke." This sends companies leaping for the exits, before they look well enough, if at all.

Sometimes there is too much smoke. Companies either end up skipping the analysis process completely, or they become discouraged and abandon the analysis effort. Then, they respond with a knee-jerk reaction to fix the problem—"Just do JIT!" or "Do teams." In this way, a company leaps to the solution without understanding why. Leaping to the solution lessens the appropriate impact of the drivers of change. It deprives the company of the richness available in a thorough understanding of the underlying "differentness" of the real drivers of change. And as events unfold, the lack of richness and understanding weakens the quality of decision making and corporate resolve.

Why is correct identification so critical? A company's response to a driver of change flows from its perception of the specific driver. False perceptions set in motion a series of responses that will be off target, wasteful of the company's resources, and potentially damaging to subsequent responses to new drivers of change.

Rather than something as simple as setting the circus tent afire, the inexorable growth of Toyota and other Japanese manufacturers who copied the Toyota Production System had the impact of razing a three-ring circus with napalm. And because the drivers of change were incorrectly identified, responses across the industry were broadly ineffective until recently.

But as important as it is to correctly identify the drivers of change, if nothing is done in the company with the information and analysis, no change will take place. The drivers of change must be communicated throughout the enterprise.

A SENSE OF URGENCY

The initial impact of the drivers of change is fearful and negative companies know change is to be forced on them (Here comes some more "broccoli." Eat it or else . . .). And correctly identifying the drivers of change is essential to create an appropriate response. The next step is to encapsulate the drivers of change in the *case for change*. This step becomes the primary vehicle for internalizing the drivers of change, and energizing the company to respond. It is the step that must be taken before making a detailed assessment of the impact of the drivers of change on your company, and before developing a suitable response.

Normally, companies deal with the case for change at the beginning of each of the two subprocesses that comprise the Process for the High Performance Enterprise. The first is the strategic case for change. It is used to initiate the Strategic Process—the process now under discussion. (Another case for change is used to kick off the

High P·e·r·f·o·r·m·a·n·c·e·s People Systems Process or other similar major initiatives. It is discussed in chapter 6.)

The strategic case for change is a full statement of the facts and circumstances surrounding the compelling reasons for change, supported by convincing arguments. It should be designed for a cross-functional team of high-level managers and staff, the leadership team who will formulate the response to the drivers of change and take the company through the Strategic Process.

But the Strategic Process is much more than convincing arguments presented to a team of managers. How much more depends on the level of understanding of the team, the degree of leadership exercised by top management, and impact desired of the case for change. Normally, top management provides the leadership for the development of the case for change. Naturally, because identifying the drivers of change and initiating a response are the domain of top management. Occasionally, the case for change comes from the "bottom-up," and when this happens, the initiators may be different, but the preparation is essentially the same.

The best way to fully define *your* case for change is by reviewing the following list of goals that it must accomplish. Then select among them for a case for change that suits the needs of your company. Here they are, and it's quite a handful.

SETTING THE "FIRE" UNDER YOUR ORGANIZATION

The strategic case for change should:

• *Create an impact significant enough to change the mind-sets of the team responsible for developing a strategic response to the drivers of change.* To become a High Performance Enterprise requires breakthrough thinking. It cannot take place when mind-sets are locked in old paradigms. It takes plenty of smoke and fire. The "fire" must be real, not just the apparent "smoke."

• *Produce a sense of urgency sufficient to create and sustain positive action.* Making breakthrough change requires enormous energy and unrelenting persistence. The sense of urgency must be palpable.

• *Identify and describe the real drivers of change in enough detail to make clear the principles and processes behind them.* This will at least ensure that the response is in the correct direction, and not back into the "fire."

CAUTION!

There is an expected open-endedness to the strategic case for change—if the company had all the answers already, it would be working on the tactical processes instead of the strategic.

• *Establish the consequences for* not *responding.* Moving away from the familiar requires a thorough knowledge of the results that the "same old way" will produce. Some people will hold out until the last, just as they did with the broccoli—"Okay, okay, okay. I'll try this little piece here. But it still *stinks.*"

• *Propose a process for developing the response.* Focus on following the Strategic Process. It will produce the productive discussions required to respond to the drivers of change. Intrusive direction will stifle the creativity of the team. Balance is required. Even at the strategic case for change, direction is necessary.

• *Empower those in charge of developing the response.* Create a sense that a solution is available, that the ingredients and resources are available in the company or will be obtained when required, and that the team will have the authority and responsibility to make it happen . . . and to live with the results. If decisions regarding the response have already been made, share those with the leadership team. Do not imply that the team is chartered to prepare a response if one has already been decided. That is dishonest.

• *Set expectations regarding the project trio—scope, schedule, and resources.* It's difficult work. Draw boundaries around the scope, propose a stretch schedule, and suggest the resources available. Request feedback from the team. Be prepared to allow at least one or two of the project trio to vary. It is impractical to "fix" all three.

· *Establish a clear challenge for the company, and the benefits of meeting that challenge.* You made the consequences of not responding clear. Now propose the future as High Performance Enterprise and its promise made a decade ago.

· *Use the communication of the case for change as an opportunity to model the likely behaviors anticipated for the new High Performance Enterprise.*

· *Outline the next steps.* Focus the next steps on processes and action plans to produce results, not on the results themselves. "Results rhetoric" is an indicator that management does not know where it is going, nor how to get there.

· *Do not just present the case for change. Win it!*

This type of case for change flies in the face of the pervasive bias toward action found in most companies. It requires a level of detail that most companies typically won't pursue. However, the failure to do so always results in the response's costing more than it should.

Creating a richly detailed case for change is much like creating a detailed design when building a new product. If you scrimp on the design, development takes longer, and the rework is always more than bargained for. On the other hand, a detailed design shortens development, and dramatically reduces rework. A detailed case for change that creates a sense of urgency will promote a more timely and effective development of the response, and will save the company time, effort, and perhaps an opportunity that could be lost in later reworking a failed response. Do it right the first time!

". . . And what is the vegetable today, Henri?"

"Today, sir, it is broccoli."

"And how is it prepared?"

"With a calamari sauce and pickled radishes, sir."

"Fantastic! That's one of my favorites!"

References:

1. Interview with Stephen J. Frangos, December 21, 1992.
2. *Teaching the Elephant to Dance*, James A. Belasco (New York: Crown Publishers, 1990).
3. *Life Was Never Meant to Be a Struggle*, Stuart Wilde (Taos, NM: White Dove International, Inc., 1987).
4. *The Machine That Changed the World*, James Womack, Daniel Jones, and Daniel Roos (New York: Rawson Associates/Macmillan Publishing Company, 1990).

CHAPTER 4

The Craft of Leadership

IT SOUNDS SO simple: leaders and managers are responsible for the company's *performance*. When leaders say the *performance* of the company they attempt to encapsulate in *one* single word what is really tens of thousands of daily p·e·r·f·o·r·m·a·n·c·e·s—countless individual daily activities, decisions, and transactions of employees at every level and in every process across the company.

The role of leadership is to bring the unity and cohesion of the boulder out of the fragmented, shifting mound of pebbles. Leaders create a context and direction to empower the people p·e·r·f·o·r·m·a·n·c·e·s, to achieve the promise of the '80s and raise the company to status as a High *Performance* Enterprise.

In *Managing for the Future*, Peter Drucker declares that leadership is not charisma, nor is it a set of personality traits. Actually, charisma can be a detriment as the charismatic become enamored of their perceived infallibility. Great leaders exhibit so many diverse personality traits that it is difficult to create a list of standard traits common to all.[1] And even if such a list could be assembled, it would be impossible to use them given our own individual, unique personalities.

Other leadership gurus in other works search for the secrets of leadership, and propose a litany of styles and approaches—from the slick to the cerebral—and label it everything from art to birth-gift. This foolishness notwithstanding, there is one thing for sure, and in that we agree wholeheartedly with Drucker—*effective leadership is work*. It's hard work—it's analyzing, synthesizing, planning, and most of all it's never-ending. But, it is still just *work*.

There is little magic or art to it. It is a craft—one to be practiced; one for which there are skills, and a process. The craft of leadership follows the flow of the Strategic Process and directs the completion of that process. It's a craft essential for simplifying the work of leadership, and in making that work more effective. It is a pragmatic approach that zeros in on the fundamental changes required to transform the traditional company into the High Performance Enterprise, and then to subject that enterprise to a habit of continuous improvement.

For those who subscribe to the philosophy of leadership-as-art, it will be difficult to conceive of a process (ugh!) for leadership. Yet leadership is work, and no less than any other work, the results of leadership-work flow from its processes. And because the work of leadership has so much impact on all the other work of the company, the leadership process must be well defined, rigorously controlled, and continuously improved.

As we begin an examination of leadership craft, we question the curious distinction between the words "leader" and "manager." What is the real difference? Frequently not much. Though in most cases leadership has been positional by tradition, it may also be situational by circumstance, and when this happens, the distinction between leadership and management becomes blurred.

Leadership is not so much a competency of a few gifted individuals, as it is a *role* that men and women at any level of the company may assume at any given time. Leaders *manage*—managers and others *lead*. Consequently, leadership should not be viewed as a gift, or the responsibility of but a few. *Leadership is a craft*—a craft with tools, processes, apprenticeships, journeymen, and only a very few master leaders. At any given time, it may become the responsibility of any one in the company:

> I was determined to have a company that was successful, not because of how much *one* or *two* people contribute, but because it has *multiple* functions and *multiple* strengths. (Our emphasis.)
>
> —FINIS F. CONNER, chairman and CEO of
> Conner Peripherals, Inc.[2]

In answering the challenge of leadership, some leaders let themselves off the performance "hook" with their acceptance of the leadership-as-art syndrome. Some trot out dry, useless "visions" expressed as this-much-profit and that-much-annual-growth or lots of rosy RONA—and then call that "leadership." Sorry, but artful exhortation and results-oriented "visions" do *not* answer the challenge.

The answer to the challenge of leadership is a process that demands a step-by-step, burn-the-midnight-oil, grind-it-out rigor and discipline with which some "leaders-in-name-only" are not familiar. Plain and simple, this is hard work! And it's hard work that can be done by all kinds of talented people committed to their companies and trained in the craft.

The work and craft of leadership can be summarized as follows:

The Craft of Leadership

1. Establish an organizational *context* for the company.

2. Establish the strategic direction for the business.

3. Translate vision into action.

4. Establish a habit of continuous improvement and renewal.

- It is based on the fact that leadership is work—that it is a craft with tools and processes.

- The craft of leadership consists of four major components, each of which provides action steps for the work to be done.

- The *primary work* of leadership is contained in the first two components:

  · Establish an organizational context for the company.
  · Establish the strategic direction for the business.

- The *follow-up work* of leadership is contained in the second two components:

· Translate vision into action.
· Establish a habit of continuous improvement and renewal.

• The craft of leadership parallels the flow of the Strategic Process. It leads to the definition of the high performance operating environment—the arena in which the High Performance Enterprise is brought to life.

THE CRAFT OF LEADERSHIP
(1) Establish an Organizational Context for the Company

The first component of the craft of leadership is the most complex. It is the heart and soul of the work of leadership. Of all the work that leadership entails, the first and most impactful work is accomplished in establishing an appropriate organizational context. This is the sister-step to establishing the strategic direction for the business. (We will spend more time developing this single step than all the others combined.)

The first component of the craft of leadership—establishing an organizational context—involves the following considerations:

A. The need for a personal context for leaders

B. A definition for the concept of organizational context.

C. An examination of the traditional organizational context; its replacement by a new paradigm, the empowered organizational context.

D. An outline of the eight characteristics of the empowered organizational context.

A. A Personal Context

The hackneyed paraphrase of the Cheshire Cat's words to Alice has become the cynics' rallying cry to describe a company's fractured context and lack of direction: "When you don't know where you're going, any road will take you there." More than just a description of the company's problem, it is also too frequently a clue to the root cause of the lack of direction. In their personal life and business life as well, some people operate out of instinct and old conditionings rather than a well-thought-out plan or set of principles. As a result, they are buffeted about by the latest craze and the most imminent fear. For those responsible for the leadership of a company, this makes for a pretty iffy and chancy kind of existence.

Before leaders can develop a context for the business, they must first develop a personal context to ensure consistency of actions and integrity of character. Business leadership is a one-on-one relationship between the leader and each follower. The basis for such a relationship is always trust. Trust results from consistency of actions and demonstrated integrity of character. Especially in cases where great change is involved, effective leaders count on trust to carry their people through the inevitable periods of stress and strain associated with change.

Effective leaders establish a personal context by developing a dynamic, principle-based philosophy consisting of fundamental operating principles for business, and their own clear personal values and principles. For a leader in today's global competition, a personal context should include at least the following six world-class operating principles. These principles form the core of an effective and successful operating philosophy. You will recognize these as the fundamental concepts that underpin the new world-class ways of differently, more effectively, utilizing people, equipment, and materials. They are the "real" drivers of change.

World-Class Operating Principles

· *Eliminate waste, excess, and unevenness*—a fundamental principle in achieving value-added services and manufacturing, and streamlined administrative processes. It's the underlying principle supporting the just-in-time manufacturing technique (lean manufacturing, cycle-time reduction).

· *Quality is defined by the customer, and integrated throughout the company*—the guiding principle of "total quality management," and policy deployment, this concept introduces us to the voice of the customer and establishes for the organization a logical and physical chain of external and internal customers.

 · *No one of us is as good as all of us*—the idea behind employee involvement, and its fullest expression, the empowered organization. This new way of looking at the organization opens the way to utilizing all the creative energies available at every level of the organization, and encourages the formation of teams.

 · *Involve everyone in a habit of continuous improvement*—this provides for incremental improvement between breakthroughs and positions the company on a higher plateau for taking advantage of the next breakthrough when it does occur. It encourages a habit of renewal and continuous improvement to preclude slipping back into the same-old-way of doing business.

 · *Practice process-orientation to improve results*—results are the "ends," and processes, the "means." If you want different results, change the processes.

 · *Measure for improvement*—new measurements for the different ways people, equipment, and materials are being managed. New measurements that provide timely feedback on individual, team, process, and company performance. Measures aligned with the objectives of the business.

Each principle appears here in its simplest form, yet carries additional richness available through countless books, seminars, and practical hands-on experience. Effective leaders increase their knowledge of these principles, experiment with them or study the experiences of others, and over time formalize a deep understanding of them.

Operating principles? For *leaders*? Doesn't sound like the ethereal and stratospheric stuff of true leadership. That's because ether and stratosphere are the stuff of *leadership-as-art*. When leadership is work, operating principles provide the underpinning for action. Eventually, when effective leaders seek an action initiative, a vehicle to carry the company to new levels of performance, they look for one that has the structural strength and flexibility of these six principles.

In looking for a vehicle for bringing about change, *ineffective* leaders jump from bandwagon to bandwagon and, just as easily, fall off the wagon. *Effective* leaders don't jump. They shop for a new "vehicle" before they buy. They research the "Consumer Reports" on World-Class Initiatives (with an especially sharp eye on *frequency of repair*), select a handful of models that meet their needs, drive one or two around the block, and then make an informed purchase. And get 100,000 miles of service and damned good mileage to boot.

Ineffective leaders talk to someone on an airplane or get excited at a seminar, and launch new programs into their companies with all the accuracy and appropriateness of an eighteenth-century mortar.

Effective leaders study their companies. They know the operating environment, its strengths and weaknesses. They study new principles and practices, learn the strengths and weaknesses of each, and plot the direction they want to take. Knowing the importance of delegation, they seek depth of knowledge to aid them in understanding when to apply tight controls, and when it's time for loose ones. At the heart of it all, they prepare for their work in the company by preparing themselves first.

B. Organizational Context

The organizational context is the mind-set that determines a company's operating environment. It is the corporate "attitude" that determines corporate behavior. Leadership creates the organizational context, and defines the rules and guidelines that determine all of the what, where, why, when, and how of the company's operating environment. It is one of the many vehicles for transmitting the values of the company.

> "[Company] results are generated by conditions, viz., the operating environment of a firm. Don't expect changes in results if you haven't changed the conditions."
>
> —RICHARD SLOMA, *No-Nonsense Management*

The desired context of a company must not be ambiguous. It must be rock solid. If it is ambiguous, the operating environment will be a by-default environment, and cannot be counted upon to produce the desired positive changes in results. The ambiguous organizational mind-set will guarantee inconsistent performance, or performance that is consistently below management expectations.

Leadership is especially hard work if leaders focus their efforts on the impossible task of improving performance by managing the one-ton boulder of *performance*. Instead, effective leaders focus their hard work on establishing a more effective organizational context to help with this work. They focus on improving performance by managing the ton of pebbles. It is through the context—the company's "attitude" or organizational mind-set—that leaders create an operating environment that makes it possible to impact performance at the level of p·e·r·f·o·r·m·a·n·c·e·s.

Listen to Ralph Stayer, of Johnsonville Foods on his leadership role:

> The debacle of ordering change and watching it fail to occur showed me my limitations. I had come to realize that I didn't directly control the performance of the people at Johnsonville, and as a manager I didn't really manage people. They managed themselves. But I did manage the context. I provided and allocated the resources. I designed and implemented the systems. I drew up and executed the organizational structure. The power of any contextual factor lies in its ability to shape the way people think and what they expect.[3]

And here is more thought from food. John Mackey is the CEO of Whole Foods, a natural-food store chain based in Austin, Texas. He refers to his 1,300 employees as "the best of the bohemian mix." (He's right. We've been in the stores, and it's Birkenstocks, braids, and brains, and excellent products and services from people who care.) And how does Mackey manage the p·e·r·f·o·r·m·a·n·c·e·s of this disparate and potentially impossible group?

> "I guess my gift to the company is that I've created a context at Whole Foods that allows people to be free," he says. "We don't

promote the managers who don't want people to have liberty. We select people who will empower other people." Team Members make most of the important decisions at their work group level; the people who work in the produce department at a Whole Foods store, along with their "Team Leader," decide what to stock, how to display it, how much to charge for it, what sales goals to set for the department and how much everyone should get paid. [4]

Both Stayer and Mackey have taken charge of the organizational contexts for their companies. They do not leave to chance or default the context that determines the ultimate operating environment of their High Performance Enterprises.

Have you, or the leaders of your company, visited the R&D lab, or the factory floor, or the accounting department, and left, on occasion, wondering if the people you met worked for the same company? When this happens, the *context* of the company is *not* under the direct tutelage and guardianship of its leaders. A by-default context is at work—a by-default context perceived individually, and responded to individually. When this happens, the resulting operating environment, with its thousands of activities, decisions, and transactions that make up p·e·r·f·o·r·m·a·n·c·e·s, will be "unmanageable."

C. A New Paradigm

The emergence of the High Performance Enterprise as a new competitive business paradigm was foreshadowed by an earlier underlying paradigm shift. The real driver of change for the High Performance Enterprise was a shift away from the traditional organizational context to one of empowerment—an empowered context that encouraged a vastly different way of working with people, equipment, and materials. The change began in Japan back in the '60s, and for the Western world, generally not until the '80s.

For most of us, prior to the '80s, our entire working experience had been in the traditional organizational context, and for many, it's still the only one in which they have ever worked. Regardless, we are all familiar with it—it sounds like this:

- "That's not my job!"

- "Look, when I want your advice, I'll ask for it!"

- "There's no way that'll work. It's going to damage the shaft . . . but if that's what the supervisor wants us to do, it's okay by me . . . it's not my equipment."

- "You folks gotta start making quality products. You gotta work harder *and* smarter . . . and start catching those defects before that stuff gets boxed."

- "Yeah, I don't give the program more than six weeks, max. That teamwork thing only lasted until we got behind during last month's ship-week."

In these few words, this is the traditional context, a context characterized by authoritarianism, entitlement, paternalism, and working to rules (working to rules supported by both old-fashioned management and old-fashioned union leadership). The traditional context creates an operating environment that does not work today and, in fact, may never have really worked well!

Now it's on its way out. How did this happen? What went wrong? The traditional context has not worked for a variety of reasons. For example, it fostered an operating environment in which the responsibility for managing thousands of daily p·e·r·f·o·r·m·a·n·c·e·s was heaped on the shoulders of a company's few managers, supervisors, and "specialists" (the trackers, the coordinators, and the expediters with their thermonuclear-white-hot *hot lists*). In this environment, companies depended on handfuls of Supermen and Wonder Women to hold together inherently ineffective systems. And then, when they wanted to promote someone, whom did they tap? You bet, good ol' Wonder Woman. Because of her incredible feats at expediting, she was rewarded by a promotion out of her "doing" expertise to a new supervision role in which she must manage her very own *unmanageable* quarter-ton mound of p·e·r·f·o·r·m·a·n·c·e·s.

In many companies, the traditional context did not work because it was responsible for a serious and counterproductive erosion of trust. How did this happen? The traditional context fosters an environment of *entitlement*. It encourages the passing upward of decisions, problems, and "it's-not-my-job issues" that would fall through the cracks if not passed upward. But a lot of it falls through the cracks anyway, because it's absolutely impossible for a beleaguered management group to either understand or handle all of that "stuff." As a result, managers end up shooting from the hip and responding to issues out of the heat of the moment—it's first-things-first, second things not at all. Inevitably, consistency of action becomes a joke, and management integrity suffers. The company's acceptance and perceived support of such a system erode the trust essential for successful leadership.

Though Western companies have accomplished much since the end of World War II, and until recently ranked number one in productivity, the traditional organizational context did not make us great. In fact, some companies became great in spite of the traditional context. And they were number one only because no one else in the world had a "better way." It only *seemed* as if it worked, and then primarily because the playing field was essentially level, with a few small bumps, here and there. The favorite game was a form of competitive leap frog—first one country or company would leap ahead, and the next year, another country or company would briefly dominate . . . and so on.

But that's all changed. At some point a decade or so ago, the cycle was broken by the first High Performance Enterprises from the Far East. These visitors from the East brought us Toyotas, Sonys, and Canons. The world-class companies vaulted ahead of the other players in such a significant way that the playing field was turned upside down. The new players changed the rules of the game. And, worse yet, because of their commitment to continuous improvement, they made up *new* rules *every* year. As soon as their competitors met one competitive challenge, the High Performance Enterprises turned up the intensity of play another notch or two, and sustained their domination of the game.

When every company was fouled up by its traditional organizational context, no company was penalized over any other—the playing field was level. But when the High Performance Enterprises got on track, other companies were bound to be in trouble. And that is what is happening today. The High Performance Enterprises employ a different way of working with people. They have established a new organizational context—an empowered organizational context that in turn creates a new high performance operating environment for their companies.

In recent years, High Performance Enterprises have shifted to the new empowered context and improved their ability to compete. This shift has increased pressure on companies with a traditional context. Working harder, smarter, longer, and with fewer people has *not* been a successful response. Some companies have exerted great effort in an attempt to implement breakthrough initiatives—management and workers alike put their hearts and souls in the programs, only to have a flawed operating environment swallow up their efforts and ultimately result in a return to the same-old-way. In other companies, similar efforts have produced "bits and pieces" of improvement, too often through the simple fact of a little more focused attention on critical problems, or the short, positive half-life impact of the Hawthorne Effect. In virtually all these companies, sustaining the *rate* of improvement has been impossible.

Is this an appropriate time for a shift in paradigms? Are the people in most companies ready for a change in the way people are managed? In his book, *Discovering the Future*, Joel Arthur Barker redefined and popularized the concept of the Paradigm Shift. If the *empowered* context is a new paradigm, we can expect it to unfold in much the same sequence of steps as that outlined in Barker's book about paradigms. Step 2, for example, says, "The affected community senses the situation, [and] begins to lose trust in the old rules." He goes on to state, "New paradigms put everyone practicing the old paradigm at great risk. And, the higher one's position, the greater the risk. The better you are at your [current] paradigm, the more you have invested in it. To change your paradigm is to lose that investment."[5]

Now, think for a moment. In the past decade, and in the past few years in particular, how many books and articles have you read that attack the "myths" of leadership, management, or the people side of business in general? How many articles (most backed by new studies) that point out forcibly that the traditional organizational context just plain doesn't work anymore?

Case in point. Let's look at the results of a study published in a 1991 *Sloan Management Review.* These results will give us an opportunity to "dispel two myths with one *Sloan.*" Here are the views from a cross-functional, cross-section of employees from companies in the automotive, electronics, steel, building products, transportation, medical, and communications industries. These people:

- "Want, appreciate, and accept autonomy, but they also want input, attention, and guidance that only their superiors can provide."

- "Need an unambiguous picture of what they are responsible for in their jobs and, just as important, what they are not responsible for."

- Need goals, but feel that goal setting requires: "Mutual input, and . . . some discussion of means and process, [because] goal setting in a cavalier manner breeds poor communication."

- Think that competition is appropriate among businesses, but not within a business. They preferred a context that created a different type of operating environment, because "collaboration and cooperation within the organization are demonstrably better strategies for improving competitiveness in the business arena."

- Desire expanded duties, authority, technical capabilities, and opportunities for more cross-training;

- Need clarified accountabilities, and "want and need regular [and ongoing] feedback."[6]

Looking at this list, you might think it was a summary of needs identified in an employee survey—the desires of a group of office employees or factory workers who felt the operating environment of their companies did not allow them to make the kind of contribution of which they were capable.

Surprise! All direct and indirect quotes are from the *managers* of these companies, not the workers. In the *Sloan Management Review* published study, "Ten Myths of Managing Managers," in-depth interviews were conducted with a group of managers from profitable manufacturing and service organizations. The managers represented a good organizational cross-section of senior-, middle-, and lower-level managers.

Now this may be a surprise to some, but in our work, often the most frustrated group we encounter in an organization is the *management team*. They feel the least empowered in terms of having the direction, tools, training, structure, trust, freedom to act, feedback, and reinforcement needed to optimize their effectiveness.

Among the myths addressed was: "Managers are self-starting, self-directing, and autonomous, or they would not be managers." Companies *assume* managers are self-managed—that they automatically understand the bosses' directives and are able to carry them out. That "managers worth their salt know what their jobs really entail." And not only do they know what their job is, but they know how well they are performing in the job. The truth is, for years managers have been dissatisfied with the operating environments in which they work. In the traditional context, managers are not *able* to perform their jobs—the environment in which they work does not fully enable, or empower, them. They are asked to manage the unmanageable.

Dual Management Myths

· *The Myth*: The traditional organizational context of authoritarianism, paternalism, and working to rules has been effective for years, but now may need some revision.

The Truth: The traditional organizational context no longer produces a high performance operating environment, and may never have. Some effective managers found ways to work around its limits, and the Supermen and Wonder Women around the world have leaped the tall obstacles and deflected the gnarly problems that laid low many a mere mortal. And, by the way, the traditional organizational context does not need revision—*it needs reinventing.*

· *The Myth*: Employee empowerment is a convenient and potentially effective soft, people side technology that management uses with lower-level workers.

The Truth: Empowerment is a context for creating an effective operating environment for *everyone* in the company. It's the right environment for workers, managers, and leaders alike. It's the only context that creates a high performance operating environment.

D. The Empowered Organizational Context

It is neither our intention to provide a new treatise on empowerment, nor to present a specific process for empowering your company. These topics have been well covered already by other books. Our goal is to establish an empowered context as the organizational context of choice for the High Performance Enterprise; and to suggest a list of characteristics of this powerful new mind-set.

Empowerment is not twentieth-century egalitarianism, nor is it a form of anarchy. It is neither Japanese nor Buddhist, nor even New Age. And, in spite of the damage done in its name by some of its more romantic proponents, empowerment is definitely not a pie-in-the-sky panacea to solve all the ills of the company.

It is a hardheaded business decision to enable everyone in the company to perform up to his or her fullest potential. The purpose of empowerment is improved performance—performance is improved because power shared is power multiplied. Its roots go back to earlier days in Western culture. Then, personal pride in workmanship flowed from hands-on experience, a sense of responsibility and control over one's work, and a feeling that your workmates and you were involved together in something bigger than just the few of you.

Empowerment is a dollars and (common) sense, practical approach at managing and improving p·e··r·f·o·r·m·a·n·c·e·s in the only truly effective way possible, viz., by having those who p·e·r·f·o·r·m become involved in and take ownership for all of their p·'s, e·'s, r·'s . . . Empowered worker and manager alike are in the best position to take action, to make decisions, and improve their performance, because they have been enabled, encouraged, and supported to do so by the organizational context of the company.

And it's not enough to empower the individual. If an empowered individual performs at 2X, an empowered team performs at 4X.

An empowered organizational context is a mind-set. The best way to describe a mind-set is by its characteristics—in this case, eight powerful characteristics:

Eight Characteristics of the Empowerment Mind-set: An Empowered Organizational Context

1. *Trust.* If there be an absolute in this context, it is that empowerment is impossible without trust. There are two essential transactions that take place in empowerment: the first is management's "letting go," and the second is workers' "accepting." Absolutely neither transaction is possible without trust. During times of great change and stress, as when a company seeks new levels of performance and commitment, trust is the belaying rope that provides a secure hold for everyone in the company.

An Empowered Context

Trust
Shared information and education
Formal Skills training
Clear roles and accountabilities
Freedom to act
Performance Feedback
Reinforcement
Resources optimized

Facilitating management's "letting-go" transaction is straightforward. It is totally in the hands of the leadership of the company. Top management must make it happen by building a sound Strategic Process, and by ensuring that all eight characteristics of the empowered context are embraced as the "law" of the company. A little faith in people, helps.

Facilitating the workers' "accepting" transaction is fairly straightforward—it, too, is pretty much in the hands of the leadership of the company. Top management facilitates the transaction for the workforce through consistency of actions, integrity of character, and having faith in the people of the company.

CAUTION!

The faith involved in the "accepting" transaction is fragile—it is generally born in the shadow of "the benefit of a doubt." When making great change, the management of a company gets only so many "benefits of a doubt." When used up, facilitating an "accepting" transaction becomes almost impossible without significant remedial work. Doing-it-right-the-first-time is important.

---

2. *Shared information and education.* Shared information is one of the first expressions of trust in the "letting go" transaction, especially shared business information. In the traditional context, not even data were made available. Now, when there are data, empowerment requires more. Data, and then, education regarding what it means, how to use it, and the form in which it is most useful. When combined, data and education produce shared information.

What is the purpose of shared information, this new knowledge? *Improved performance!* Managing in the empowered organization is based on shared information directed to the point where p·e·r·f·o·r·m·a·n·c·e·s take place. In the new operating environment, "workers will be called upon to act on that knowledge to continually improve their own performance, the performance of their work group, and the performance of the company as a whole."[7]

C A U T I O N !

Business education should not be entirely focused on the financials of the company. People need to understand competitors, customers, markets, industry, international issues, etc.

3. *Formal skills training.*   Too frequently, training has been the silver bullet for empowerment and the company's people efforts. Its timing has been inappropriate, and its content wasted because it was not formally linked to business objectives. As a result, the operating environment never changed to permit the application of the new skills.

The correct focus and chief purpose of training in the empowered context is *improvement.* All training must be (1) aligned with the objectives of the business, (2) evaluated regarding its applicability to improving performance, (3) sensitized to the actual needs of the people, and (4) committed to reinforcing the new mind-set required of the empowered organization. And, then, the timing of training will be appropriate.

C A U T I O N !

Training is an ongoing process—prioritization of needs is essential. When it makes sense in the empowered organization to utilize the services of outside training companies, ensure customization where appropriate to align packaged materials with the context and resulting empowered operating environment of your company.

4. *Clear roles and accountabilities.*   An empowered context produces an environment that *expects performance* at every level of the company. Why is this important? As Judith M. Bardwick points out in *Danger in the Comfort Zone*:

Quite simply, American business and industry can no longer afford to sustain Entitlement. We cannot continue to carry under-productive people. Today, as the rate of change grows continuously faster, we need people who are confident enough to cope with tomorrow's unpredictable problems. . . . Uprooting Entitlement is not easy. It's hard to get people to give up the warm blanket of protection. People who have been accustomed to years of Entitlement will resist increments of risk. They will resist accountability and flee from evaluations. . . . To make things even tougher, wherever Entitlement exists it is usually codified in the organization's rules and enshrined in its culture.[8]

Because entitlement is as alive and well in the executive suites as it is on the factory floor, clear roles and accountabilities are an issue at *every* level in the empowered organization. While it's important for leaders to effectively communicate the challenge of the new organization, it is equally important for them to put "teeth" into the changes required by holding people at every level accountable for their performance.

In the empowered organization, new roles must be defined; it's best done from the bottom of the organization upward. In the process of defining roles, accountabilities and boundaries are most naturally established. (The process for doing this is described in detail in chapters 9 and 10.)

CAUTION!

Because change in the High Performance Enterprise is ongoing and evolutionary, roles will change in the same ongoing, evolutionary manner. Create clear expectations about these changes in order to keep managers and workers focused on the tasks at hand.

---

5. *Freedom to act.* No longer is initiative stifled—employees at every level are encouraged to take action to improve performance. Freedom to act, yes!—within a framework of boundaries that establish individual and team responsibilities and accountabilities. Boundaries that identify what decisions may be made independently, and those occasions on which only input is requested.

This is a freedom to act within new broader job definitions and value-added policies and procedures. Earlier, we quoted John Mackey of Whole Foods, the nation's largest natural-foods supermarket chain, on his role in creating a context. Here are those words again, this time showing how clear boundaries and policies have been institutionalized as part of the empowered context he created:

> Team Members make most of the important decisions at their work group level; the people who work in the produce department at a Whole Foods store along with their "Team Leader," decide what to stock, how to display it, how much to charge for it, what sales goals to set for the department, and how much everyone should get paid.[9]

CAUTION!

Avoid a "romantic" view of empowerment. Unbounded freedom to act, coupled with an unrealistic sense of the evolutionary nature of empowerment, can produce an environment in which management becomes paralyzed and workers disenchanted.

---

6. *Performance feedback.* The purpose of the empowered context is to improve performance. Regular, ongoing feedback on whatever the individual, team, work group, or department has been empowered to do has a positive impact on performance. No one likes working in a vacuum—people want and need feedback, they learn from it. Consistent and visible feedback also helps maintain a sense of just how important the work is on which performance is being measured.

CAUTION!

Existing performance monitoring and evaluating tools may be modified to provide feedback, but this should be done only as an integral part of the redesign of the company's people systems. (More on this in chapter 12.)

7. *Reinforcement.* The move to an empowered organizational context means utilizing people differently. It also means that changes in mind-set and behavior will be required from top to bottom. Reinforcement through pay and reward is among the more powerful change agents available to a company.

A key part of creating reinforcement is establishing both positive and negative consequences for performance. No company can any longer afford the guaranteed across-the-board increases of the entitlement mind-set of the traditional operating environment. There can no longer be increases without a connection to the performance of the individual, the team, or the business.

CAUTION!

Traditional managers are frequently uncomfortable asking their people to change and to contribute more fully without first holding out a monetary carrot. It is easy for companies to move too quickly in their use of pay and reward to "solve" this problem. Changes in pay and reward will come, but only after other steps are taken. (More in chapter 13.)

8. *Resources optimized.* It's called "putting your money where your mouth is." Empowerment without the resources is like having the car keys but no permission to use the car. The empowered context requires that resources be aligned with the acknowledged priorities and business objectives of the company. Frittering away the company's resources on anything less erodes trust, impairs the freedom to act, and jeopardizes the performance committed upon by the empowered workforce.

CAUTION!

There is no free lunch. Almost invariably, some "seed money" or a "grubstake" of some kind is required to get started, and, almost invariably, this is where management faith is required. (Having a good performance improvement plan helps, too.)

We began with the idea that leaders need a personal context—a principle-based operating philosophy that serves as the foundation of their work. We defined "organizational context," and explored the failure of the traditional context and its replacement by a new paradigm—the empowered organizational context. The first component of the craft of leadership is complete. No mystery, no magic— just detailed hard work. Just the work of leadership.

THE CRAFT OF LEADERSHIP
(2) Establish the Strategic Direction for the Business

The finest empowered organization without direction is like the proverbial ship without a rudder. Now, it's rudder time. Direction in the High Performance Enterprise is not a single entity. Strategic direction unfolds. It is developed over time in an increasingly more specific set of documents.

A key to success for the High Performance Enterprise is avoiding the fragmentation and lack of integration that plagues so many traditional companies. In those companies, employees see a flurry of seemingly unrelated activities—activities not linked to the strategic thrust of the company, and with no apparent linkage to each other. As a result, the flurry of activity saps their personal strength and wastes the scarce resources of the company. Avoiding this trap is a vital responsibility of the leadership of the High Performance Enterprise.

Strategic direction is reflected in the mission and vision statements created for the company, two documents we sometimes bundle as the mission/vision package. This process requires a sense of balance at the leadership level. There are times during the process when breakthrough thinking is required—the environment must be free and open to thinking the unthinkable. At other times, the cold reality of the company's core strengths and weaknesses must be frankly addressed. The Leadership Team must have the "freedom to act," appropriate boundaries, and the direction to help maintain that balance.

The Leadership Team

Your company may have its own process for the work that lies ahead. Regardless of what you use, the backbone of the process should be the equivalent of the Strategic Process. It provides the focus, alignment, integration, and system required to take a "hard" process approach to strategic direction.

For our purposes, we will continue with the Strategic Process where we left off in the previous chapter, when the case for change was communicated to the Leadership Team. They were chartered with the responsibility to develop a strategic direction for the company, and to follow the outline of the Strategic Process for the High Performance Enterprise. They begin their work with a self-education process focused on the business both internally and, especially, externally. A few practical considerations for the team are:

- The Leadership Team takes a formal project approach with defined scope, schedule, and resources (the project trio). In their charter, the team received tentative scope, schedule, and resources. With a feel for the actual requirements for the project, they will either validate those or request a change.

- The team uses a structured problem-solving approach. Teams use a variety of approaches, such as Kepner-Tregoe or the 7 Management Tools. Your team should stick to familiar tools if at all possible. (Although, for some teams, this is an opportunity to learn new tools anticipated for use in the new operating environment.)

- Build on the strengths of the company, and create performance expectations beyond the usual.

- Expect the process to take time. How much? Depends . . . at least on the readiness of the organization to take on the task, the strength of leadership behind the project, the sense of urgency, and the balance between expediency of results and an "empowered" process.

- Allow for soak time. Education, newly shared information, and the process of creating the High Performance Enterprise stretch the envelope of any company. A little time is required for all the pieces to fall into place.

The Mission Statement

The mission statement defines the company's purpose. From the company's view, it says: who we are . . . what we do . . . for whom we do it . . . why we do it. Effective mission statements:

- Are concise, easy to understand, and short enough that the essence of the message presented can be recalled by people at every level.

- Specify the customers to be served, and how the company will serve their needs.

- Reflect those core competencies and/or technologies that differentiate the company from the pack.

- Focus on the main strategic thrust of the company.

- Establish significant but attainable general goals.

- Serve as a focal point expression of the company's operating principles and its empowered organizational context.

- Provide both a well-focused direction, and the flexibility to take action as required.

The Vision Statement

The vision statement defines the organization of the future. From the company's view, it says: With our empowered context as a base, how will we feel, look, and operate when we are a High Performance Enterprise? What are our ideals, hopes, and dreams? What kind of a company will we be?

A well-crafted vision statement is based on the assumption that a person or company can achieve whatever they can conceive and believe—that believing is seeing. The Leadership Team will focus on creating an effective vision statement that will:

- Provide breakthrough possibilities for the company of tomorrow, because it is not tied to the company of today. This is an opportunity to "think the unthinkable." The team will not limit its view of the future because of current circumstances.

- Establish goals for tomorrow that do not take into consideration the exact possibility or impossibility of achievement. The truly impossible will fall by the wayside farther along in the process. This is the time to dream.

- Focus on the processes that produce the results, not on the results themselves:

  - On the behaviors that will exemplify the empowered context.
  - On the processes that will make things different, produce improved results, and ensure the growth and prosperity of the company and its people.

- Impact people viscerally, because it establishes the principles and values that will guide the p·e·r·f·o·r·m·a·n·c·e·s of people at every level of the organization.

- Is descriptive—its richness and detail help the company

through the hard times and changes required of the company striving to become a High Performance Enterprise.

The specific content of vision statements varies from company to company. Some include more detail than others, and all reflect the particular style of the authoring company. Regardless, there is a shared purpose for the mission/vision package: to provide strategic direction for the empowered organization. The payoff for the mission/vision package comes from what it does *for* the company:

· Creates a purpose-driven company, i.e., provides constancy of purpose.

· Builds a foundation for shared responsibility—sharpens the focus, and provides alignment and integration of activities at every level of the organization.

· Provides a meaningful, useful framework for action and decision making.

· Establishes a challenge for all employees.

· Increases enthusiasm, commitment, and pride in the company.

The vision/mission package is a critical step in establishing the strategic direction for the company. This is not a time for the Leadership Team to waste their effort on risking small, incremental changes in the company. A vision without breakthrough thinking— a vision limited in potential because it is rooted to current circumstances—is a waste of time. No company can afford to waste time on a mediocre vision. Richard Sloma, in another of his maxims, says to managers:

Important results are never generated by trivial undertakings involving insignificant risk of failure. Get involved, therefore, only in activities where there is a risk of significant mistakes. It is only in such activities that you'll find the opportunity for significant achievement. [10]

"We never took the development of a mission and vision seriously until we understood how to translate it down into the daily activities of the organization—down to p·e·r·f·o·r·m·a·n·c·e·s. Now we know they are a critical element of our work." This is a typical comment of executives who are learning the craft of leadership, and dedicated to change in their organization.

Wishing upon a star may have worked for Walt Disney, but for most companies, a different, more rigorous process is more effective. It's hard work, but the payoff is worth it. With a commitment to the empowered organizational context, and now mission and vision statements to provide a strategic direction, we've reached the point in the craft of leadership where it's time to translate vision into action.

THE CRAFT OF LEADERSHIP
(3) Translate Vision into Action

Exhortation will not make the vision real to your company. The pompom and megaphone approach may work at the football stadium, but not on the assembly line, at the computer, or in team meetings. Only through a "hard" process approach can the Leadership Team bring focus, alignment, integration, and system to the translation of vision into action.

Translating vision into action at the strategic level is a time-consuming, detailed, and difficult iterative process for the cross-functional Leadership Team. It is here that their operational experience and knowledge of the company become truly essential, because they have the responsibility for *three critical deliverables*:

A. Strategic success factors.

B. Operational business objectives.

C. Initiatives for the High Performance Enterprise.

It is not our intention here to cover "strategic planning" *à la* Michael Porter *et al.* Rather, it is to provide a sense of the *leadership work* involved, and to establish that this is all part of the craft of leadership. We will provide a master format for use by Leadership Teams in all companies. The unique approach that your company takes will reflect its own combination of people, products, processes, technology, and "situation."

Before the Leadership Team begins the actual work on its three deliverables, it has preliminary work to complete, the products of which will be tools for the team to use in translating the vision of the company into action. Drawing on the case for change and the mission/vision package, the team begins the process by creating two business profiles: one of the future, or targeted, business; and another of the today, or baseline, business. The degree of detail to which teams take these profiles is a function of their awareness of the company and competitive issues involved; their commitment to productive planning; and the degree of severity of their bias toward action. (Those suffering from severe bias-toward-action will be lucky to fill the back of a cafeteria napkin.)

The targeted business profile will describe the business of the future in outline form by way of categories of desired characteristics for the business three to five years into the future—characteristics that will permit the company to become a High Performance Enterprise, and to respond positively to the real drivers of change. These characteristics should span the functions, products, processes, technologies, people, etc., issues: for example, flexibility requirements, cycle times of major processes, teams and teamwork, quality levels, product and market approaches, to name a few.

For each characteristic, the team will then develop detailed, descriptive statements to qualify, quantify, and to enrich their understanding of exactly how the targeted business will perform or appear in each characteristic. The final product will be a reflection of the way the team "thinks" about the business of its future.

The team will then develop a contrasting profile of the business of today, the baseline business profile. For each characteristic and descriptive statement of the targeted business profile, a corresponding characteristic and descriptive statement reflecting today's status will be prepared for a baseline business profile.

Using the two profiles, the Leadership Team will then conduct a gap analysis between the targeted and baseline views, and express the gap in terms of "action items" to undertake to fill the gap. The gap analysis provides an assessment of the work required to move the company from the baseline business to the targeted High Performance Enterprise. It provides a working "migration strategy" for use in developing the three deliverables for this component of the craft of leadership.

A. Strategic Success Factors

Using the profiles and a working "migration strategy" as a base, the team searches for groupings of common action items that, when combined, will produce a concentrated impact on the ability of the company to achieve its target. This process will yield a handful of common groupings of action items called "strategic success factors": major themes or areas of change and improvement; or broad, general goals that identify the major achievements that over time will enable the company to complete its mission and fulfill its vision . . . to become a High Performance Enterprise.

For most companies, strategic success factors will focus on broad areas such as quality improvement, reduced cycle-time or processing time, improved delivery commitment, elimination of waste and reduced costs.

B. Operational Business Objectives

Using the business profiles, the working "migration strategy," and the groupings of strategic success factors, the leadership team focuses on establishing operational business objectives: the specific goals necessary to fulfill the strategic success factors. Operational business objectives will be:

· Concrete, measurable, and operationally oriented.

· The annual expression of what may be a three- to five-year strategic drive to accomplish the strategic success factors.

- An expression of *incremental* direction and progress toward the mission, vision, and strategic success factors.

For example, a strategic success factor of "quality improvement" might produce operational business objectives of: (1) improve first-pass yields by 7 percent; (2) reduce defects at final inspection to < 0.5 percent; and (3) reduce scrap by 40 percent.

C. Initiatives for the High Performance Enterprise

The leadership team must choose action plans, or initiatives to carry out its operational business objectives. The initiatives chosen will provide a framework of action for the High Performance Enterprise. There are plenty of "ready-made" initiatives available: self-directed teams, TQC/TQM, JIT and its variants (lean manufacturing, demand-flow manufacturing), and work cells to name a few.

Unfortunately, there seem to be as many versions of each as there are users, academics, authors, and consultants to recommend them. Rather than overwhelm yourself, use the following guide to assist you in the selection of initiatives that support *your* strategic direction.

Selecting Initiatives

- Develop a general understanding of the world-class principles mentioned earlier. These are the underlying principles for most of the world-class initiatives. A critical selection criterion for any initiative should be how well it accomplishes the fundamental changes promised by these principles:

  - Eliminate waste, excess, and unevenness.
  - Quality is defined by the customer, and integrated throughout the company.
  - Involve everyone in a habit of continuous improvement.
  - No one of us is as good as all of us.
  - Practice process orientation to improve results.
  - Measure for improvement.

- Select one "working initiative" that seems to offer the potential of accomplishing the improvement required by your business objectives. Learn about it. Read, study, and find out what the different gurus have to offer. Evaluate its attributes, principles, and processes; contrast them with the operational business objectives you must accomplish, and the empowered organizational context embraced by the company. Then move on to other initiatives, as required.

- Build on the strengths of the company. There is a core of resources in every company: people, technology, geography, facilities, equipment, etc. When properly energized and focused, they are capable of producing the same kind of sustained improvement as the world-class companies. The initiatives selected should build on these core strengths, and through the processes the initiatives employ, leverage the company through the improvements required.

- Every company is unique . . . in a way. But companies should not fool themselves into thinking that they must customize every off-the-shelf program, or reinvent the wheel just because they are unique. In a session with George Fisher of Motorola, he told us to unashamedly: "Borrow, adapt, and otherwise [use] the ideas of good companies." No company has time to "reinvent the wheel." Learn from the successful practitioners.

- Do not corrupt the initiative you select, i.e., do not cherry-pick the elements that are *easy* for you to do; and then "adapt" or "modify" those that are not. An effective initiative has focus, alignment, integration, and system. Too much modifying can cut the heart out of any initiative. This is particularly dangerous because the perception becomes one of "Oh, yes. We tried self-directed teams, but it didn't work."

The team will develop a list of selection criteria, prioritize its operational business objectives, evaluate possible initiatives or combinations of initiatives, and select the initiative(s). Make sure the selected initiative(s) provides the focus, alignment, integration, and system, or process, to work in the empowered context and to pull together the activities of an involved workforce into a unified force for improvement. This will provide the "hard" process approach required to translate vision into action.

How long has it been since we reminded you that leadership is hard work? Okay, it's hard work. At this point, Leadership Teams generally face the Paradox of Previously Ignored Detail. The two verbal symptoms go something like this: "Oh, my God! I didn't know there was so much detail, so much to do to become world-class! We'll *never* get all this done!" And the paradox: "Oh, my God! I didn't know there was so much detail, but when we get this done, we're gonna be dynamite!" The bias toward action has its place. However, companies that fight the temptation to "get on with it," and truly dedicate the time and resources to an effective Strategic Process, significantly increase the likelihood of achieving status as High Performance Enterprise.

THE CRAFT OF LEADERSHIP: (4) Establish a Habit of Continuous Improvement and Renewal

In Costa Rica, a *jardinero*, a gardener, will cut your front and back yard by hand with a machete and a sharpening file. From inside the house, you hear the sound of swish-swish-swish-swish-swish . . . rasp-rasp. A rhythm of cut-cut-cut . . . sharpen . . . cut-cut-cut . . . sharpen. A rhythm of working the process . . . improving the process . . . working the process . . . improving the process. This is the rhythm that people and companies use to become effective, and to retain their effectiveness.

The striking phraseology from Richard Schonberger's book, *Japanese Manufacturing Techniques*, still rings true: "A *habit* of continuous improvement." Not improving every once in a while, or when the mood strikes, but a *habit* of *continuous* improvement. This is a significant component of the craft of leadership. This work of renewal is at the heart of a leader's craftsmanship. His tools are the people and processes of the company. As with all fine tools, they regularly and lovingly need a *new* edge to cut cleanly and sharply through the work to be accomplished.

We began this discussion with the thought that leadership is neither charisma, nor personality traits. It is work. Hard work. We end with that same thought, but now you have a process to use to develop your own personal craft of leadership. In the next chapter, you will have an opportunity to work on your craft. There we will define the high performance operating environment—an empowered environment in which p·e·r·f·o·r·m·a·n·c·e·s are managed in the only effective way, viz., by having those who p·e·r·f·o·r·m become involved in and take ownership for their p·'s, e·'s, r·'s, f·'s. . . .

References:

1. *Managing for the Future*, Peter F. Drucker (New York: Truman Talley Books/Dutton, 1992).
2. *Electronic Business*, March 18, 1991.
3. "How I Learned to Let My Workers Lead," Ralph Stayer, *Harvard Business Review*, November–December 1990.
4. *Austin Chronicle*, August 14, 1992.
5. *Discovering the Future*, Joel Arthur Barker (St. Paul, MN: ILI Press, 1989).
6. *Sloan Management Review*, Fall 1991.
7. *Workplace 2000*, Joseph H. Boyett and Henry P. Conn (New York: Penguin Books, 1991).
8. *Danger in the Comfort Zone*, Judith M. Bardwick (New York: American Management Association, 1991).
9. *Austin Chronicle*, August 14, 1992.
10. *No-Nonsense Management*, Richard S. Sloma (New York: Macmillan Publishing Company, 1977).

CHAPTER 5

A New Work Covenant

Sally believes she is "entitled" to her allowance. The concept of "The harder you work, the more money you should make!" does not mean much to her. She "expects" to get her allowance and, even though she doesn't come right out and say so, you can tell she *expects* to do little to earn it. After all, she's *entitled* to that allowance.

When Sally grows up and goes to work, it's likely she will take that same attitude with her into the workplace. And if she goes to work at a company with a traditional operating environment, her entitlement mentality will be reinforced. Today, Sally is comfortable just sitting in front of the television set waiting for her allowance—tomorrow, she'll be at her workstation just waiting for her company "allowance." She'll be putting in her time, waiting for the ol' weekly paycheck to which she is entitled.

THE TRADITIONAL OPERATING ENVIRONMENT

Let's take Sally out of her traditional company, and send her to work at one of the High Performance Enterprises. A year or two later, when she's had a chance to work in that different environment for a while, let's send her back to the old traditional operating environment and have her make some observations from her new perspective. When Sally looks around at the traditional operating environment in which she used to work, what will she see?

Sally's observations—attributes of the traditional operating environment.

Entitlement. Generally, an environment in which there is no relationship between performance and payoff—a pervasiveness shared at all levels by management and employees alike. It's the "allowance ethic" of Sally's youth raised to industrial-strength potency—it's getting paid for "time spent."

After a while, entitlement becomes an addiction. Everyone becomes hooked on the "security." Managers and employees "enable" their own addiction by not rocking the boat, by sweeping problems under the carpet rather than solving them, and by avoiding risk—everyone becomes a "safety player." The company "plans" great and glorious futures, and sadly the plans become ends in themselves, with no real action taken. Not surprisingly, making fundamental change in such an environment is difficult, and sometimes impossible.

Conflict avoidance. Can you imagine what would happen if young Sally did not get her allowance as expected, perhaps because she hadn't done her one or two chores? Right!—a screaming, heel-kicking, fist-banging fit. And what do you suppose would happen, then? Right!—she would get the allowance anyway, because Mom and Dad couldn't tolerate the conflict. In the traditional environment, performance suffers as a result of conflict avoidance. Managers are hesitant to confront poor performance not only among employees, but also among other managers. Too often it is the senior managers or the board of directors who are the most unwilling to deal with management performance problems. (By the way, it's not that Sally didn't hear plenty of yelling and raised voices—what she found was not really conflict . . . it was incredible frustration.)

Informal "lifetime employment for mediocrity." The traditional company eventually takes care of its extremes—it rids itself of the vocal agitator for change, and the *grossly* incompetent. Occasionally, it takes a little time. Who's left? The employees who know how to play the system; who don't make waves; those who show up, put in their time, and collect their "allowance." A form of corporate Darwinian selection results in a company that, by default, favors mediocrity. This natural selection includes an appropriate percentage of genuinely mediocre managers and employees—and that's bad enough. The real tragedy, though, is that a larger percentage of these managers and employees is capable of better-than-expected performance, but the performance-numbing effects of the traditional environment keep them at the mediocre level (Sally felt sad about this observation. She remembered what it was like on the assembly line—she'd felt sort of "dead.")

Combine avoidance of conflict and the performance-numbing effects of the work environment with the litigious way of life in some countries, and it is not surprising that nearly every company carries a group of employees considered by both management and employees to be "dead wood." An employer is required to provide reams of written documentation of poor performance before an employee can be let go—documentation not available because "problems" are swept under a carpet of indifference.

Not even downsizing or "rightsizing" fully impacts the environment of mediocrity. Many companies use "early retirement opportunities" to reduce head count, encouraging those with creativity and a desire for a better work life to jump at the opportunity to leave. And because many companies have no effective performance management, these companies have no rational or legal way of sorting out the good performers from the poor. So, barring getting caught in a layoff or downsizing, the mediocre employee who "keeps her nose clean" has "lifetime employment."

Hierarchical deference. In the traditional operating environment, decision making is usually pushed up to higher levels of the hierarchy, and opinions are deferred until the opinion of a more senior person is made known. This hierarchical bureaucracy lengthens the cycle-time for decision making and dilutes the integrity, urgency, and accuracy of the information passed upward. And it's not unusual for a slant or spin given the information to affect its basic honesty, precluding management from even having a shot at making a sound decision.

"Problem solving is the province of the 'experts.'" This is not a surprising phenomenon when hierarchical position carries the authority for getting things done. It effectively takes problem solving and process improvement out of the hands of those who have the best "feel" for the process. It also takes the *burden* of improvement from their shoulders and places it squarely on management and its "experts." These actions then concentrate the responsibility for improvement on the *few* rather than the *many* . . . and promotes *mediocrity of process* as well as mediocrity of personnel.

Risk avoidance. Human nature dictates a direct correlation between how much control and influence over an issue people have, and how much risk they are willing to take regarding it. (The less empowered, the less risk taking.) We said it before: the traditional operating environment favors the safety player. Even with control and influence, taking risks requires trust, a fragile commodity.

A multi-billion-dollar company was spending hundreds of thousands of dollars on empowerment programs and work cells, and was moving extraordinarily slowly in doing so. A newly appointed work cell leader confided that the work cell team members felt senior management must not trust the work cells because they were being so cautious with the implementation.

Narrow jobs. "I put the baseplate on the bottom of the widget, and then screw them together with these four screws." The job: baseplate assembler. One of 175 individual jobs at a company of 400 hourly employees. Unusual? Not really. To some degree or another, for most traditional companies work has been fragmented into a myriad of narrow, confining jobs. "That's not my job" becomes an almost palpable barrier to movement.

Working to rules. Doing exactly what one is told to do . . . and displaying no initiative to do anything additional—a stultifying mind-set among both management and employees. And it's not a "union thing" either. "Working to rules" is as pervasive a mind-set as its partner, "entitlement." Together they enable and support the climate of mediocrity inevitable in both the traditional union and nonunion operating environment. "Keep your head down, your shoulder to the wheel, and your mouth shut" is the management *and* employee response when working to rules is the order of the day.

Working to rules is also a good way to avoid taking risks. There it is in black and white! All the "shoulds" and "should-nots" are spelled out. Follow the rules, and you cannot be blamed for problems. Conversely, if the "rules" are always followed, the problems will never go away.

Inflexible workers. In the traditional operating environment, workers are practically chained to their workstation, whether its a machine or a desk. Shackled partly by their own fear of moving about—it's risky! Jobs are normally so poorly defined that moving around could set a person up for failure. Or forbidden to move by supervisors whose processes would collapse if unskilled workers were allowed to move about freely in the process. (Sally had hated this part of the traditional operating environment—moving around really made things interesting.)

Outdated rules. Rules are designed to control, and mostly, it seems, to tell people what they *cannot* do. Companies have exhausted countless resources developing volumes of rule books, only to then require additional resources to maintain and enforce the rules. Often the rules were put in place to address a problem caused by a percent or two of the workforce. The other 98 percent were not exhibiting the problem, nor were they so inclined. Yet, to control this minority, the rules were put in place.

Once in place, rules seem to take on a life of their own. People laugh at the stories in the newspaper about an obscure rule, still part of the law of a modern state, that forbids the slicing of whole wheat bread on Saturdays. But company rule books and policy manuals are full of equally inappropriate rules.

Competition for resources. Because the traditional operating environment is to some extent the result of either poor direction or direction by default, the people who work there are in a constant battle for resources critical to their survival. Battles royal take place regularly, because without the prioritization inherent in a sound strategic direction, it's "every man for himself" and "the devil take the hindmost."

A soft approach to the people side of the business. The importance of the people side of the business—its importance to the success of the business is neither acknowledged by the company nor felt by its employees. People issues suffer from poor focus, lack of alignment, fragmentation, and little systematization or process. Because it is people who make change happen, and who bear the brunt of change, a soft approach to the people side of the business virtually guarantees that change and improvement will not take place.

Poor Sally! We started her out in the traditional operating environment, gave her a taste of the environment of the High Performance Enterprise, and now we've made her go back and observe the traditional. Her observations paint a pretty bleak picture. If most companies still have a mostly traditional operating environment, is this picture what it's like in those companies? Is it as bleak as we've painted it? It probably doesn't seem as bleak, because it is the place where most people have worked for most of their lives. They've learned to cope with the idiosyncrasies of the traditional operating environment.

But, you can be sure that the bleakness was obvious to Sally— bleakness made obvious by its contrast with the high performance operating environment where she has spent the last couple of years. Less obvious, but also made apparent to Sally by the same contrast, was a saddening fact: her old traditional company would not be a survivor in the war against the High Performance Enterprises, and neither would her friends, its employees.

In stark contrast to the traditional company, the operating environment at the High Performance Enterprise is alive with promise, energized by a vision of what can be, and actively working toward a future far different from Sally's old company.

Though this is not a new promise—it's the same promise from the '80s—it is a promise so rich in its rewards to the company and the employee that it is a promise worth continued effort. Companies have learned, however, that it is not a promise to be taken lightly, nor is it one for which companies can expect instant, magical fulfillment.

THE NEW WORK COVENANT

How does a company begin to define its unique high performance operating environment? For most companies, the process begins back when the leadership of the company makes a commitment to an empowered context, and creates a vision of the company as High Performance Enterprise. What's left is to build on these components and to formally define the high performance operating environment as a new work covenant between the *company* and its *employees and managers*. This is the work of a Leadership Team.

The High Performance Operating Environment
Key Elements of the New Work Covenant

- *Performance counts*—it is a performance-driven environment.
- The context for performance is *empowerment*.
- There is a *focus on the customer*—external and internal.
- A unified *sense of purpose* provides direction and a focus for p·e·r·f·o·r·m·a·n·c·e·s.
- There is a high level of *involvement*, and, therefore, *ownership*.
- There is a sense of *shared responsibility*.
- The hierarchical *structure is flatter.*
- Workers and managers are *skilled* and *flexible.*
- Organizations and activities are *team-based.*
- *Success* for individuals, teams, and the company is a *corporate mandate.*
- It's a fun place to work!

Why a new work covenant? The High Performance Enterprise demands a shift from the entitlement mind-set to a new expectation mind-set—a mind-set that expects performance from every person in the company. Moving to an expectation mind-set is such a radical shift that a new two-way working relationship between the company and its people is required. The key elements of this new work covenant define the high performance operating environment:

- *Performance counts*—it is a performance-driven environment. "Welcome to the High *Performance* Enterprise! 'Performance' is our middle name, and the attribute that differentiates us from ordinary companies. If you work here, you can expect to be given the skills, tools, and the opportunity to perform. Your performance counts! Performance is important because, as the saying goes, 'Lead, follow, or get the hell out of the way.' We *lead*, and to ensure that we continue to do so, *High Performance* is our first name. Our last name is *Enterprise*. We, the people, are the Enterprise . . . we are the business. We don't just make things or provide services. We are an economic entity that makes a contribution to our world: to our customers, to our stake-holders, and to us, the employees of this Enterprise. *We* are the High Performance Enterprise!!"

For the High Performance Enterprise, there is no such thing as a laissez-faire approach to performance. Performance is not a sometimes/maybe kind of thing. The comfortable, good ol' days of the *entitlement mind-set* must give way to a new *expectation mind-set*—a mind-set characterized by a heightened level of insistence on *performance*, and a persistence in seeking *improved* performance. Managers and employees alike will feel an unrelenting pressure for performance. But this is only one side of the new work covenant between the company and its people.

- *The context for performance is empowerment*. This is the other half of the new work covenant. Performance counts—but the context for performance must be empowerment. An insistence on perfor-mance, and a persistence in seeking improved performance become reasonable and productive only when there is:

- Trust.
- Shared information and education.
- Clear roles and accountabilities.
- Skills training.

- Feedback.
- Reinforcement.
- Freedom to act.
- Resources.

· These are the eight attributes of the empowered context. The new work covenant is an expression of the expectation mind-set. The new work covenant establishes an expectation of performance, in response to an expectation of empowerment. Empowerment is part of the "glue" that binds the thousands of p·e·r·f·o·r·-m·a·n·c·e·s into *performance*.

· *There is a focus on the customer—external and internal.* Customers are anyone impacted by a company's processes or products.[1] This may be "customers" in the classic *external* sense, or those *internal* to the company impacted downstream by upstream processes or "products."

Listening to "the voice of the customer" ensures that the quality of a company's products and services is defined by the customer. The concept of internal customer is not merely a clever way of thinking about the impact of one employee's products or services on another's. It is a fundamental operating principle of the High Performance Enterprise. It is to be observed internally at every level of the company, because it ultimately ensures that all the company's p·e·r·f·o·r·m·a·n·c·e·s are focused, aligned, and integrated to satisfy *external* customers.

· *A unified sense of purpose provides direction and a focus for p·e·r·f·o·r·m·a·n·c·e·s.* There is a network of linkages among the company's business objectives, its initiatives, and the daily work of people at every level. It provides a focus for the thousands of activities, decisions, and transactions taking place every day.

· *There is a high level of involvement, and, therefore, ownership.* Because those who p·e·r·f·o·r·m are truly empowered, they are able to significantly increase *their* influence and impact over what they do. This leads to a natural sense of responsibility and ownership for "their" products and processes. And to a special ownership in which employees at all levels take responsibility for their actions, and choose not to be victims.

· *The sense of shared responsibility permits a flatter hierarchical structure.* It is impossible for a handful of managers and supervisors to effectively manage p·e·r·f·o·r·m·a·n·c·e·s. However, it is only when those who p·e·r·f·o·r·m share this responsibility can effective "management" take place, freeing up the fewer managers and supervisors to "coach" their teams to higher performance and to persist in seeking improved performance.

· *Workers and managers are skilled and flexible.* Flexible, skilled people at every level expand the options available to a company across a broad range of activities, decisions, and transactions. The free movement of skilled workers is the foundation of the agile High Performance Enterprise.

· *Organizations and activities are team-based. Teams* of people outperform *groups* of people. In the High Performance Enterprise, teams with defined purposes, scopes, and boundaries will consistently outperform the ragtag work groups and departments of the traditional company. Teams operate with the focus, alignment, integration, and system required to reinvent the people side of the business.

· *Success for individuals, teams, and the company is a corporate mandate.* What will motivate the high performance operating environment? Success! And not just success viewed as a result, but also success as a process, because much of a person's daily success comes from the "doing" of what they do, rather than the "did" of it. Working in a job for which you are well trained, following defined processes with quality built in, and having the opportunity to improve the work you do—that makes for a successful and rewarding day. The new work covenant with its focus on the two-way street of performance and empowerment is also a focus on success—success for the individual, the team, and the company.

· *It's a fun place to work!* Helen Keller said, "Life is a grand adventure, or it is nothing." Grand adventures are always fun. Perhaps not all *parts* of them—getting eaten by crocodiles or chased by tigers. But in the newness of things, the sense of teamwork, and the knowledge that you conquered something difficult—those parts *are* fun. Working at the High Performance Enterprise will certainly be a grand adventure after working in the traditional operating environment. And it should be fun because the dark, personally stultifying aspects of the traditional environment will be lifted. There will be opportunity to make a personal contribution, and be personally successful.

Fun or not, there is a nagging question about this issue. If the high performance operating environment is such a great place to work, and its performance is so great, why isn't every company jumping at the chance to make the change? Practically nobody says, "Don't change!" In fact, most business leaders say, "Boy, do we need to change!" So, for most people, it's not a question of whether or not to change to a high performance environment. The real question is: How does a company change if it wants to? *Most companies simply don't know how to make the change*—they don't know where to begin, and they don't know where to go from there.

Second question. How does a company make the change to a high performance operating environment? In general, the reason companies don't change is because they don't know *how* to change— they don't have a process to follow to make significant change, much less make the change gracefully.

When asked "where to begin," Winnie the Pooh had the best answer: "Why, you begin at the beginning!" For most companies, that means beginning at the same Strategic Process followed by our Leadership Team. It means they must begin by acknowledging and identifying the drivers of change, and responding to them with a commitment to an empowered context, and a vision and mission for a renewed company—the High Performance Enterprise. Then, after translating vision into action through strategic success factors and business objectives, the company selects initiatives as a framework for action. And, finally, from a new expectation mind-set the company defines its high performance operating environment—the environment in which initiatives will be undertaken, and the success factors and business objectives achieved. The final task of the Leadership Team is to define their *unique* version of the high performance operating environment, and to document it for future use in the company, specifically for use in the 10-Step Process.

Where does the company go from here, to move from the *perfor-*

mance level to that of p·e·r·f·o·r·m·a·n·c·e·s? What does the high performance operating environment look like at the level of daily activity? What does it look like in Marketing, in Manufacturing, or in Product Development?

There is a tactical level process that can be used for each of the different areas of the company, for Marketing, Manufacturing, Product Development, and the people side of the company. . . . The process is the same for all areas in all companies, but the resulting designs and developments will differ—they will be "organic" to both the functional area and particular company. Why? Because the process is designed to focus, align, and integrate the p·e·r·f·o·r·m·a·n·c·e·s of the company with *that* company's particular business objectives and its unique high performance operating environment.

We will not address *all* functional areas of the company in this book, but we will address that part of the company that brings success or failure to the rest of the company. Our focus is on reinventing the people side of the business through a process called the High P·e·r·f·o·r·m·a·n·c·e·s People Systems Process—a 10-Step Process for reinventing the people side of the business.

Reference:

1. *Juran on Planning for Quality*, J. M. Juran (New York: The Free Press/ Macmillan Publishing, 1988).

Section II

REINVENTING THE PEOPLE SIDE OF YOUR BUSINESS

In Section II, our intent is to take you step-by-step through the 10-Step High P·e·r·f·o·r·m·a·n·c·e·s People Systems Process. We have balanced the requirement for technical information for the Design Team level with the general readability of the material. The "how-to" nature of the information to be covered dictates the following format for each chapter:

- Overview—sets the stage by defining terms and establishing a rationale for the particular step.

- Benefits—discusses the benefits that accompany that particular component of the people systems.

- Process—the meat of every chapter covering the 10-Step process. Here step-by-step instructions are given to guide a Design Team for a High P·e·r·f·o·r·m·a·n·c·e·s People Systems project through the completion of each Process Step. Within each Step, we point out potential problems and helpful hints. At the end of each Process step, there is a synopsis for those who are not members of a Design Team or steering committee but want a quick overview of the step.

· Wrap-up—each chapter ends with a brief wrap-up that includes a list of results obtained when completing that step. The wrap-up also includes ancillary information not necessarily part of the step-by-step process.

There are 10 major Process Steps covered in section II. Within each are "substeps" referred to in the book as "Action Steps."

This 10-Step Process is a structured but "open" process. It may be applied to product and service companies alike—union and non-union—and across blue-collar, white-collar, and professional organizations. Most examples come from the manufacturing sector.

CHAPTER 6

Reinventing the People Side of Your Business

. . . AND THEY LEAPT into the air, wings beating strongly they struggled toward the sky. They were free! Higher and higher they rose, their blood coursed faster, they were consumed with exhilaration. Leaving Daedalus behind, Icarus soared even higher. Then, as he felt the growing warmth of the nearing sun on his face, a strange, ominous sensation crept through the nerves in his arms and exploded in his mind with a shock that literally tore him from the sky—his wings, so perfectly crafted of the finest wax, were melting. And in less than a wing beat or two, he plummeted toward the sea. Daedalus watched in horror. Helpless.

For the most part, mythology covers very well the story of Daedalus and Icarus. It tells of their plan to escape from the Labyrinth; the wings of wax so beautifully made by the master craftsman, Daedelus; and Icarus's ultimate death as the heat from the sun melted the wings of wax, and brought him crashing into the sea.

Not reported in mythology, however, were Daedalus's words as he watched Icarus zoom by—the same words also uttered by more than a few of us as our wings of wax melted and we came crashing to earth: "Oh, well. Back to the drawing board." How many times have *you* heard that expression? Or uttered it yourself? And shared the heartfelt exasperation, and the resigned acceptance, that failure was brought on by a flawed process of invention.

Today, we see companies exasperated with a people side of their business that has kept them from realizing the promise of the '80s. And a growing resigned acceptance of the fact that they themselves are responsible, because they failed to reinvent the people side of their companies to match the requirements of the High Performance Enterprise.

"Reinventing the people side of *your* business" is more than a catchy phrase. It is a mandate for you to pick up where the high-level strategic process left off. It requires your company to move beyond that level, and to bring its efforts down to ground level where the company's daily activities, decisions, and transactions take place— down to the level of p·e·r·f·o·r·m·a·n·c·e·s .

"Reinventing" is not an easy process. For most inventors, the process requires them to scrap some or all of their old ideas completely, and begin anew with a new product definition to guide them. This is okay for inventors working in isolation, because they probably aren't forced to actually use their inventions. Most companies intent on reinventing the people side of their business, however, are faced with the fact that their current "invention" is still in daily use, and will have to be used until the new, *re*-invented model is available. And while an inventor may be able to maintain some distance from the actual use of his inventions, companies are faced with reinventing the people side of their business while being involved in it on a daily basis.

And, by the way, just what *is* the "people side" of the business? And how do you "reinvent" it?

Most effective inventions begin with an accurate product definition, which includes a description of what is desired and how it is to be used. The actual "reinvention" of a company's people side begins when the leadership of that company follows the Strategic Process outlined in the previous section of this book. Within that process, the company establishes a strategic direction and a high performance operating environment, both of which *are* the product definition for the new "invention," i.e., they provide a description of the desired people side of the business, and how it is to be used.

In its broadest sense, the people side of the business is any part of the business where people impact or are impacted by the activities, decisions, and transactions of the company. In a narrower sense, it is *people*, the *work* they do, and the environment in which they operate. In its most narrow sense, it is the Human Resources programs, policies, and practices.

The High P·e·r·f·o·r·m·a·n·c·e·s People Systems Process is a 10-Step Process designed to reinvent the people side of the business in its broadest sense. It is done so by specifically addressing the people side at its most critical point: the work people do and selected Human Resources programs, policies, and practices. Together, these are the backbone of the people side of the business. By concentrating on reinventing the *work* people do and selected Human Resources programs, policies, and practices, the 10-Step Process is your "drawing board" for reinventing the people side of your company.

This 10-Step Process is a *hard* technology approach to the *soft*, people side of the company. The High P·e·r·f·o·r·m·a·n·c·e·s People Systems Process provides:

- *Focus*: on the "backbone" of the people side of the company; on *work* and selected HR programs, policies, and practices.

- *Alignment*: with the company's strategic direction; and with the high performance operating environment of the envisioned company, a High Performance Enterprise.

- *Integration*: step-by-step along the "backbone," and out to the body of initiatives, the framework of action for the strategic direction.

- *System*: through a defined, proven process for reinventing the people side of the company.

OVERVIEW

The 10-Step Process focuses on the "backbone" of the people side of the business: the work people do and selected HR programs, policies, and practices that impact people most directly. The following description will provide a feeling of the flow behind the High P·e·r·f·o·r·m·a·n·c·e·s People Systems Process.

High P·e·r·f·o·r·m·a·n·c·e·s People Systems Process

1. *Create the target and baseline organizational profiles.* Translate the new high performance operating environment and the company's initiatives into meaningful profiles that reflect how the organization will look at the p·e·r·f·o·r·m·a·n·c·e·s level.

2. *Define "flexibility."* Define "flexibility" in real terms—in terms of the free movement of skilled workers necessary to support the needs of the company.

3. *Redesign work: redesign jobs, and define teams.* Use flexibility requirements to move from restrictive, narrow jobs to broader JOBs that promote flexibility; and define teams properly to promote their growth and performance improvement potential.

4. *Define roles and scope of supervision.* Redefine the role and scope of supervision to bring it in line with the new way work will be done in broad JOBs, by individuals working in teams.

5. *Design skills development process.* Design a skills development process to make sure that people are trained and certified in the skills necessary to permit free movement of high-quality workers within the broad JOBs of the team-based workplace.

6. *Design P·e·r·f·o·r·m·a·n·c·e·s Feedback System.* Now link p·e·r·f·o·r·m·a·n·c·e·s back to the quantitative measures of the strategic direction of the company and the observable behaviors required by the high performance operating environment, and provide performance feedback to teams and individuals.

7. *Design NewComp.* Reinforce p·e·r·f·o·r·m·a·n·c·e·s as defined by the first six Process Steps, designing pay and reward programs that link the new design back through the six Process Steps to the company's strategic direction and defined high performance operating environment.

8. *Prepare blueprint, and develop major design components.* Complete the design blueprint; if necessary, complete and docu-

ment the detailed development of Process Steps 3, 5, and 6, based on the framework created in those steps.

9. *Plan for implementation, and implement.* Plan for a *successful* implementation, and then implement.

10. *Monitor, evaluate, and continuously improve.* Finally . . . acknowledge there is no "finally," and build in continuous improvement and renewal.

When these Process Steps are complete, you will have restructured the way work is done and designed a new "People System" according to the requirements placed on you by your company's strategic direction and high performance operating environment. You will have provided focus, alignment, integration, and system to the *soft* side of the business. You will have reinvented the people side of your company.

The Strategic Process provided the product definition for a desired new people side. Now, the High P·e·r·f·o·r·m·a·n·c·e·s People Systems Process provides a 10-Step Process to design, develop, implement, and continuously improve the people side of the company as it is expressed in the company's *"work"* and key HR programs. See figure 6a on the following page.

THE PROCESS IS THE SAME—THE RESULTS DIFFER

Companies of every kind—manufacturing and service, union and nonunion, small and large—all use the High P·e·r·f·o·r·m·a·n·c·e·s People Systems Process. The same 10-Step Process is applied in each company, and in each organization in that company. It is a *defined* process, but it is an "open" process—it provides structure and direction, but it also facilitates the tailoring of a design to the unique features of each organization.

Though the Process Steps are the same for all organizations, the results differ—the results will be "organic" to each particular organi-

Figure 6a
HIGH
P·E·R·F·O·R·M·A·N·C·E·S
PEOPLE SYSTEMS PROCESS

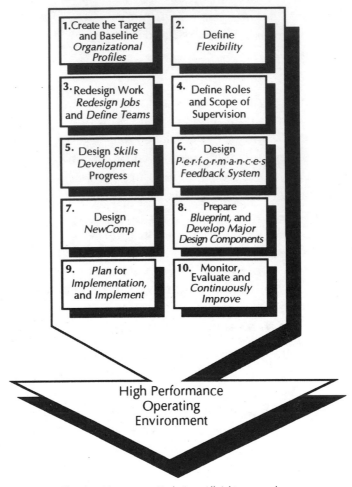

1. Create the Target and Baseline *Organizational Profiles*	**2.** Define *Flexibility*
3. Redesign Work *Redesign Jobs* and *Define Teams*	**4.** Define Roles and Scope of Supervision
5. Design *Skills Development* Progress	**6.** Design *P·e·r·f·o·r·m·a·n·c·e·s Feedback System*
7. Design *NewComp*	**8.** Prepare *Blueprint,* and *Develop Major Design Components*
9. *Plan* for *Implementation,* and *Implement*	**10.** Monitor, Evaluate and *Continuously Improve*

High Performance
Operating
Environment

zation. One telecommunications manufacturer applied the same process to each of four different facilities. Although similar work processes were in place in each factory, each of the resulting People Systems was slightly different. What made them different? Results vary from organization to organization because of . . .

DESIGN VARIABLES

- Differences in the nature of work;

- Whether the design is in a white-collar or blue-collar organization;

- The organization's existing or desired operating environments;

- The initiatives selected by the organization;

- Whether it is a union or nonunion environment;

- The functional area of the company involved in the design;

- And the country in which the company operates.

The last three differences on this list warrant a comment. First, a few of the detailed differences in a union environment:

- A difference between union and nonunion environments is the emphasis on performance management. Generally, there is not even a traditional performance appraisal in the unionized environment, whereas the nonunion environment is more likely to have something (as ineffective as it may be). This does not mean that the performance feedback should be omitted from the 10-Step Process in a unionized environment. It can be used, but perhaps not linked directly to pay.
- Because there is often less flexibility in changing the base pay system in a union environment, alternative base pay approaches may be limited. Conversely, in a union environment, there may be more opportunities for performance-based reward programs such as goal sharing or gainsharing.
- Successful design and implementation of new People Systems in unionized companies have occurred because union leadership and company management agreed to take the design process *outside* the collective bargaining process. The change to a more neutral venue reinforces an alliance between the union and management to jointly create a "win/win" design. The 10-Step Process works especially well

in a union environment when a joint union/management design team is formed around shared information, a desire for mutual trust, and a commitment to an empowered operating environment.

   Though differences in design may result from whether or not the company is union or nonunion, the same differences can also show up between two nonunion shops. And in some union environments, because union leadership is acutely aware of the impact of the drivers of change on the employment of their membership, the union becomes a powerful change agent, and provides surprising and impressive leadership for reinventing the people side of the business.

   Next is the issue of differences that arise because of the functional area of the company in which the 10-Step Process is being used. For this book, we illustrate the process with manufacturing examples, because that is where most companies start. However, the logic applies across *all* functional areas of the organization. Follow the logic from profiling the strategic direction and high performance operating environment in the function; to redesigning the way work is done in broader JOBs by skilled workers with increased flexibility; to the relationship between performance and "new" compensation; and finally a commitment to continuous improvement and renewal. The High P·e·r·f·o·r·m·a·n·c·e·s People Systems Process works in Sales, Marketing, Engineering, and Finance. The process is the same; the results differ.

   The differences among designs done in different countries are caused by different labor laws, cultures, and indirect compensation such as health care, time off, and the like. These do not cause fundamental differences in the resulting design. The "open" process nature of the High P·e·r·f·o·r·m·a·n·c·e·s People Systems Process facilitates incorporating each country's unique laws and culture into the design. The 10-Step Process was designed for the company that wants to become world-class—wants to become a High Performance Enterprise. The globalization of competition gives companies in different countries more similarity of "situation" than it does difference.

GETTING STARTED

Getting started involves three major elements:

- A *readiness assessment* to determine the state of the organization and its people, and their preparedness to begin such a project.

- A *formal managed project approach* is required because of the magnitude of a PeopleSystems project. Such an approach consists of a formal project management structure; defining the objectives, scope, schedule, and resources required to complete the project; and a means to track progress.

- *Education* for the entire project staff.

READINESS ASSESSMENT

It is best to conduct a readiness assessment before beginning a project of this magnitude. The High P•e•r•f•o•r•m•a•n•c•e•s People Systems Process will reach into many sensitive corners of the organization. The more you know in advance, the better prepared you will be and the better the design you will produce. A useful assessment should include:

- An evaluation of the state of management's development of:
  - The case for change; a mission and vision for the company;
  - Identified success factors and business objectives;
  - Initiatives selected;
  - The degree of definition of the desired high performance operating environment;
  - And an evaluation of how well this has been communicated to the different levels of the organization.

- Observations of inconsistencies, obstacles, and potential conflicts with the organizational activities and systems of the current operating environment, and with the planned mission/vision package and the desired high performance operating environment.

- A brief assessment of employee and supervisor/manager attitudes and morale.

- Review of the major components of the existing Human Resource programs with an eye toward their ability to support the planned strategic direction of the company and its desired high performance operating environment.

- A recommendation for an overall approach is established using the 10-Step Process as a format for action.

A written assessment report should be prepared containing: all *observations;* an *assessment* of the readiness of the organization for the work ahead; and recommendations regarding how best to apply the 10-Step High P·e·r·f·o·r·m·a·n·c·e·s People Systems Process to the organization.

This is an appropriate occasion for outside assistance. In fact, for many companies, this is not a Saturday afternoon, do-it-yourself task. It is frequently more complex and comprehensive than a company can do alone. (Many do not have the expertise, experience, or resources to pull it off alone.) And an arm's-length assessment by outside practitioners skilled in the use of the High P·e·r·f·o·r·m·a·n·c·e·s People Systems Process provides a more objective assessment than one completed by in-house personnel.

FORMAL PROJECT MANAGEMENT

A typical project structure will consist of several teams or task forces, each serving a different role. This type of project includes Steering Committee, Design Team, and Project Task Teams (to work on specific tasks or to plan for implementation). We'll examine each of these, explore objectives for the project, and develop the concepts of scope, schedule, and resources for the project.

Steering Committee

Steering Committee members often remark at the conclusion of the project, "We had no idea of the amount of work, and the detail it took to do this thing right, but we now see that had we *not* done it this way, we'd have done it wrong!" For most of them, the process provided insight (not previously available) into the people side of the company—insight that helped ensure the success of other major projects, too. The Steering Committee's efforts are critical in ensuring alignment and integration with the business strategy, and in "steering" the Design Team through organizational politics.

Role The Steering Committee provides leadership—direction and context—for the High P·e·r·f·o·r·m·a·n·c·e·s People Systems Process. The committee establishes an "umbrella framework" within which the design and implementation teams operate.

Membership Membership of the Steering Committee should include top management of the organization involved in the project, as well as key corporate-level managers who are part of the decision-making process. In a union environment, the steering committee can include representatives of the union leadership. Steering Committee members, in addition to their position in the company and its decision-making process, should have a stake in the future of the design.

Responsibilities

- Establish and document the business context for the project, for their own use, and as the basis for educating the Design Team. Include as reference such things as:
  - The case for change, supported by enough detail to provide an accurate context and a sense of urgency;
  - Mission and vision statements (reviewed and enhanced, if already developed);

- · Documented strategic success factors and measurable business objectives;
- · Major initiatives for quality, cycle-time reduction, work cells, etc.;
- · The definition of the desired high performance operating environment.

- · Establish a "charter" for the design team that sets forth major objectives, including the project parameters of scope, schedule, and resources.

- · Periodically review and guide the work of the Design Team, particularly at major milestones of the project, or at points in the project where a go/no-go decision is required.

- · Define the "empowerment" of the Design Team—what can they do, what decision-making authority do they have, and when must they defer to the Steering Committee (this provides the Design Team's "bounded" freedom to act).

- · Remove organizational obstacles from the path of the Design Team.

- · Work with other senior-level managers to ensure consistency and alignment in goals and objectives with other organizational initiatives.

- · Grant final approval on design blueprint.

- · Participate when appropriate in communication and education activities.

The state of readiness of the Steering Committee, and the company in general, will dictate how the committee carries out its responsibilities. For Steering Committees just beginning the journey to becoming a High Performance Enterprise, their first responsibility might be to define the case for change and the elements of the mission/vision package. Some committees educate themselves before educating the Design Team. Other Steering Committees make education a joint activity with the Design Team.

In their charter to the Design Team, the Steering Committee will spell out the suggested scope, schedule, and resources for the People Systems project. Among the Design Team's early responsibilities will be to assess the appropriateness and accuracy of the suggested scope, schedule, and resources based on their work in Process Step 1 of the 10-Step Process. Once they have a handle on this, the Design Team will report back to the Steering Committee, either accepting these as suggested, or recommending modifications based on their assessment. (This will be part of a formal Migration Strategy package developed in Process Step 1, and presented to the Steering Committee as the first go/no-go decision point for the project.)

Design Team

"This has been one of the hardest but most rewarding challenges of my career. I never dreamed we would tackle all the issues we did— and that management would listen to our recommendations." This quote from a Design Team member, as the seven-month design process wound to a close, illustrates the growth potential to team members assigned to the project, as well as the degree of hard work and effort involved.

Role   The Design Team responds to the charter presented to them by the Steering Committee. The charter will establish *scope* (to "reinvent the people side of the company" by addressing the work people do and selected HR programs, policies, and practices); *schedule* (to get the job done in a specified time frame, perhaps linked to the timing of a specified future event); and *resources* (including the Design Team itself, and other resources available to the team, both inside and outside the company).

Membership   This is a cross-functional, multilevel team usually comprised of middle managers, first-line supervisors, employees, Human Resources staff, and other technical staff as appropriate (Quality, Finance, Technical Support, Materials, etc.). In a union environment, the Design Team must include members of the union leadership and employees from the bargaining unit. NOTE: Always put your *best* people on the Design Team. The better the design, the better the results, the smoother the implementation.

Responsibilities

- Fulfill the charter presented by the Steering Committee.

- Educate themselves on the case for change; the mission/vision package; on the work of the people and the selected HR programs, policies, and practices; and on the details of the 10-Step Process.

- Follow the design process established by the 10-Step High P·e·r·f·o·r·m·a·n·c·e·s People Systems Process.

- Report regularly to the Steering Committee to confirm incremental direction and progress of the project, and specifically when go/no-go decisions are required by the Steering Committee in their charter to the Design Team. (The first major go/no-go will occur when the Design Team has completed Process Step 1, and returns to the Steering Committee with the Migration Strategy for the People Systems project.)

Leadership   Clear, effective leadership is essential for the Design Team. The ideal team leader should be organizationally astute, and respected by top management, peers, and employees, in general. The team leader must be able to keep the Design Team focused and calibrated. Most often, the team leader comes from the operations side of the business, not Human Resources. Occasionally, Operations and Human Resources will co-lead the project. When a union is involved, a union member usually co-leads with a management member.

Depending upon the scope of this project, the team leader position may be part-time or full-time. If full-time, the team leader will be placed on temporary assignment to manage the project. An outside facilitator with extensive hands-on experience with the 10-Step Process can assist the team leader in expediting the process and avoiding the usual traps and pitfalls.

Practical Guideline

The High P·e·r·f·o·r·m·a·n·c·e·s People Systems Process is the responsibility of "operational" management, not Human Resources. "Operations" cannot dump this responsibility on HR. "Operations" is the user of the People Systems created by this process. HR provides guidance, and has administrative and technical responsibility.

Project Task Teams

Role   At various times during the People Systems project, the Design Team will augment its efforts by creating Project Task Teams to take on specific assignments. Task Teams are used most often during the *development* and *implementation* stages of the project (Process Steps 8 through 9). These teams collect data or develop the detailed documentation for a particular segment of the design. For example, Project Task Teams develop skills training and certification documentation, or collect departmental data on specific performance *sub*factor measures to support major performance factors selected by the Design Team. Task Teams also work on planning and executing the implementation, including developing a communication strategy, ensuring documentation is in order, revising policies and procedures, etc.

Membership   Project Task Team membership will vary depending on the nature and size of the organization. There may be multiple Teams representing different departments or facilities. Each team of employees, supervisors, and managers and their Task Team leader will be accountable to the Design Team for successfully developing, planning, or implementing, as the case might be.

Project Task Teams are an excellent opportunity to increase the involvement of employees, supervisors, and managers in the 10-Step Process, and broaden the contribution and "ownership" for the project. These teams also keep the Design Team from "getting in over their heads" in the technical aspects of jobs, skills, and compensation.

Practical Guideline

A Design Team member or two on each of the Project Task Teams serving as facilitator or coach is a good way to maintain continuity and direction.

Responsibilities   Project Task Teams respond to the direction of the Design Team in contributing to the development, planning, or implementation of specific aspects of the 10-Step Process, especially those Process Steps associated with jobs, skills, performance, and compensation. They are responsible for completing their specific "tasks," and for maintaining the integrity of the design by adhering to the design blueprint.

Objectives

The Steering Committee begins its development of the Design Team's charter by establishing specific "objectives" for the team to accomplish. Such objectives might highlight elements of the high performance operating environment that the Steering Committee deems essential. Or objectives might specify that the new people systems design must increase the flexibility of the workforce to support specific world-class initiatives. In general, the Steering Committee spells out objectives for the design that will directly support the business objectives such as improved quality, reduced costs, and reduced cycle time. These objectives complement and place emphasis on the broader range of the project as expressed in the project's scope.

Scope

"Scope" is the range or extent of a project. Generally, the scope of a People Systems project is a function of: the structure provided by the 10-Step People Systems Process; the size, complexity, and nature of work of the organization for which a People Systems project is planned; and the state of development of the company's strategic direction and the definition of its high performance operating environment.

Rules for Scope, Schedule, and Resources

Rule 1: You may anchor any two of these, and the third becomes a dependent variable, i.e., its "value" will be determined by the other two.

Rule 2: If you anchor one of these, the other two must vary accordingly.

Rule 3: If you unrealistically anchor all three, you need to check your sense of reality.

The 10-Step Process is not a pick-and-choose, mix-and-match, kind of process. Each Process Step builds one on the other—a relationship that creates the focus, alignment, and integration necessary to reinvent the people side of the company. Skipping Process Steps or Action Steps does not save time—it weakens the focus, alignment, and integration of the design.

This said, however, you will see as we get into the details of the 10-Step Process, the total time of the design phase may be shortened. There are ways to enhance the concurrency of the process, and points at which the development of specific design issues may be time-phased to accommodate the needs of your company.

Schedule

From an overall schedule viewpoint, there are four major stages in a People Systems project: design, development, implementation, and continuous improvement. The design stage is often the most time-consuming and is the responsibility of the Design Team. The Design Team is involved in the development stage, but generally off-loads the bulk of development to Project Task Teams. The implementation stage is usually a combined effort of the Steering Committee, Design Team, and Project Task Teams. Finally, the continuous improvement stage is ongoing, and becomes the responsibility of a Continuous Improvement Committee established by the Design Team as it plans for implementation.

In a practical sense, the time spent on this type of project "depends." Schedule may be fixed, for instance, to coincide with the required roll-out of a specific program. With the schedule therefore fixed, meeting the schedule will "depend" on scope and resources. If the scope is also fixed, then the company must provide the resources necessary to meet the schedule, or the fixed (?) schedule will inevitably slip. If the schedule is not "fixed," then it may vary according to the scope of the project and the availability of resources. In this case, the scope and resources will determine the schedule.

At first glance, this sounds complicated. However, scope, schedule, and resources are tied together in a simple mathematical relationship that far too many companies ignore. They fail in projects such as this because early in the project, top management "fixes" the schedule, and also unrealistically fixes both the scope of the project and the availability of resources. It simply won't work!

A *proactive approach* at scheduling is helpful. Look out into the calendar ahead. Is there a pay increase coming up, a bargaining session with the union, or a strategic initiative such as TQM, JIT, work cells, or self-directed teams to be implemented? If so, get started early enough to allow for time to design, develop, and implement the new People Systems.

Figure 6b
HIGH P·E·R·F·O·R·M·A·N·C·E·S
PEOPLE SYSTEMS PROCESS

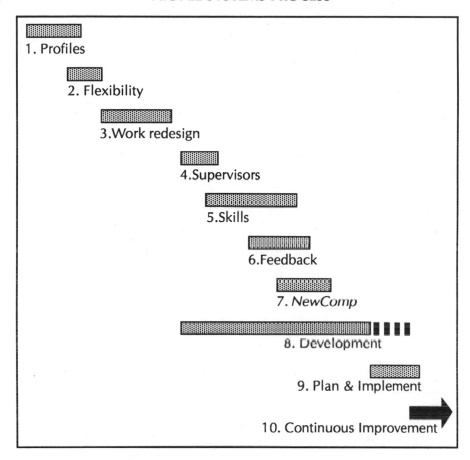

1. Profiles

2. Flexibility

3.Work redesign

4.Supervisors

5.Skills

6.Feedback

7. *NewComp*

8. Development

9. Plan & Implement

10. Continuous Improvement

As a rule of thumb, for companies who pretty much have the front-end strategic direction completed, and at least a fair picture of the desired high performance environment, and commit a reasonably dedicated Design Team plus occasional help from external resources, the High P·e·r·f·o·r·m·a·n·c·e·s People Systems Process will take from 9 to 18 months. Some parts of the system may be time-phased later, in order to make others available earlier.

Resources

Always put your best people on this project. Your goal is to accomplish nothing less than reinventing the people side of your company. It doesn't make sense to put people on the project whose only qualification is that they are "available." The best people are always the busiest, but they also produce the best designs in less time.

Because you will want your best people on the project, resources will be the toughest hurdle to overcome. Here are the kinds of resource issues you will face in completing the High P·e·r·f·o·r-·m·a·n·c·e·s People Systems Process:

Internal resources

- The time spent by Operations, specialists from functional areas and HR management and staff;
- The time spent by Design Team members to concentrate on the design and to have the soak time essential for a good design;
- Time and money for Design Team training;
- The availability within the company of people with appropriate skills and experience;
- Time and money for skills training development of employees once the design blueprint is complete.

External resources

- Finding consultants with hands-on experience to facilitate the design process, and help guide and focus the Design Team's efforts.

A special note to small to mid-sized companies. If you are in a small to mid-sized company, you are probably already thinking, "How do we go about a project of this magnitude with our limited resources?"

Companies like yours *are* doing this with limited resources. They use a modified-Marine approach: "Just a few good men and women!" (Five to eight people, minimum.) But because your resources are "fixed," scope and schedule must then vary.

The scope of the High P·e·r·f·o·r·m·a·n·c·e·s People Systems Process is essentially the same for companies large and small, and the actual design *effort* is similar for companies of all sizes. Complexity and number of skills can increase development effort. For openers, though, small to mid-sized companies still must commit to the *initial* design effort. However, here are a few ways to get the job done with your limited resources (not all of these ways will make complete sense until you have gone through the details of the 10-Step Process):

- Complete the design phase. That's a fundamental priority.

- Your Design Team should complete what development work it can, along with the design, while they are actively involved and information is still fresh.

- Focus on completing the development and implementation of the basic People Systems components that impact the way people work: flexibility, broad JOBs, defined teams, and new roles for supervision.

- Then, complete the development and implementation of the balance of the remaining components on a prioritized, time-phased basis.

- Get outside help. No one can actually *do* the design but you and your company. Qualified consultants can help with valid short-cuts, and advice regarding traps and pitfalls.

A $60 million furniture manufacturer has formed a Design Team of four managers (including a vice-president and the HR manager), one supervisor, and three hourly employees. They meet every Monday and for two or more hours. Their schedule for completion is longer than they'd like— ± 12 months—but it's the realistic time line they can meet given the time and people they have to devote to the project.

This Design Team has committed to periodic outside assistance, but as the vice-president on the Design Team says, "No one else can do this for you. We have to do it! It's not something we can delegate or hire out." No one—no person, no giant consulting firm—has available a canned program to deliver superior People Systems. As the HR manager says, "The 10-Step Process offers a structured approach to dealing with the complex people issues, rather than just jumping in."

If you are with a large company, all of the above comments for the smaller companies apply just as well to you and your organization. The rules that govern the relationship among scope, schedule, and resources apply to all companies equally . . . and, today, *no* company has unlimited resources.

Practical Guidelines

· The success of each step depends on input from the previous step. There is a building-block sequence. Follow it.

· The People Systems project should be structured as a *joint project* between "operations" or the "function" and the Human Resources Department.

· Curb the bias for action and disdain for detail. The design work is the majority of the process. The more detailed the thinking on each Process Step, the more sound the design.

· Set aside the initial concerns and issues about workforce acceptance and reaction. Make a list of these as the design progresses. Use the list at the point of implementation planning. You will then discover that the design has provided many of the answers to these concerns.

· Communicate the plan to the organization. Educate them on the 10 Steps of the process and how it is linked to the company's strategic framework. Keep the organization updated on progress through the 10 Steps.

· Inject plenty of humor and occasional celebrations into the process. Consider the process a positive learning opportunity for all involved and recognize the learning.

Project Tracking

Formal project management requires formal project tracking. There are numerous project management software programs on the market to assist you with organizing and managing the project. However, many companies do a satisfactory job with a simple project book in which they hold documentation of the design, minutes of their meetings, an actively maintained Gantt chart, and an ongoing, unfolding blueprint of the design.

EDUCATION

Most companies are not prepared to "reinvent" the people side of their business. Educating those involved in the process is a critical step, especially when the company seeks to involve people heretofore completely disregarded.

At this point, you probably think we are speaking of line workers or clerks when we reference "people heretofore completely disregarded." Not so. In an amazing number of companies, only top-top management *really* knows what's going on in the company's "world." Only *they* know the extent of competitive intrusion, the impact of too-long cycle-times on the company's bottom line, and who the customers really are and what they think of the company and its products and services.

Two kinds of education are required to ensure the success of the 10-Step Process: education about the company, and education on the 10-Step Process. The participants should include at least the Steering Committee and the Design Team. The curriculum is determined by the results of the readiness assessment. Delivery and facilitation of the training are handled by a combination of internal and external resources. (NOTE: Sometimes the readiness assessment points out that the company needs to do more homework on its strategic direction and definition of its high performance operating environment before education takes place.)

Those companies who invest in the up-front education of the

Steering Committee and Design Team stay more focused on the critical issues, progress more quickly through the process, *and* operate more independently than those companies that begin the 10-Step Process without the benefit of education.

COMMUNICATING THE CASE FOR CHANGE

Setting up a major project, and pulling some of your best people away from work, is going to generate interest and rumors within the organization—especially when people learn the People Systems project has something to do with jobs and compensation. From the beginning, it is critical that an effective communication strategy is developed and followed.

At this point in the process, the top management team has likely already developed and communicated the strategic case for change to key managers. The strategic case for change would have thoroughly explained the real drivers of change and outlined the impact of the drivers if *no* change were made. The strategic case for change was *open-ended*—not all the answers were available at this initial communication. Its focus would have been on developing action plans and "next steps," not on detailed tactical processes and results.

Expanding the communication of the case for change to the general population of the organization is a different proposition. It demands a more closed-ended approach, an approach with less left hanging, and a more positive, more "*real*-istic" appraisal of the consequences of *not* changing. It will be the communication of perhaps the same information, but in a manner to strike at the p·e·r·f·o·r·m·a·n·c·e·s level—to elicit a response to the "What's in it for me?" question, which says, "My future's in it, that's what!"

Mike H. Walsh, the CEO of Tenneco, recently made the following statement about leading major organizational change.

Does all this change make employees feel insecure? Of course. But anybody who recognizes what is going on in this world and isn't somewhat insecure, I would argue, is not awake. And I think the biggest enemy of progress is happy talk. You need to tell your people that if we do not change, and change fundamentally, we are going out of business. And that will create insecurity. The trick is to turn that insecurity into constructive tension. My experience is that people in companies can deal with reality and facts much better than their management gives them credit for. If you talk straight to them, tell them what's required, and tie it together with the rewards, there is an enormous capability well beyond what any of us traditionally believe.[1]

Walsh is right. Managers frequently underestimate their people and the people's ability to comprehend and respond to the plain, unadulterated truth. Sugar-coating the case for change, or mentioning it once a year, is a major disservice to all members of your organization.

The communication of the tactical case for change may be made in conjunction with the roll-out of a High P·e·r·f·o·r·m·a·n·c·e·s People Systems project, or in conjunction with the roll-out of other company initiatives. (If the communication is being made solely in conjunction with the 10-Step Process, it's preferable to wait until the Design Team has completed Process Step 1, and its Migration Strategy.) Figure 6c illustrates a general outline of the flow of information that should be included in the communication: "not only is there a real need for change, but here's *how* we're going about it."

The communication will include the mission, vision, strategic success factors, operational business objectives and major initiatives, of which the High P·e·r·f·o·r·m·a·n·c·e·s People Systems project is one. The purpose of the communication is to create a compelling case for change, to describe the major components of the company's response to the drivers of change, and provide information on the initiatives.

It's critical that this communication truly grab people's attention, concern, and interest. In the analogy of the elephants "chained" to no-longer-existing stakes in the ground by powerful conditioning,

Figure 6c

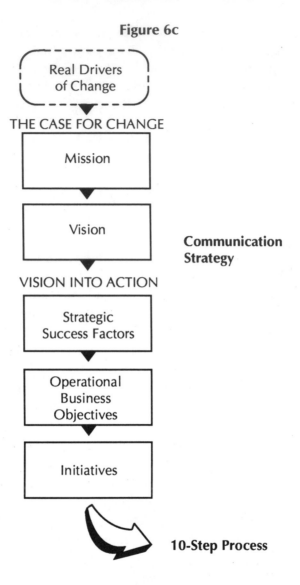

Belasco says the secret to getting companies and their people to change is to "set a fire so your people see the flames with their own eyes and smell the smoke with their own nostrils—without burning the tent down." Sounds a bit radical, but the case for change must serve as smoke and fire for the members of your organization.

Care must be given to ensure the concepts delivered are translated to a meaningful level of understanding and relevance to the general population of the company. Too often, executives try to make the case for change with a barrage of financial data. While the financial situation is relevant to the company's need to change, the impact is frequently lost on the general audience. The terms, calculations, and numbers lack relevance. People cannot relate them to their daily work at the company.

One year, the CEO of a major publishing firm delivered his annual "state of the company" address to an audience of his employees. During the speech, he announced the major goal for the coming year was to "increase ROI." He was so intent on delivering the message that he failed to notice the blank stares. Much to his chagrin, he later found the majority of his employees had no understanding of ROI. His message failed because no compelling case for change was communicated.

The need for communication just begins with communicating the case for change. From that point forward, every opportunity in front of employees is another opportunity to communicate the core information of the case for change, progress on the company's initiatives, and its performance against objectives.

The senior management of a division of a *Fortune* 50 company were incredulous when a readiness assessment indicated their employees were not aware of "the case for change," and as a result were resisting critical new manufacturing initiatives. The general manager continued to probe the data. After all, he remembered communicating the "case for change" nine months before. And, besides, people knew what was going on with the company's markets, because they read the paper, didn't they? What the general manager failed to realize was, though he and his staff lived and breathed the "case for change," hearing the information once a year in a 90-minute presentation didn't have the same impact on his employees. The case for change must be repeatedly communicated to make it a "living, breathing" case for change.

As you explore the 10-Step Process in the chapters ahead, take the case for change for your organization, put it together with your strategic direction and your ideas for a high performance operating environment. Keep these thoughts in the back of your mind. Remember, it's your drawing board. The High P·e·r·f·o·r·m·a·n·c·e·s

People Systems Process provides focus, alignment, integration, and system—it provides the *structure*. You have to provide all the lines, the textures, the colors, the shadings, *and* the central theme. *You* have to reinvent the people side of your company.

Reference:

1. "Leaders of Corporate Change," *Fortune*, December 14, 1992, p. 110

CHAPTER 7

Consuming the 500-Pound Enchilada

Process Step 1: Create the Target and Baseline Organizational Profiles

IMAGINE YOU ARE at the company picnic. The special treat this year is a 500 pound enchilada that the cafeteria folks made the day before. The idea is to consume the enchilada in record-breaking time to warrant an entry into the *Guinness Book of World Records*. As the general manager, you are expected to take the lead in this event. You ponder your approach. Should you organize teams of beefy bodies and assign them to strategic points along the enchilada? Or should you line up individuals on both sides for an all-out attack?

There are other details you hadn't thought of until you are standing there facing this Sequoia-sized log of chili and cheese. How do you instruct people to go about this so they don't ruin their summer picnic clothes? No one thought about "protective clothing." What is the proper, safe utensil to use that will permit warp-speed ingestion of sloppy enchilada material? Do you have enough stomach antacids available for participants when finished? How do you eat a 500-pound enchilada?

*   *   *

For most projects, the difficult period is getting started. Project leaders are feeling their way into their new roles. Questions have arisen to which they do not yet have answers. The size of the project is overwhelming. Team members are becoming acquainted with one another, the norms of behavior are perhaps not yet normal, and new team dynamics get in the way of even basic communications. *And* the project schedule and efficacy can be impacted negatively if the team gets off on the wrong foot.

For the High P·e·r·f·o·r·m·a·n·c·e·s People Systems Design Team, they've barely been chartered and educated on the process they're to use, and they're already faced with a mountain of information to "consume." Here's their 500-pound enchilada:

- A charter to redesign the company's people systems—part of reinventing the people side of the company;

- The mission/vision package;

- A set of goals established by the strategic success factors and operational business objectives;

- A list of the various strategic initiatives to be undertaken by the company;

- The charge that they ensure that the people systems of the company are linked to all these other elements through a network of linkages;

- And an unfamiliar 10-Step Process with which to work.

It's the same for most project teams at this point: the magnitude of the project appears larger than life because its scope and boundaries are not yet fully understood; the process appears overwhelming because it's new; and the schedule appears unrealistic. The question is, "How do you consume a 500-pound enchilada?" The answer is, "One bite at a time."

For the People Systems Design Team, the first bites of their 500-pound enchilada are the "profiles process"—a process that gives them a method to begin nibbling away at the significant task before them.

The organizational profiles set the stage for the remainder of the design process by translating the high-level definition of the high performance operating environment into a detailed picture of what it will look like. The process continues by developing the necessary action items to make the new operating environment a reality, and organizing them into a Migration Strategy to reinvent the people side of the business.

In essence, creating and processing organizational profiles are other techniques for translating vision into action. This time, the "vision" is expressed in an assortment of concepts or documents: the case for change; the defined high performance operating environment; and the specifics of the People Systems redesign spelled out in the charter for the Design Team.

Here is the process for taking the first few bites. Going after the profiles process one section at a time is an easy way to get started:

Profiles Process
Action Steps

1. Create a profile of the organization of the future—the targeted profile The profile defines the detail of how your future high performance operating environment will look.

2. Then create a contrasting profile of the organization of today— the baseline profile. This is your starting point.

3. Perform an analysis of the gap between the two profiles to produce action items that identify both the *item* missing (the gap) and the action (work) required to fill the gap.

4. Assign each action item to a step in the High P·e·r·f·o·r-·m·a·n·c·e·s People Systems Process or to one of three other options.

5. Develop from this information a Migration Strategy—a framework of time-phased action items.

The purpose of the profiles process is threefold: (1) to initiate the tactical-level response to the case for change; (2) to begin the application of a process approach to the people side of the company; and (3) to create a framework for putting vision into action.

Simply put, the benefit of the profiles process is getting started on the right foot—with focus, alignment, integration, and system. Getting started correctly has a powerful impact on finishing correctly. The results of the People Systems design project will be enhanced by the effectiveness of the "hard" process approach of this vision into action translation process.

A business on the East Coast had been struggling to harness the power of the people side of the company. Finally, they elected to use the 10-Step Process. Top management maintained a lackadaisical attitude until they had an opportunity to review the profiles prepared by the Design Team. For the first time, the task ahead became clear and real and its importance evident. Then the Steering Committee and Design Team received the interest and support they needed.

PRELIMINARY WORK

Before creating the profiles, however, there is important preliminary work to be done. As a group, the Design Team should:

- Gather the data, viz., documents such as the case for change; the mission/vision package; input on the high performance operating environment; information on the strategic success factors, operational business objectives, and the strategic initiatives; statements of the company's values and principles; articles and books that support the activities of the Design Team.

- Conduct interviews with key decision makers.

- Analyze the current initiatives and their impact on the organization. For example: reducing cycle or processing time often requires greater worker flexibility. As a result, workers are asked to learn and perform other jobs. Flexibility or a flexible workforce will be a required characteristic in such an environment.

· Explore "best practices" at other companies (benchmark).

· Review the profiles process as presented here, and select the problem-solving tools to be used: will you use the 7 TQC management tools, or an approach such as Kepner-Tregoe, or . . . ?

· Use consistent formats such as those suggested here for recording and presenting the information developed in this Process Step of the 10-Step Process.

· Review the data in light of the profiles process that lies before you—anticipate where and when parts of the data will be useful during the process.

· Affirm two critical issues:

. . . the empowered context: its role in the high performance enterprise, and the requirement that participation in the process on which you are embarking should reflect that context.

. . . and that the redesign process is an opportunity for breakthrough thinking to support the company's desire to become a high performance enterprise . . . this is a time to think the unthinkable!

THE PROFILING PROCESS

1: Create a profile of the organization of the future—the **targeted profile**.

To create the *targeted organizational profile* for your company, you must answer the question "On this date,————, what will be the characteristics of the targeted organizational profile required by our (1) new mission/vision package, (2) by the new high performance operating environment, and (3) to support the initiatives to be implemented?"

The words used in this "profiling question" are important. Asking the wrong question will develop a profile that leads the Design Team away from the focus, alignment, and integration that make the profiles such a useful tool.

In some companies, the targeted date may be predetermined by how the People Systems redesign is aligned and integrated with other initiatives. If at all possible, set the date for a medium-range, rather than long-range, target. A medium range of 18 to 36 months provides for a more rapid implementation of the supporting and reinforcing effects of world-class people systems—a more rapid "reinvention" of the people side of your company.

A medium-range target also places the company's people systems in a more responsive cycle—planning a company's people systems 5 to 10 years in advance does not acknowledge either how fast things are changing or how the rate of change is accelerating. And the medium range emphasizes the requirement for ongoing renewal and continuous improvement of the People Systems.

The "Profiling" Question

"On this date,————, what will be the characteristics of the targeted organizational profile required by our (1) new mission/vision package, (2) by the new high performance operating environment, and (3) to support the initiatives to be implemented?"

With the preliminary work done, and the targeted date decided, it's time to develop a working list of characteristics for the targeted profile. The new operating environment may include existing characteristics that are desirable to retain and nurture in the future. The list will include new characteristics not currently developed in the organization, but which are believed to be imperative to the alignment of the environment and its people with the business strategy.

The strengths of High Performance Enterprises flow from a common set of underlying principles and practices, and one would expect a similarity among characteristics in the targeted profiles of most companies. Typical characteristics are:

- Flexible workforce.

- Team-based environment.

- Customer-focused.

- Continuous improvement.

- Simplified pay and grade structure.

- Employee involvement/empowerment.

- Information sharing.

These examples provide a feel for the breadth and critical nature of the type of characteristics. In selecting the key characteristics for the future, zero in on what counts, what is imperative. Not just what "sounds nice" or is a copycat "me too" characteristic. If teams are really not part of your business strategy, then don't put them in just because a lot of other companies are doing teams. Teams, for the sake of teams, will fail.

After developing a working list, the Design Team should review and discuss each of the proposed characteristics, and reach a consensus on the *key* characteristics of the targeted organization. Keep the list to a manageable six to eight characteristics. The goal is to paint a picture of the future that can be easily understood by people at all levels, but with enough detail to be useful to the Design Team.

Now the fun part. For *each* characteristic, develop brief descriptive statements that will illustrate the characteristic in action in your targeted organization. An effective format for listing the descriptive statements is shown in figure 7a. For example, if the characteristic is "flexible workforce," then the descriptive statements might include:

Figure 7a

ORGANIZATIONAL PROFILES (WORKSHEET)	
CHARACTERISTIC: *Flexible Workforce*	
BASELINE PROFILE	TARGETED PROFILE
	• Flexibility is defined along the work process˙
	• Employees have multiple skills and use them at a number of different positions
	• Employees move easily up and down the process for "their" products

When you've completed one characteristic, move on to each of the other characteristics on your list and repeat the procedure, developing descriptive statements of a similar detail level for each.

2. Create a contrasting profile of the organization of today—the baseline profile.

Your target is in view, but how far away from it are you? One way to find out is to create a contrasting profile of your organization as it is today. This will be a *baseline organizational profile*, and is part of what you need to assess your distance from the target.

The baseline profile process is a customized version of the process for the targeted profile. This time, the Design Team selects one of the targeted characteristics, picks the first descriptive statement for that characteristic, and then asks the question, "If this is how we describe the organization in the future, how does our organization look today for that same descriptive statement?"

Continue with each descriptive statement for each targeted characteristic, until there are corresponding baseline descriptive statements for each. Develop at least one baseline statement for each targeted statement, with a limit of two to three per targeted descriptive statement. If you have more than this, use one of your problem-solving tools to prioritize and reduce the baseline statements to the two to three recommended. For example, for the targeted characteristic of "flexible workforce" and its targeted descriptive statements, a company might establish baseline descriptive statements as shown in figure 7b.

Figure 7b

ORGANIZATIONAL PROFILES (WORKSHEET)	
CHARACTERISTIC: *Flexible Workforce*	
BASELINE PROFILE	TARGETED PROFILE
• Flexibility is not defined— accidental when it does occur • Everything is *functionally* defined	• Flexibility is defined along the work process
• Only utility operators have multiple skills and use them • Cross-training is informal and ad hoc; few opportunities to practice multiple skills	• Employees have multiple skills and use them at a number of different positions
• Employees do the same work day after day • There is no movement unless directed by supervisors	• Employees move easily up and down the process for "their " products
• Most employees are "specialists" • Supervisors are reluctant to move empl~~oyees aro~~und	• Employees are more "generalist" than "specialist"

Suppose for a particular targeted descriptive statement, a company's contrasting baseline comment is "Nothing going on" or "Not a current program"? For all practical purposes, there is a "hole" in your current operating environment. In a sense, this is positive. While the company may have a long way to go, there may be no same-old-way conditionings to slow down the transition.

Once descriptive statements for all of the characteristics of the baseline organizational profile are completed, you will have a comprehensive, contrasting baseline organizational profile. With both profiles in hand, the Design Team will be able to develop an accurate picture of the "distance" between "today" and "tomorrow."

The profile format used so far isolates each of the characteristics individually. A more holistic format (see figure 7c) presents all of the characteristics and descriptive statements for one profile together on a single page. Having both the baseline and targeted organizational profiles available in this format is especially useful as a reference tool for the Design Team, and for when it's necessary to compare the two environments in their totality.

3. Perform an analysis of the gap *between the two profiles to produce action items that identify both what's missing (the gap) and the action (work) required to fill the gap.*

The gap analysis is performed by examining the contrasting descriptive statements from the baseline and targeted profiles and asking the question, "What's missing?" The answer to this question should reveal both the item that's missing and the action required to provide it—in other words, a gap with two qualities:

A. A defined and quantified statement of the items missing between the characteristics of the baseline and targeted profiles:

What process(es) is missing?

What skills are needed?

What information or education is lacking?

What boundaries are absent or wrongly placed?

What resources need to be added?

People? Time? Money? Facilities? Equipment?

Figure 7c

TARGETED ORGANIZATIONAL PROFILE

Customer Satisfaction	Continuous Improvement	Culture	Self-Directed Teams	Flexible Workforce
Quality is defined by the customer and t... custc... satisf view even job	Continuous improvement is an integral	We operate from a shared	Teamwork is second nature	Flexibility is defined along the
Ever empl know exter inter custc and comr freel them Ther a res effec and used custc supp feedl syste All empl unde the relati betw doin job v total custc satisf				

BASELINE ORGANIZATIONAL PROFILE

Customer Satisfaction	Continuous Improvement	Culture	Self-Directed Teams	Flexible Workforce
There exists no concept of internal customer	No standard problem-solving/ continuous improvement tools available or in use at any level of the organization	We have a culture by default, not by design	Employees do what they are told to do–a "high control" environment	A narrow concept of "job"–"that's not my job!"
No notion of how *what I do* affects customer satisfaction	Continuous improvement not reinforced through the performance management process	Internal competition among functional, departmental "silos"	Employees seldom have input into decisions, even on the work they do every day	We have a well-skilled and highly technical workforce whose full potential we do not fully utilize
Only sales talks to the customer	Lots of good ideas, but no process to address them and incorporate them for improvement	Poor linkage between what we want/expect and what we actually measure	Team concept is ill-developed and/or non-existent– "what's in it for me," is the general concern	Cross-training is haphazard, informal, and not of guaranteed quality
Little if any feedback from either the external or internal customer	Fire-fighting is more fun and easier to do than planned fire prevention	Wide gap between what we say and what we really do	Most processes are informal and transmitted by word of mouth	Product and process are sub-optimized because of the narrow job focus and informal process documentation
			All performance measures are oriented to the individual–no incentive to be an effective team member	

B. A rough idea of the actions required to modify, improve, or replace the "missing ingredients" identified.

The answer to the "What's missing?" question then contains both "item" and "action." In other words, the answer to the gap analysis question is an action item—an expression of the work to be done.

There are two major approaches to asking the question, "What's missing?" Use the partial Organizational Profiles Worksheet in figure 7d. The detailed, bottoms-up approach begins with the first set of descriptive statements to be compared and asks "What's missing?" between each of the baseline descriptive statements and its targeted

Figure 7d

ORGANIZATIONAL PROFILES (WORKSHEET)	
CHARACTERISTIC: *Flexible Workforce*	
BASELINE PROFILE	TARGETED PROFILE
• Flexibility is not defined— accidental when it does occur • Everything is *functionally* defined	• Flexibility is defined along the work process
• Only utility operators have multiple skills and use them • Cross-training is informal and ad hoc; few opportunities to practice multiple skills	• Employees have multiple skills and use them at a number of different positions
• Employees do the same work day after day • There is no movement unless directed by supervisors	• Employees move easily up and down the process for "their" products
• Most employees are "specialists" • Supervisors are reluctant to move emp~~l~~ ~~nd~~	• Employees are more "generalist" than "specialist"

counterpart. The answers for each are recorded as an "action item" (as in figure 7e). And so on, until each set of descriptive statements is dealt with one by one, producing a list of action items for that characteristic. The action items shown provide a sense of the level of detail expected. The bottoms-up approach tends to produce a lengthy list, with redundant or overlapping action items. The Design Team will have to sort through the list and group similar or common action items (it is not unusual for one action item to resolve the "What's missing?" for several different descriptive statements).

The *top-down approach* takes a more macro-oriented view. First, the Design Team roughly groups common targeted and baseline descriptive statements for each characteristic, proposes a few *key* action items, and only when those don't bridge the gaps are more detailed action items created. For some, this is a more holistic approach. Working through the statements group by group, this approach will tend to produce fewer action items, but action items with more alignment and integration. The proponents of both ap-

Figure 7e

GAP ANALYSIS . . . ACTION ITEM (WORKSHEET)
CHARACTERISTIC: *Flexible Workforce*
"What's missing" is: Take "*Action*" on this "*Item*"
• Define flexibility as it relates to the movement of employees
• Define major processes and establish and document the boundaries of flexibility to support work along the process
• Identify the new skills required for new job definitions and support by creating a formal skills training program
• Develop a formal skills training and certification program
• Develop and maintain an employee skills inventory for use by supervisors and the team, and the training department

proaches will want to use the problem-solving tools in which they've been trained to facilitate the approach selected.

When the gap analysis is complete, by whatever approach, you will have a list of action items, as in figure 7e, that outlines the differences between the contrasting baseline and targeted organizational profiles—action items that establish a free-flowing, but not yet organized action plan for closing the gap.

4. Assign each action item to a Process Step in the High P·e·r·f·o·r·m·a·n·c·e·s People Systems Process or to one of three other options.

In a typical project, at this point the project team would take the list of action items, and begin the process of creating a project schedule. They would group and organize the items, create additional levels of detail, and establish timing relationships (dependencies).

However, because the focus of this project is on the redesign of a company's People Systems, there is an easier and more straightforward approach. The baseline and targeted organizational profiles were developed from a profiling question focused on the high performance operating environment. Because the purpose of the 10-Step Process is to reinvent the people side of that environment, quite naturally most of the action items would fall under one or more of the Process Steps of the High P·e·r·f·o·r·m·a·n·c·e·s People Systems Process.

So, instead of taking the standard project approach, the Design Team may use the 10-Step Process as a template, and group and organize the action items under the appropriate Process Step. This will provide a much quicker start at organizing the action items, and allow the Design Team to take advantage of the built-in levels of detail and timing relationships incorporated in the 10-Step Process.

If the Design Team takes the action items resulting from the gap analysis of the profile characteristic "flexible workforce" (figure 7e) and assigns the action items to the appropriate Process Steps, here is how those action items fall out:

PROCESS STEP 1. PROFILES

Not applicable. This is the Process Step in use.

PROCESS STEP 2. FLEXIBILITY

- Define flexibility as it relates to the movement of employees.
- Define major processes and establish and document the boundaries of flexibility to support work along the process.

PROCESS STEP 3. REDESIGN WORK

- Identify the new skills required for new job definitions and support by creating a formal skills training program.

PROCESS STEP 4. ROLES AND SCOPE OF SUPERVISION

- Develop and maintain an employee skills inventory for use by supervisors and the team, and the training department.
- Ensure managers and supervisors are committed to cross-training program.
- Clearly define roles for supervisor, assistant supervisor, team member.

PROCESS STEP 5. SKILLS

- Identify the new skills required for new job definitions and support by creating a formal skills training program.
- Develop and maintain an employee skills inventory for use by supervisors and the team and the training department.
- Establish consequences for achieving or not achieving minimum skill requirements.
- Establish rotational training procedure to support cross-training and skill certification and recertification.

PROCESS STEP 6. P·E·R·F·O·R·M·A·N·C·E·S FEEDBACK

- Establish consequences for achieving or not achieving minimum skill requirements.
- Ensure managers and supervisors are committed to cross-training program.

Not surprisingly, most of the action items would be dealt with as part of one or more Process Steps. Of all the action items, only one was not assigned to the 10-Step Process: set cross-training parameters to ensure schedules. This is an item to be handled by supervision and scheduling. This action item lies outside the scope of the 10-Step Process—it is an "outlier." For this outlier item, and others outside the scope of the process, there are at least three options available:

· Expand the scope of the People Systems project to include the specific action item(s);

· Outsource the action item(s) to project teams working on other initiatives;

· Create a new project to address the action item(s).

In such cases, the Design Team should recommend appropriate disposition for the outlier action items at the next presentation to the Steering Committee, or as part of the Migration Strategy.

5. Develop from this information a Migration Strategy—a framework of time-phased action items.

As part of its charter, the Design Team was tasked with presenting to the Steering Committee an overall project plan for the redesign of the company's people systems. The Migration Strategy outlines a medium-term project plan to move the company toward the targeted organizational profile. This project plan, or Migration Strategy, for the company's People Systems design is presented in a format centered on the High P·e·r·f·o·r·m·a·n·c·e·s People Systems Process. The Migration Strategy would include the following elements:

MIGRATION STRATEGY ELEMENTS

· A narrative establishing the Migration Strategy presentation as the first validation review (go/no-go review) for the Design Team. It roughly outlines the scope of the project, and establishes the High P·e·r·f·o·r·m·a·n·c·e·s People Systems Process as the methodology to be followed.

· A Gantt chart and/or PERT chart representation of the project schedule in the format of the 10-Step Process. This would provide the Steering Committee with an idea of major milestones and alert them to dependency and critical path issues.

· An explanation of the resources required (time, money, facilities, and the people both directly and indirectly involved).

· An outline of the project management approach to be followed by the Design Team, including a schedule of routine reviews and planned validation or go/no-go reviews.

· A documentation package including:

  · The case for change;
  · The mission/vision package;
  · An outline of the strategic success factors, operational business objectives, and strategic initiatives to be supported by the new design;
  · The macro-level high performance operating environment;
  · The baseline and targeted organizational profiles;
  · A list of the major action items generated in the gap analysis;
  · A presentation of the action item assignment to the 10-Steps.

· Recommendations regarding the disposition of outlier action items that fell into the categories of scope expansion, outsourcing, and new project creation.

· The recommendation by the Design Team that based on the package presented, the Steering Committee authorize the Design Team to proceed with the project as presented.

A formal Migration Strategy presented in this manner (figure 7f) is a critical tactical element in any company's drive to become a High Performance Enterprise because (1) it outlines a controlled, evolutionary plan for managing the revolutionary change called for by status as a world-class competitor; (2) it provides a focused, aligned,

Figure 7f

MIGRATION STRATEGY PACKAGE

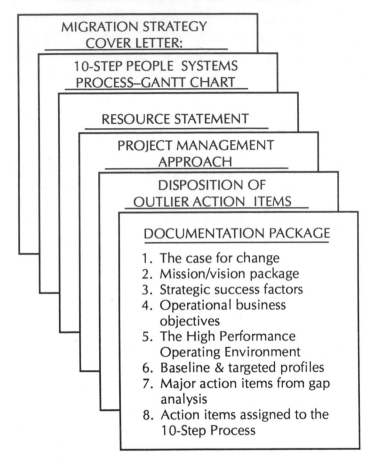

MIGRATION STRATEGY
COVER LETTER:

10-STEP PEOPLE SYSTEMS
PROCESS–GANTT CHART

RESOURCE STATEMENT

PROJECT MANAGEMENT
APPROACH

DISPOSITION OF
OUTLIER ACTION ITEMS

DOCUMENTATION PACKAGE

1. The case for change
2. Mission/vision package
3. Strategic success factors
4. Operational business
   objectives
5. The High Performance
   Operating Environment
6. Baseline & targeted profiles
7. Major action items from gap
   analysis
8. Action items assigned to the
   10-Step Process

integrated, and systematic approach to reinventing the people side of the company; (3) it increases the likelihood of success because it is the result of an appropriate level of productive planning; (4) it establishes a direct line of sight from the action items of the project back to the strategic direction of the company, and its desired high performance operating environment.

The promise of the '80s was unfulfilled because most companies did not have a process with which to address the people side of the business. Not having such a process precluded their creating the

**Synopsis: Process Step 1
Create the Target and Baseline Organizational Profiles**

Objective: Translate your company's vision of a high performance operating environment into an action plan, and create a Migration Strategy to achieve it.

Process: 1. Create a profile of the organization of the future—the targeted profile. The profile defines the detail of how your future high performance operating environment will look.

2. Then create a contrasting profile of the organization of today—the baseline profile. This is your starting point.

3. Perform an analysis of the gap between the two profiles to produce action items that identify both the item missing (the gap) and the action (work) required to fill the gap.

4. Assign each action item to a step in the High P·e·r·-f·o·r·m·a·n·c·e·s People Systems Process or to one of three other options.

5. Develop from this information a Migration Strategy— a framework of time-phased action items.

Results: The Design Team has detailed documentation that describes the targeted and baseline organizational profiles, and a Migration Strategy to move the company to the target.

high performance operating environment, and reinventing the people side of the business. In the profiling process and the creation of a Migration Strategy, the Design Team has translated the vision of the high performance operating environment into a plan of action to reinvent the people side of the business.

WRAP-UP

· The effort put into Process Step 1 sets the tone for the remainder of the project. Superficial treatment, avoidance of potential conflicts or sensitive topics, and lack of interest will be a bad sign of things to come. On the other hand, healthy discussion, attention to detail, and the rigorous pursuit of the targeted and baseline profiles and the completion of a strong Migration Strategy will be a sign that the Design Team has taken more than a few bites out of their 500-pound enchilada.

· The results at the end of Process Step 1: Create the Target and Baseline Organizational Profiles will be:

  · A detailed picture of the key organizational characteristics of the future—a targeted profile that reflects a response to the "case for change" and a detailed picture of the high performance operating environment;
  · An equally detailed picture of the organization today that serves as a baseline for tracking improvement;
  · A gap analysis between the target and baseline profiles that results in a list of action items that define "What's missing?" and the action to be taken;
  · A Migration Strategy that provides a framework for action for the Design Team.

CHAPTER 8

Value-added Movement

Process Step 2: Define Flexibility

"HERE's THE GOOD news: American business's campaign to improve quality is paying off so well that in many areas the Japanese no longer enjoy a clear lead. Now the bad news: While the quality gap narrows, the world's best competitors are suiting up for an even more challenging contest. It's called *flexibility*, and its watchwords are change fast, keep costs low, and respond quickly to customers." [Our emphasis.][1]

The recent *Fortune* article did not spell out the *really* bad news: flexibility is not a new strategic weapon for the world's best competitors—the High Performance Enterprises. Flexibility has been an integral part of JIT, work cells, TQM, and Kaizen for decades.

Fortune went on to regale its readers with such sophisticated examples of flexibility as the Nissan Intelligent Body Assembly System (or IBAS, with its cluster of 51 robots that can assemble, weld, and inspect three or more different car models interchangeably on each IBAS line); and at KAO Corp., the soap and cosmetics company's information system's collection and distribution of 10 gigabytes of data (which enable it to distribute average orders of only seven items within 24 hours to any of 280,000 shops).

The "gee whiz" systems mentioned are only the "latest" manifestations of a basic employee-level flexibility that began in the crude assembly lines of the '60s and '70s. The flexibility addressed here is not the gee whiz, 10-gigabyte variety. It is that same basic employee-level flexibility that is an essential ingredient of the people side of the High Performance Enterprise.

The IBAS assembly line and 10-gigabyte information systems may not be a part of every company's future, but there are impressive potential benefits of flexibility for every company. None of these benefits will materialize if it fails to first define flexibility, and then make flexibility a part of its high company performance work environment.

What is this "new" competitive weapon, flexibility? What does it look like? Why is it important? And how does a company move from traditional inflexibility to a concept of flexibility, and then put that into practice on a daily basis?

It's easy to provide a clear basic definition of the concept of flexibility, but almost impossible to provide a single, definitive path for the application of flexibility. For better or worse, *flexibility is in the eye of the beholder!* Because each company is a unique "beholder," we can only provide a process for seeking *your* company's "flexibility." What the actual flexibility map looks like when you get there will be up to you.

A quick way to understand flexibility and its benefits is to take a look at the environment of the traditional organization. Traditional organizations and workforces tend to be inflexible.

CHARACTERISTICS OF INFLEXIBILITY

- Employees work at the same position or station day after day.

- In both union and nonunion environments, working to rules is a stultifying way of life.

- Movement from one position or job to another is regulated by rigid policies spelling out job bidding, bumping "rights," or seniority-based transfers—all requiring disruptive moves that may or may not meet the needs of the organization.

- Daily work assignments or work scheduling is directed by a person with authority, such as a supervisor.

- Manufacturing battles with master scheduling for the longest possible "fixed production schedule."

- Problem solving is always the responsibility of the "specialists" or someone in "authority."

In many companies, inflexibility crept innocuously into the organization under the guise of "good organizational management," and in the form of policies and procedures designed to ensure control and consistent treatment of employees. Unfortunately, a focus on control and consistency has led *to* inflexibility, and led *away* from meeting the business objectives of the company.

A special irony can be found in the organizations where management says, "We have a flexible workforce. Over the past 10 years we've had so much movement among our employees, that everyone's worked in almost every department." Even if department-to-department movement did take place, current rules and practices more than likely make it impossible for management to take advantage of the potential flexibility. Sometimes the encumbrance results from a "What's in it for me?" attitude among employees that makes movement essentially impossible. Regardless, "potential flexibility" that is unusable or heavily encumbered is still inflexibility.

Inflexibility is not free. It's difficult to document the exact dollars and cents cost of inflexibility, but there is a broad consensus among management gurus: inflexibility, as epitomized by working to rules or doing only what you are told, is among the chief culprits of the Western world's failure to match the productivity gains of the High Performance Enterprises.

Inflexibility inflicts obvious, ongoing costs on an organization. These costs are results of:

- Lost production or services due to the absence of a workforce with shared critical skills.

- Lower productivity as a result of the significant non-value-added movement associated with the control and consistency environment.

- The poor quality and rework that result from a reliance on ad hoc, informal on-the-job skills training.

- The lost sense of ownership for customer satisfaction that used to be found when employees in small companies moved naturally up and down the line to fill in for absent co-workers.

- Low employee morale and job satisfaction resulting from being unable to move freely and confidently up and down the process.

This is *inflexibility*. What about flexibility?

Flexibility is a mind-set. It is an expectation shared by managers and employees that movement from position to position by skilled workers at every level of the company is a vital element of the high performance operating environment.

Flexibility is a response to the requirements placed on a company and its workforce by management's decision to seek status as a High Performance Enterprise. The typical strategic direction and world-class tactical initiatives selected by such companies hold flexibility as an essential ingredient of the high performance operating environment. JIT, work cells, TQM—all value and take advantage of the role of the flexible employee. Flexibility means people have the essential skills, and can work effectively within a broad segment of the work process. As a result, flexibility allows managers to accommodate fluctuating capacity requirements.

We looked at the inflexibility of the traditional work environment. What are the traits of a flexible, high performance work environment?

TRAITS OF A FLEXIBLE WORK ENVIRONMENT

- The mind-set is "No one of us is as good as all of us"—that employees are capable of ongoing learning, of creativity, and a growing, increasing contribution.

- An employee's day-to-day activities vary depending on the organization's needs.

- Processes are standardized as the basis for improvement, and to enable flexible employees to move easily from position to position.

- Employees receive standardized and documented skills training, and are able to work within/up and down the process.

- All employees and teams have the skills and knowledge to solve problems, make decisions within their boundaries, and to practice ongoing process improvement.

- Disruptions to work due to absenteeism, vacations, are minimized by the movement of skilled workers around the work process—a movement that is either directed or self-directed.

- People are able to work within defined, broader boundaries with minimal direct supervision.

- The appropriate People Systems are in place to define, recognize, and reinforce flexibility

FLEXIBILITY IS THE NAME OF THE GAME

Both the company and its employees benefit as a result of a flexible work environment. It's the best of all worlds—a true win-win situation. Success stories abound where companies have dramatically improved performance following increased workforce flexibility. The IBAS assembly lines and the 10-gigabyte information systems are validation of the High Performance Enterprises' early and continued efforts at employee-level flexibility.

At Toshiba, a manufacturer of a diverse array of products, a slogan was instituted in 1985: "Synchronize production in proportion to customer demand." Evidence of their creed is obvious in their computer factory at Ome, outside of Tokyo. Toshiba has instituted flexible production lines designed to avoid shortages of the current "hot" products and overproduction of "cold" products. The production lines have their full content of "gee whiz" technology, but underpinning it all is a flexible workforce that assembles multiple models of products in small batches: a workforce trained to make as many as 20 different models of laptop computers. They are supported in that effort by visually displayed method sheets at each operation to provide the correct detailed assembly information as models change on the line.[2] For Toshiba, flexibility supports the strategic direction of the company. A flexible workforce enables Toshiba to synchronize production in proportion to the demand of their customers.

The Toshiba production line is an example of agile production—a production environment in which companies produce many different products on the same line, with the same workers performing the different tasks required for each different product passing down the line. Agile production begins with *employee-level flexibility* and matures with *process* and *technology flexibility*. All three elements must be integrated and aligned if organizational agility is to be achieved. Too much focus on one element over the others can lead to costly investments with disappointing returns—witness GM's $40 billion technology and automation binge, hamstrung by inflexible workers and processes. State-of-the-art flexible technology will not sharpen a company's competitive edge if its workforce is inflexible. The return on the investment made on state-of-the-art technology may not be as high as the return on an investment made in the people.

Flexibility saves money, especially when it is utilized in its most powerful expression, the self-directed work team. When team members move around the work process, they develop a heightened sense of "customer"—an awareness of how their work impacts that of others. And they enhance their ability as a team to improve the processes in their work areas.

At the San Diego Zoo, the Tiger River department is staffed by a flexible workforce. A team of unionized "flexible" specialists manage the display. Though they represent a variety of scientific disciplines, maintenance, and construction, there is a blurring of roles that fosters a heightened sense of responsibility. "Seven people run Tiger River; when it started there were 11, but as team members learned one another's skills they decided they didn't need to replace workers who left."[3] Flexibility saves money.

Flexibility leads to improved performance. Other companies have redefined flexibility as an integral part of their implementations of world-class initiatives (JIT, work cells, TQC, etc.) and experienced significant performance improvement in lead times, labor costs, and work-in-process (WIP) inventory. As in the example above, a more flexible workforce may lead to fewer workers required for the same work. The position taken by the High Performance Enterprise is that the opportunities provided by a flexible workforce allow the company to increase its capacity without a directly proportional head count increase.

Tellabs Operations, Inc., a Midwest manufacturer of telecommunications equipment, was able to manufacture the same products in half the space, cut lead times by 95 percent, and reduce work-in-process inventory by 95 percent as they implemented JIT and a flexible workforce. Tellabs also found they were much better positioned to respond to peaking fluctuations in the production schedule with less significant increases in employment.

Companies find their employees benefit from becoming more flexible. Employee satisfaction tends to increase because there is more variety to the work; they see more of the "big picture" and can directly link their contribution to it; and through increased personal and organizational performance, employees also obtain increased monetary rewards as a result of their flexibility. At first, not everyone likes "being flexible." Once they experience the benefits themselves and understand the benefits to the company, most employees say they never want to go back "to the old ways." Being part of a flexible workforce is exciting.

Finally, in today's job market, and increasingly in the future, a key benefit for those with increased skills will be enhanced employability through flexibility. The multiskilled employees will be the most valuable to their companies, and if forced to leave and find work, will be the most quickly reemployed. In describing *Workplace 2000*, Boyett and Conn say, "Within business units of large organizations and within small companies, the most valued employees will be those who are flexible and can perform a wide range of functions. Breadth of knowledge concerning business operations and customer needs is likely to be more highly valued than depth of knowledge in a narrowly defined specialty."[4]

DEFINING FLEXIBILITY MAPPING AND BOUNDARIES

Before you can achieve the kind of flexibility described above, you must begin by defining "flexibility" for your own operating environment. What does it look like? Flexibility can range from each employee's mastering one additional position or operation to a situation in which all employees are capable of performing in all positions or operations within a team, department, or facility. For your company, flexibility depends on the nature of your processes and the needs of your business.

Defining flexibility has an important impact on a company's operating environment. Part of that impact takes place on the people side of the business because defining flexibility is a critical step in developing a company's People System. To assess the impact of flexibility on a company's major People Systems, follow this thumbnail sketch of the impact of process improvement on the company's major People Systems:

1. The High Performance Enterprise seeks improved performance by changing the fundamental way work is done—changes accomplished by modifying or creating new work processes, which in turn require that jobs are more broadly defined (to facilitate the movement of flexible workers).

2. More flexible workers require that a company implement a means for acquiring and maintaining the additional skills to ensure quality performance in the new, more broadly defined jobs.

3. Both individuals and teams need regular feedback on how they are performing in the more broadly defined job.

4. The entire People Systems approach of process, jobs, skills, and feedback is anchored and reinforced through pay and rewards.

If flexibility is in the eye of the beholder, how does the "beholding" company take the step of describing "flexibility"? A successful, proven approach is called "flexibility mapping." Flexibility mapping is a generic tool that any company can use to set a direction for defining flexibility—the path they actually follow, and "flexibility" as they define it will be organic to each company. Each company that performs flexibility mapping will create a definition for flexibility that flows from the company's fundamental requirements for a flexible workforce. The flexibility definition is reflected in the characteristics of the targeted organizational profile.

Unlike other Process Steps, defining flexibility is not accomplished through a strictly sequential series of Action Steps. It is an iterative, discussion-oriented step that generally requires a fair amount of give and take among Design Team members. It requires the assistance of those who know the company's processes particularly well—the "doers" sometimes know best.

To help you understand this step we will lay out before you a series of (1) questions to explore, (2) process hints for flexibility mapping, and (3) design considerations. When you have worked through these, we will discuss (4)—how to draw a flexibility map—and then use a case study to demonstrate how an actual company used this process to define flexibility for their manufacturing operations.

1. Questions to explore.

• *"Assuming flexibility is an essential characteristic of our targeted profile, what are the boundaries for freely moving skilled people without barriers?"* The Design Team will defer to functional, process, or product management for the answer to this fundamental question.

• *What are the objectives of our world-class initiatives and how will flexibility help achieve them?* For some world-class initiatives, flexibility is an underlying principle. This can dictate the degree of flexibility required of the workforce.

• *Should the boundaries be drawn around processes or products?* Regardless of which, the more effective boundaries are drawn horizontally along the flow of the process rather than vertically cutting across the process.

• *To what degree does product/process commonality, mix, and volume impact how work is done?* At Tellabs Operations, Inc., the

Remote Align/Data Station Termination product line consisted of roughly a half dozen models, all of basically the same design, using similar parts, requiring the same equipment, and of sufficient volume as a group that the product line was treated almost as a mini-focused factory within a larger focused factory. Though similar to other products in the larger factory, flexibility boundaries were drawn around the RA/DST work cell, with all employees trained and expected to move up and down the line with a minimum amount of direction.

· *Are processes equipment-driven?* Is equipment dedicated or shared? Is a relay-out of the factory possible to support a desired flexibility boundary or is the relay-out either impossible or necessarily delayed? Management's answer to these questions is a factor in setting flexibility boundaries. Management must decide the relationship of employees and equipment—are employees to be specialists and/or generalists; are employees to be dedicated to machines or move freely among them in a group technology approach? Should a flexibility boundary be drawn around all of the equipment in a highly sophisticated fabrication area?

· *Not only "where" should flexibility boundaries be drawn, but "when"—at what point in time?* Is it more appropriate to work on flexibility boundaries for the processes or products as they will appear in the time frame of the targeted organizational profile, or to have a series of evolving boundaries begin with today and evolve toward a future target? Set the boundaries for the targeted profile of the future.

2. Process hints for flexibility mapping.

· Flexibility mapping is trial and error; it is iterative, and a deductive process. It is a process in which the work done up front determines how well the first few steps are taken. It is a tool for examining the processes of the company in light of the objectives the company wants to accomplish, and establishing logical boundaries of flexibility to support those objectives.

· Although establishing flexibility boundaries is part of the People Systems redesign process, this is not a Human Resources issue. It is clearly an Operations, or Manufacturing, issue and the leading question must be asked by them. (Or an issue for the particular functional area in which flexibility mapping is being used.)

> "Given that flexibility is an essential characteristic of our targeted profile, within what boundaries do we want to be able to freely move skilled people without barriers?"

• Sometimes when flexibility boundaries are drawn, the workforce and current operating environment put a severe damper on the process—"There's no way our people would be willing to learn new skills and move around into every position in the work cell!!" Companies can avoid this problem by setting aside all current workforce issues and envisioning how to create flexibility for a new hire, "generic" employee. Later, the design team can address the issues of an incumbent workforce and develop action items to move to the targeted flexible environment.

• Occasionally, when under time pressure, there is a temptation to map only a part of the process or a few products. This should be resisted. Map all processes or products. Only when all major processes or products have been mapped for flexibility is it possible to see the overall impact of flexibility, and how flexibility will support the initiatives to be implemented.

3. Design considerations.

• If a decision has been made to implement work cells, or self-directed teams, that decision itself may be the most significant consideration in setting boundaries. If the boundaries of the teams have already been thought out as part of the work cell design, they become the *de facto* flexibility boundaries. If not, flexibility mapping may in turn then become a basic design issue for the proposed work cell or team.

• Occasionally, existing group, section, functional, or department organizational boundaries can become the initial flexibility boundaries (they are organic to the current operating environment of the company). If nothing else, they serve as good working models for continued discussion.

· There *is* an evolutionary consideration to flexibility boundaries, in the sense that they may expand over time. An initial flex boundary might be "the cell" with an expansion over time to "between cells" to an eventual boundary of "department" or "anywhere in the process" or "anywhere for this product." Even in this case, the boundaries should be set at the targeted time frame and not time-phased through each expansion.

· It is unlikely there will be one single flexibility boundary for the entire operation. There are likely to be several flexibility boundaries around various parts of the process or around various products. Each will define the areas of the process or products within which unconstrained movement is desired and expected.

4. Drawing the map.

With these considerations in mind, we can move to flexibility mapping itself. Flexibility mapping begins with an approach similar to "process mapping," but does not normally go to the level of detail attempted with that tool. How detailed? The flexibility map should be just detailed enough to permit the concept of flexibility to be fully defined.

Working with transparency and whiteboard, the Design Team, assisted by Operations/Management, begins the mapping process with a review of the questions mentioned above, followed by the preparation of a process map to be used by the group. The typical mapping approach involves a "horizontal map," i.e., it follows the process of the product or service in and out all of the functions and/or departments through which it passes. Many companies begin with a simple map outlining the flow of key products through the major functional areas. A second time through may contain more detail, such as specific areas or machine cells in each of the functional areas. The final version might include a level of detail to expose all of the inspection, material handling, and expediting that accompanies the process.

The Design Team takes an iterative approach, developing a series of initial flexibility maps, always testing each against the fundamental question: "Given that flexibility is an essential characteristic of our targeted profile, within what boundaries do we want to be able to freely move skilled people without barriers?"

CAUTION!

Avoid the two potential boundary extremes: the "all people can do all things" boundary, and the "if each employee could only do one more thing" boundary. Both may be appropriate at a given point in time. However, the first extreme sets up expectations greater than may be desired or realized in a reasonable period of time. Though initially appropriate, the second extreme may be far too limiting—it significantly underestimates the flexibility of which people are capable.

When a decision has been made, and a final flexibility map selected, only one step remains: identify all of the actual current job titles that reside in each of the targeted flexibility boundaries. List them within each flexibility boundary—randomly, or in whatever manner is easiest for the team. This listing of jobs within flexibility boundaries is the foundation for Process Step 3.

HOW FLEXIBLE CAN WE BE?

How does flexibility mapping work in a real company? This medium-sized consumer products company manufactured a broad range of products in a traditional work environment—employees stayed within narrowly defined jobs, and "got ahead" by continually bidding on higher-graded jobs in whatever department they became available. Here is the thought process through which the company's Design Team went to draw its flexibility boundaries.

The Design Team included senior management from Operations and Human Resources. Initially, they outlined a few major objectives and criteria they wanted to meet with an increased flexibility among their people.

• It was important to minimize the frequent non-value-added movement of employees from one department to another—movement institutionalized by the company's job structure and personnel policies. Management was concerned that skills were being wasted as employees "hopped around" the job classification system from department to department in search of more money and advancement.

• They wanted to increase flexibility by increasing the number of skills held by each employee and the depth in each of those skills.

• And when employees were more flexible, management wanted to be able to move them more easily within a specified area without being required to post a job opening, or working through the constraints of old personnel policies no longer required in the new work environment.

• As a process business, production lines were long, complicated, and expensive. Management wanted to avoid moving equipment to accommodate a flexible workforce; therefore, little change to the actual process flow was anticipated. Opportunities for improvement focused on an enhanced appreciation of quality, implementing JIT, and better utilizing the skills of a flexible workforce.

• Historically, people were reluctant to move from one plant to another. This would be more likely required as a result of a product-focused flexibility than from a process focus.

The mapping process began by displaying the current flow chart of how product moved through operations (see figure 8a). Essentially, two major product groups were produced: liquid products and tablet products.

The discussions on where to draw the boundaries narrowed and began to reflect the following question: Will the company gain more by focusing on flexibility by product or by process? The reasoning went as follows:

• If we select a *product* focus, as depicted in figure 8a, employees are going to be faced with movement from a front-end process that relies on reading "recipes," weighing, and mixing, to a back-end process that is totally equipment-intensive. The two areas require different skill sets, and a different mind-set. Employees transferring from front to back or vice versa would require new skills and abandon others. This is movement between two distinct skill sets.

· If we select a *process* focus, i.e., a front-end process and a back-end process, as depicted in figure 8b, employees will be able to develop more skills in their part of the process and to develop more depth in each of those skills. And when they move *within* the front or back, the company will not lose skills already developed. And this will require less movement from plant to plant.

After much discussion of the pros and cons of both, a *process* focus as outlined above was selected. Ultimately, six flexibility boundaries were drawn, as shown in figure 8c, with each flexibility mapping following the same basic process.

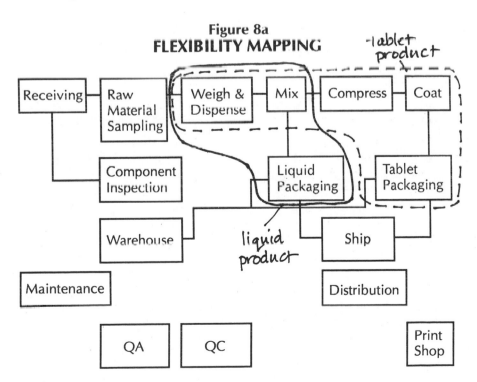

Figure 8a
FLEXIBILITY MAPPING

Figure 8b
FLEXIBILITY MAPPING

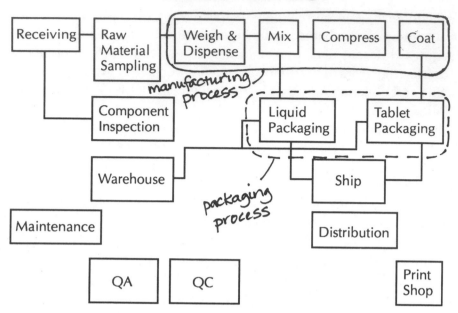

Figure 8c
FLEXIBILITY MAPPING

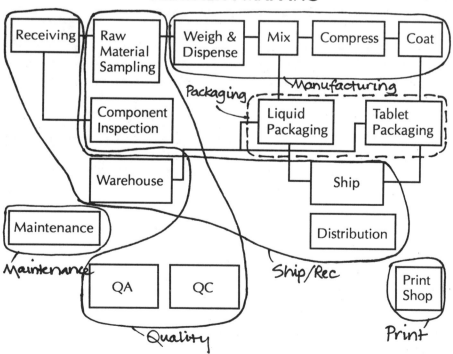

Finally, the Design Team listed all job titles and grades that resided in each of these six areas. The team made sure *all* job titles were included. There is a tendency to "forget" those positions not directly involved in the work, but indirectly supporting the work. In this case, jobs like material handler, inspector, and expediter were included within several of the boundaries.

A typical list might look like this one of the kinds of jobs bounded by the flexibility map for shipping/receiving/distribution/warehouse:

Warehouse

Job Title	Grade
Janitor/sweeper	2
Data entry clerk	3
Material handler	3
Forklift driver	4
Shipping clerk	4
Receiving clerk	4
Senior material handler	4
Distribution clerk	4
Senior forklift driver	5
Senior shipping clerk	5
Senior receiving clerk	5
Yard driver	6
Distribution order clerk	7
Cycle counter	7
Truck driver	7

For the company in our case study, flexibility is becoming a competitive weapon. They don't compete against Nissan and its 51-robot assembly line, nor do they compete against KAO Corp. and its 10 gigabytes of data, but they do compete in an industry where it is difficult to establish differentiations among competitors. As part of their design work with the High P·e·r·f·o·r·m·a·n·c·e·s People Systems Process, they have added a significant differentiator in the form of flexibility.

Synopsis: Process Step 2
Define Flexibility

Objective: To determine the work process areas in which the company needs to move skilled employees without barriers; and to minimize non-value-added internal movement of employees from one work area to another.

Process: Defining flexibility is an iterative process best accomplished by working through a series of questions, process hints, design considerations, and trial-and-error flexibility mapping. The discussions generated by the question will lead the Design Team to flexibility maps that set the stage for job and team design. The general areas to explore are:

- What are the boundaries for freely moving people without constraints?
- What are the objectives of our world-class initiatives and how will flexibility help achieve them?
- Are boundaries to be drawn around products or processes?
- What impact does product/process commonality, mix, and volume have on how work is done?
- Are processes equipment-driven?
- Not only "where" are flexibility boundaries drawn, but "when"—at what point in time?

After the initial flexibility boundaries are drawn, the Design Team lists all current job titles and grades existing within each of the boundaries. This last step is preparatory work for the next Process Step.

Results:
- A series of flexibility maps for the entire operation.
- A list of existing jobs and grades for each flexibility boundary.
- An outline of time-phased expansion of flexibility boundaries.

WRAP-UP

The results from Process Step 2: Define Flexibility include:

- A series of stabilized flexibility maps of the entire operation. Each map outlines an area in which management expects the movement of skilled employees to take place as needed without barriers—either under direction, or when appropriate, under self-direction.

- A list of existing jobs (and their grades) currently being performed within each flexibility boundary.

- And, if appropriate, an outline of the time-phased expansion of flexibility boundaries.

References:

1. *Fortune,* September 21, 1992.
2. *Fortune,* September 21, 1992.
3. *Fortune,* May 18, 1992.
4. *Workplace 2000*, Joseph H. Boyett and Henry P. Conn (New York: Penguin Books, 1991).

CHAPTER 9

New Work

Process Step 3: Redesign Work: Redesign Jobs and Define Teams

SITTING AROUND THE table, listening to managers talk over their salads, was an eye-opener. Here at a large conference on "self-directed" work teams, the war stories were spewing forth during an animated luncheon discussion. "Our CEO literally said, 'Go do teams,' and we went off in a blaze of glory only to discover four months later we had lost the troops somewhere back behind us, at the first turn," said one vice-president for a large service company. "I wish that had been our only mistake," sighed a woman who had been a breakout leader earlier in the day. "We poured thousands of dollars into training our employees on being good team members; we even included some special training for the supervisors. Yet, after nine months of up-and-down results from the teams, our supervisors informed us that people didn't really like the teams. They spent all this effort on trying to solve problems, and couldn't even get tech support to answer their phone calls. Everyone thinks teamwork isn't really changing anything and they want us to disband the work teams."

For every success story about teams reported in the business press, there is at least another unwritten story about teams that failed. No one knows exactly how many companies have failed with teams, but it is a frequent topic of discussion when managers from different companies get together. As these lunchtime conversations continued, they centered on can-you-top-this horror stories of experiences these managers had lived through when implementing teams. Some recounted how their companies were still facing an employee mind-set that things such as problem solving and team activities are "not my job." Other managers complained of "losing" the ability and right to manage because they had "empowered teams."

Employees were trained on teamwork and on the management continuum between control and commitment—they had been told control is bad and commitment is good. Though the company had just begun their team efforts, and were a long way from the potential of a strictly commitment environment, the result was a management group afraid to manage because decisions, "leadership," and direction of any kind would be labeled "controlling."

These problems will continue until companies take the time to first define teams and redefine jobs before jumping directly from the concept of teams to the training of teams to the expectation of immediately self-directed teams.

The High Performance Enterprise is in a mode of constant change. It changes the way it does business, and changes the way products and services are produced. The changes in process lead to changes in the design of work, and today that generally means that the redesigned work is done by teams. It also means that work done by the individual changes. None of these changes occur easily or automatically.

Work must be designed or redesigned to support process changes, to facilitate the functioning of teams, and to develop flexibility in the workforce. Work redesign includes two major concepts: job redesign and team definition. Both concepts require that action be taken early in the People Systems process. New "jobs" and team definitions are to be aligned and integrated with the requirements of the Targeted Organizational Profile developed in Process Step 1, and especially to encourage the flexibility bounded by Process Step 2.

In Process Step 2 of the High P·e·r·f·o·r·m·a·n·c·e·s People Systems, the Design Team drew flexibility boundaries around major work processes. Drawing the boundaries was only a start. The *jobs*

Tales of Team Failures . . .

Snippets of stories from managers recounting their mistakes with teams . . .

• "Training was provided, but we didn't really do much to change the operating environment. Without opportunities to apply what was learned, the effect of the training eventually faded. In fact, morale was lower as a result."

• "We turned team leadership over to the teams too early, before they were really ready."

• "We realized in retrospect that we didn't apply enough initial direction and structure for teams, we didn't really define boundaries. We just said, 'Go do teams.' "

• "The top execs at our company hadn't thought through what their expectations were of teams, what the bottom line benefit would be. That process was begun *after* teams were headed in a variety of different directions, some of which we felt were inappropriate. Trying to get the teams realigned with new direction and objectives was a nightmare."

• "In our company, we emphasized the term 'self-directed' teams. We spent a lot of money on training our employees and supervisors. Six months into the project, we discovered that our supervisors were resentful and fearful about the program. We had assumed they were on board all along."

• "I took the approach that it was a project that could flourish as a 'grass roots' effort. I did not realize that for teams to succeed, it required a different way of managing that affects the entire organization, and that it needs to be driven top-down."

---

within these boundaries must be changed. Many companies take an initial approach to increasing flexibility by cross-training employees among several existing narrowly defined jobs. Most managers still perceive "jobs" the same narrow way. As a result, job *content* itself has been ignored. Managers just want their employees to be able to do more "jobs." When this approach is taken, employees inevitably take the position that they are doing more than one "job." This mind-set results in resistance to the "additional work" and/or the expectation of additional compensation.

Rather than move employees among narrow jobs, and maintain the "specialist" perspective, today's managers have the opportunity to create a new, broader paradigm of "job"—where flexibility can take on real meaning. Broadening the concept of "job" is an opportunity and a requirement to change the mind-sets of managers and employees alike about the individual's role within the company and the relationship between the individual and the company.

The concept of "job" reflects a division of labor, and how actual work is to be accomplished. In the good ol' days when companies were small, the division of labor was relatively broad. Employees had to know how to do many different things, and often took a "whatever it takes" attitude to deliver products and services on time to the customer. It was not unusual to see little differentiation between managers and workers. However, as companies grew and management became a "science"(?), layers of management were added, communication became complex, and the division of labor narrowed significantly as a result of Frederick Taylor's principles of scientific management. Today, we have developed cadres of specialists who work insulated from the "big picture," and with little "feel" of the business.

The team concept is being implemented as a way to reinvolve employees in problem solving, to communicate the realities of the business, and to share the complexity of work among groups of people, among teams. Too often, however, companies launch into teams for the sake of teams. They neither think through objectives for the teams, nor how the teams are to be structured to ensure success in meeting the objectives. They don't consider the ways team effectiveness will be evaluated, and they ignore the potential impact or collision with other programs or the company's human resource systems. The result is often frustration and fizzle, and, finally, failure.

In the High Performance Enterprise, the concept of "job" radically changes—it no longer represents narrow divisions of labor. The American Compensation Association (ACA) suggests the traditional definition of "job" is being replaced by a much broader description, "such as all the work done by a group or members of a productivity team.' "[1]

People in traditional companies think of their jobs as something they "have" or own. They have operated, perhaps for years, within the narrow bounds of the job description. In the High Performance Enterprise, however, an individual will work in a job, but may not have or own all of the job. What used to be defined as a job in the traditional organization will now be an operational skill, or a work assignment, or a team position, or workstation. The standard disclaimer found in small print at the bottom of traditional job descriptions—". . . performs other duties as required"—will become the primary description of jobs in the future.

The same "job" in the High Performance Enterprise might be held by all team members or by all employees in a particular department. Tellabs Operations, Inc., a company that designs and manufactures telecommunications equipment, has redesigned work so that there is only one job for all production employees. The *one* job is called "electronics associate"—the job description basically says the job of electronics associate is building a high-quality product, on time. Within that one "job," there are defined "team positions" into which employees rotate to increase their skills and flexibility—and, once trained, team positions into which they freely move to perform the work required.

The majority of job classification systems today are towers of numerous hierarchically segmented jobs, and job families. The progression upward within a job family rarely represents substantive difference in actual job content, making many systems little more than institutionalized devices to control time-in-grade progression—the kind of progression characteristic of an entitled environment.

The job classification system in the new work covenant of the High Performance Enterprise, on the other hand, contains relatively few levels. Progression is well defined and typically based on performance aligned with and contributing to the objectives of the business. Rather than progression up the organizational ladder, breadth of skills and knowledge is recognized and rewarded. Progression is redefined to include not only upward, but also lateral, movement within a broad band or grade.

ADVANTAGES OF WORK REDESIGN

"Radically redesigning work, which invariably means simplifying it, is perhaps the best way to ensure that you get more work done better with fewer resources."

—"Thriving in a Lame Economy,"
Fortune, October 5, 1992

Redesigning work is rethinking about how to organize and manage people to optimize the organization's process capabilities, and meet the objectives of the business. A major element of redesigned work is more broadly defined jobs. Broad jobs create a refocused workforce, where employees perceive their job as "meeting customer expectations," rather than performing a narrow set of tasks. Another advantage of broadly redefining jobs is its simplifying effect on organizational structure. One result of this process is a reduction in the number of job titles from scores or more to 10 or less. And it is not uncommon for this to be accompanied by a two-thirds reduction in the number of pay or labor grades. Compared with the traditional organization, the appearance and activity in an organization where work has been effectively redesigned are very different:

- Few broadly defined job titles for each major employee group;

- Flatter organizational structures with fewer grade levels;

- Reductions in non-value-added internal movement, with job postings much diminished;

- Greater flexibility with free, unencumbered movement of people within large areas such as departments or processes;

· An emphasis on "doing it right" the first time, and on improving the way work is done.

There are two components of redesigning work—job redesign and team definition. Though we'll look at job redesign first, the processes are not necessarily sequential. Some companies find that completing team definitions contributes to the job redesign process. Others find that having redesigned jobs allows them to build teams around the new jobs. Yet others work both processes concurrently.

The following approach to work redesign greatly increases the freedom to act—a new-found freedom to act offset with boundaries. Boundaries are addressed in both job redesign and in team definition. Depending on what your organization's focus is at the time the Design Team is in this Process Step, you may concentrate on job boundaries, team boundaries, or both. Because of the importance in properly establishing boundaries, it is covered in both job redesign and team definition.

If you have already implemented teams and your experience has been unsatisfactory, or if you are currently involved with teams and are disappointed with current team function and contribution to the business objectives, the process outlined in this chapter is an opportunity for mid-course correction.

CHANGING WORK CONTENT THROUGH JOB REDESIGN

In a High Performance Enterprise, jobs are redesigned to support the organization's needs for flexibility. Because the changes are so fundamental, job redesign drives all remaining People Systems components such as training, individual and team performance requirements, compensation, etc.

The approach taken in the redesign of jobs for a High Performance Enterprise is broadening the content of a job. Broadening a job involves increasing the total number of possible tasks that may be performed within the boundary of the newly created, more broadly defined job. For example, a manufacturing company may take all assembly jobs and look for ways to consolidate and identify the actual skills used in the assembly process. The broadening of task content takes place on the basis of increasing the total possible skill content of the job. The skill content of a number of existing narrow jobs is going to be reorganized and consolidated into one new broad job to reflect the organization's flexibility requirements. Every individual occupying one of the new jobs will not be expected to perform every task within the entire new broadened job boundary, or even learn all the new skills. Over time, a majority of employees will be able to effectively perform a greater variety of tasks based on mastering a number of the new skills included in the broader job definition. In very broadly defined jobs, few employees will be expected to master and maintain every new skill.

Employees in traditional companies have a distinct view of "their" job. It is to run this machine, or attach this part, or process this claim. In contrast, for the employees of a world-class company, "their job" is to produce quality products or services, and that may involve any number of tasks utilizing any number of skills and may take place at different positions along the process of the product or service. And the world-class company uses the broadened job structure approach to create and reinforce that new mind-set that an individual's "job" is now to build product or deliver services that satisfy customers, not just operate a single piece of machinery. The goal is simple: give people greater flexibility, more exposure to and ownership for the work process as a whole.

CAUTION!

By simply changing job nomenclature, it is unlikely you will achieve desired results. One company in the British Isles went from 27 job titles to *27 team positions* and one job title. In reality, employees still considered *their team position, their job.*

As we move back and forth between the old and new concepts of job, it's easy to confuse the traditional and High Performance Enterprise notion of "job." (We will use the all-lower-case term "job" when

referring to the narrow "jobs" of the traditional operating environment, and the all-upper-case "JOB" for the broadly defined jobs
found in the high performance operating environment.) The Action
Steps of the job redesign process are as follows:

Redesign Jobs
Action Steps

1. Identify major similarities and differences among *existing* jobs
   within the selected boundary, and analyze for commonality at the
   process level.
2. Define new JOBs role, scope, and boundaries.
3. Identify skill content of new JOBs.
4. Title new JOBs.
5. Evaluate new JOBs.
6. Apply the common sense test.

---

1. Identify significant similarities and differences among existing "jobs" within the selected boundary, and analyze for commonality at the process level.

Traditional job analysis, where detailed task analyses are conducted,
is not necessary for this job redesign approach. Rather than focusing
on discrete tasks, the emphasis changes and expands to focus on the
skills present in a broader view of the work flow.

The objective of this part of job redesign is to identify skill similarities among jobs, and look for opportunities to combine different
skills or skills sets in the previous narrow, discrete jobs into one or
more new broad JOBs. This is a rough-cut approach. With this
objective in mind, the Design Team will take several passes at
reviewing the jobs in each flexibility boundary with an eye toward
how the jobs and the skills relate to one another. The following
questions provide a useful framework for this analysis:

· What are the common skills among these jobs?

- What are the common qualifications for these jobs?
- Is there a common technology represented by these jobs?
- Are there common working conditions among these jobs?
- What is the approximate time it takes an employee to be able to work independently in each of these jobs?
- Do any of the jobs require a significantly different or specialized knowledge?
- Do any of the jobs require specialized training that cannot be learned on the job?

On the first pass through each flexibility boundary, the Design Team will look for an opportunity to combine all of the current jobs into one JOB. This may or may not make sense—the nature of the work may present too wide a gap in skills requirements among the jobs within this boundary. If not, they make another pass at the initial flexibility boundary, this time setting aside those jobs that contain elements of "uncommon" skills, qualifications, technology, working conditions, etc., as candidates for separate JOBs within each flexibility boundary.

Practical Guideline

When thinking about how the new JOBs should be designed to support the work process and flexibility requirements, use a generic, new hire employee as a model for filling the new JOBs. Avoid using the incumbent workforce, or even specific incumbents as a model, because there is a tendency to unnecessarily limit the scope of the new JOB based on the perceived limitations of incumbent employees.

This iterative process usually stimulates a lively discussion among Design Team members, a discussion that should be pursued until the team has combined a few jobs whose basic skills and characteristics meet the commonsense test into one or more broad new JOBs.

At this point, the team should list the characteristics and process commonalities among the individual jobs that make up each tentative new JOB—this will be input for the next closely related action step. Then they take each remaining flexibility boundary, and perform the same analysis of skills on the jobs contained within each, until all boundaries have received the same treatment.

2. Define new JOBs role, scope, and boundaries.

As the Design Team works its way through the first Action Step of the job redesign process, the shape of the new broad JOBs begins to take form in their minds. In this second Action Step, the team solidifies that "shape" by defining the new role, scope, and boundaries for each new JOB. Using the list of characteristics and process commonalities developed for each JOB in the previous step, the team enriches its description for each tentative JOB by defining its role and scope according to the following guidelines:

1. *Role*. Prepare a brief statement outlining the part the JOB plays in meeting the performance standards for the affected products or processes. Include a brief explanation of how this JOB will support the strategic direction and high performance operating environment of the company.
2. *Scope*.

- *Activities*. Outline how people in this JOB will spend their time in supporting the business objectives. What are some of the primary activities that will require their focus?
- *Major accountabilities*. List those elements and objectives specified to be within the scope of the JOB, and on which the individual has significant influence or impact.
- *Key interfaces*. Outline the routine contacts and communication links required between the individuals in this JOB and the other specialists or organizational entities required in meeting objectives.

3. *Boundaries*. Regardless of JOB structure, boundaries of empowerment must be established to provide levels of authority. Not

only boundaries to grant permission to act, but also to identify areas
that are off limits. For example, new JOB content typically includes
expanded responsibilities for costs and budgets. Make sure that the
proper expectations are set regarding the kinds of decision making
permitted in this area. Whatever the beginning boundaries, they will
likely change and expand, synchronized to the actual evolution of the
JOB. The following is an area which companies acknowledge the
freedom to act within the JOB is bounded by clear limits:

· *Decision making*:

"*Independent*" *decisions*—those decisions individuals can
make independent of external review. Normally, these decisions
concern the work process itself, and are made within parameters
or boundaries spelled out clearly, and in advance.

"*Chain-of-command*" *decisions*—are within the boundaries of
the JOB, but because of budgetary or oversight issues require
the approval of another layer(s) of management. In an effort to
enhance decision-making speed, team effectiveness, and productivity, these should be gradually moved toward the "independent" category.

Input only—not really decisions, but issues on which the
individual is required to provide information for decision making
to take place at another level of the organization.

Another type of boundary should be considered: the physical or
locational confines of the JOB, e.g., all of "assembly," or all of a
specific group of machines, or the "front end" of product XYZ—an
area of JOB consistent in skills and characteristics, an area that
provides the company with the breadth of flexibility sufficient to
ensure achieving the goals of the company's initiatives, and its business objectives.

NOTE: Avoid including inspection responsibilities in one job and
then maintaining inspection as a separate job in another area, unless
the nature of inspection work is significantly different to warrant a
separate job designation in the second instance.

Continue the process until all the flexibility boundaries for the
entire work flow have been addressed, and a handful of broad new

JOBs has replaced a potful of narrow jobs. The typical result? Examples of what some companies have achieved are: from 57 jobs to 1 JOB; from 72 jobs to 10 JOBs; from 68 jobs to 8 JOBs; from 28 to 3; from 190 to 5, etc.—JOBs within which skilled workers move freely without constraints . . . at first under direction, and finally self-directed.

Practical Guideline

Beware the traditional mind-set regarding the complexity or difficulty of certain jobs. Certain jobs may have been historically considered difficult for reasons that may no longer be valid. For example, in one company, the job of mixing operator had always been rated more difficult than others because of the requirement to lift 100-pound bags of raw materials. Although new material-handling equipment had been installed that minimized lifting requirements, the perception still prevailed that it was a difficult job because of the lifting requirement.

---

3. Identify the skill content of new JOBs.

The redesign of jobs is an opportunity to develop not only breadth of skills, but also depth of skills. A good example of increasing depth of skill is to require machine operators to know both the operation of multiple machines, and the setup and preventive maintenance. And not only does the depth of operational skills increase, but also a requirement for depth in other "core or support" skills such as teamwork and problem solving with its data collection, analysis, and presentation requirements.

Once the Design Team has reviewed all the work being done within the entire work process, and has established broader JOBs to support the work in each flexibility boundary, the Design Team then applies more detail and definition to the new JOBs. For each JOB, the Design Team creates a skill model by identifying the individual skills that make up the JOB. The skills are grouped by how they apply to the job and the type of training required. The following is a framework into which the actual skills that constitute a JOB may be organized for both job redesign and skills development purposes.

Skill Model for JOB Content and Required Training

Knowledge Transfer Only
• *Core skills*—those skills that are common across all the JOBs, e.g., safety and housekeeping, teamwork, communication, etc.
• *Support skills*—those skills that are JOB-specific and represent peripheral effort in the overall execution of the JOB, e.g., material handling, inspection, etc. NOTE: Some support skills require more training, practice, and evaluation.

Knowledge Transfer, Training, Practice, and Evaluation
• *Operational skills*—those skills that represent the majority of JOB content, that reflect the "work" being done, e.g., machine operation, setup, or preventive maintenance on multiple machines.
• *Technical skills*—for some JOBs, these are the highly technical skills that require a base knowledge of operational skills, but represent specialized aspects of the "work" being done, e.g., major machine repair, the use of highly specialized technical test equipment, etc.

---

4. Title new JOBs.

In this Action Step, you will name each of the new JOBs. Naming new JOBs is important to the people in these JOBs. They want the JOB title to communicate their worth. With only a few JOBs to title, the names are often almost generic-sounding. Many companies take the approach of including the word "associate" in all new JOB titles. The functional or process area represented in the new JOB is then added as a qualifier or description of the nature of work. Wal-Mart calls all their sales personnel "sales associates." Tellabs calls their manufacturing employees "electronics associates."

Other companies use the term "specialist" rather than "associate."

Ironically, the new JOBs represent generalist rather than specialist skills, yet, the *term* "specialist" denotes higher skill levels. Some companies have used the work process captured by a JOB to qualify or describe the specialist JOB, for example, assembly specialist, packaging specialist, maintenance specialist, etc. Others have used qualifiers that describe the nature of the skills or work, such as "technical specialist." Employees tend to be positive about the word "specialist" as part of their identity.

The key is to create broad titles to fit the broad nature of the new JOBs. The title or language used around the JOB is critical in reinforcing the desired mind-set of broadly viewing one's role in the organization.

5. Evaluate new JOBs.

Job evaluation has traditionally used a variety of approaches in establishing equity between jobs and to the external market. These methodologies created the traditional narrow, hierarchical job classification systems. Currently, most companies use some combination of point-factor and market pricing methods—both have some value when modified to accommodate the broader concept of JOB. Choosing an appropriate method is usually up to the Human Resources Department in each organization. Regardless of the method chosen, look for opportunities to simplify the evaluation process by consolidating the multiple factors employed to include the basic evaluation categories of skill, effort, responsibility, and working conditions. With these as a base, a new JOB evaluation process might include:

- The simplified, broadened categories of skill, effort, responsibility, and working conditions.

- For each JOB, a JOB summary that includes role, scope, and boundaries.

- A skill model, and the documentation from skill training requirements and performance expectations (these items will be covered in succeeding chapters).

- Documentation on mental and physical requirements to perform the JOB.

NOTE: Companies should check with their legal counsel to determine additional documentation requirements.

This documentation will provide a package suitable for developing the "defensible logic" for both general and compliance issues. And, by the way, the fact that there will be far fewer JOBs to evaluate helps in simplifying the process.

When developing a traditional job classification system, the next step normally would be to convert job evaluation results into a new pay or labor grade structure. In the High P·e·r·f·o·r·m·a·n·c·e·s People Systems, this step is delayed until later at Process Step 7: Design *NewComp*. Two essential ingredients for establishing the new JOB structure are still to be developed: a skills development process (Process Step 5) and a P·e·r·f·o·r·m·a·n·c·e·s Feedback System (Process Step 6). Both are tightly integrated with the "new" compensation system, and it is not until Process Step 7: Design *NewComp* that grades are developed, pay rates or ranges are established, and pay delivery guidelines created.

All that's left to complete job redesign is to review the new JOB definitions and their groupings by applying the "common sense test." Final documentation of each new JOB is usually completed during the development phase of the project.

6. Apply the Common Sense Test.

After all the arguing and hard work, it's time for the Design Team to step back and take a look at the new JOBs they've created. Does the design make sense? Is it defensible? Can the team visualize the JOBs in action? Does the design stand a hardheaded, common sense review? Though some members of the team may not be totally comfortable with the new JOB definitions, is there a strong consensus to proceed?

Frequently, a little soak time is needed. Remember, also, this is just the beginning of the design process. Each subsequent step provides opportunities to return to the job redesign step and make modifications. If in general the Design Team believes their work reflects work redesign that is appropriate for the needs of the company, it is time to move on.

Occasionally, a review of the new JOBs will reveal broader organizational issues. On the one hand, new JOBs facilitate the formation of teams because there are fewer barriers. On the other hand, eliminating these barriers can have other organizational effects. Companies that operate with numerous "functional silos" are likely to find the new JOBs cross departmental lines. Implementing the new JOB design may require a reorganization. For one multi-billion-dollar organization, their key objectives were to develop product focus and accountability in those areas most critical to assuring the availability of products to their customers. When jobs were redesigned, and a new JOB included aspects of several different functions, the design ran smack into the functional silos: business units for the major product families, and separate, centralized manufacturing and quality functions. After completion of the work redesign step, it became obvious that a reorganization was necessary, and manufacturing and quality were decentralized into the various business units.

DEFINING TEAMS

In the High Performance Enterprise, the role of the "individual contributor" changes dramatically. The employee is still valued and recognized as an individual, but, more importantly, is also recognized as a contributor to a team.

Teams, in and of themselves—teams for the sake of teams—are not an organizational mandate. Teams are a result of managing differently, managing from a process orientation. Teams represent a different way of doing things, and can take on various sizes and configurations in an organization, depending on the work to be done. Teams are here to stay. The Ages of Information, Automation, and Discontinuity, combined with the globalization of competition, have made the nature of work more complex. There is intense pressure for increased flexibility, to continuously improve products and services, and to deliver at faster and faster speeds. Companies can no longer

Synopsis: Process Step 3
Redesign Work: <u>Redesign Jobs</u> and Define Teams

Objective: To directly support the business objectives by redefining work through the broadening of each job's role and scope *and* the clear definition and purpose of teams. To ensure accountability for meeting these business objectives, as they are defined within the work of each individual and team.

Process: **Redesign Jobs**

· Using the previously defined flexibility boundaries, the Design Team reviews the lists of existing jobs and grades to identify similarities and differences among these jobs within each flexibility boundary.

· To meet the flexibility objectives and consolidate many of the jobs, new, broader JOB boundaries and scope are defined. Each new JOB is defined by:

Role
Scope
    Major activities
    Accountabilities
    Key Interfaces
Boundaries and decision making

· The key to flexibility is multiskilled people. The skill content of each new JOB is identified by the following skill categories:

Core skills
Support skills
Operational skills
Technical skills (optional)

· The approach then taken to titling and evaluating each job will differ among companies. Most will use a modified version of their current approach.

· Finally, a common sense test is applied to ensure the new JOB structure makes sense.

Results: A reduction in the dozens of narrow jobs, to a few broad JOBs that are redesigned to support the key business objectives.

sustain a work environment for the individuai Wonder Woman or Superman—they can no longer rely on the individual "hero" to make their processes work. This is the Age of Teams.

THE EVOLUTION OF TEAMS

More and more companies are instituting teams in response to changes in work processes, to the increasing complexity of work, and to required increases in productivity and quality. The most successful companies are those who *prior* to implementation take the time to plan and define the nature of teams that best suit their needs. Unfortunately these companies are the minority. With all the talk of teams during the past 10 years, you'd think the process would be well defined. But that's not true! Over and over again, companies derive little benefit from teams because they launch into teams before they define teams—they create expectations that are not met, and this results in frustration and failure. The benefit of defining teams before launch is in minimizing the problems that companies experience with teams.

Defining Teams

To establish team purpose, objectives, evolution, structure, leadership, role, and boundaries.

Teams are evolutionary. No organization moves from an individual-based environment to a team-based environment in a single bound. Creating a team-based environment is a process, and like most processes, the successful teams pass through all stages of the process in an evolutionary manner. Acknowledging and understanding this evolution are extremely important.

Different types of teams evolve differently, and there are numerous models that describe team evolution. Though especially appropriate for a specific type of team with a specific purpose—the self-directed work team—the following model is useful in understanding team evolution.

Team Evolution

Stage 1: Conception
The notion of organizational change to self-directed work teams is being conceived. The organization is still operating traditionally.

Stage 2: Incubation
The organization begins the planning and design work for redesigned work flow and processes. Many of the team activities are geared toward information gathering, planning, and designing. Process mapping occurs in this stage. The traditional roles of supervisor and employee still exist, but are starting to change with the significant increase in information sharing.

Stage 3: Implementation
The work from Stage 2 is implemented in Stage 3. The new work processes and structures are implemented. Roles and responsibilities undergo significant change.

Stage 4: Transition
The teams are working through and experiencing their new work system. There may be occasional trips and falls as the teams master new skills and responsibilities. The supervisor is much more a facilitator of the new work process than in the past.

Stage 5: Maturity
Teams have mastered all of the basic requirements for a self-managed work team. They focus on process improvement for their area of work.[2]

Estimating when and how teams will pass through the different stages of team evolution helps calibrate managers' expectations and helps manage employee expectations. Everyone sees teams as a process—as evolving through different stages over time.

The actual evolution of a team is determined by its purpose. For example, if the purpose of the team is a specific project, then the evolution of the resulting team is rapid, focused, and when the project is completed, the team is disbanded. For significant projects, such as the redesign of a company's People Systems, project teams can change shape and membership over time. A Design Team is no longer needed after implementation, but the need for an ongoing continuous improvement team may be required, in which some Design Team members may be asked to participate. Regardless of the type of team or duration of its life cycle, the evolution of the team should be spelled out before its inception.

When the purpose and objectives reflect ongoing process improvement effort through work teams, the evolution will more likely follow these five phases of team evolution. Work teams tend to result in longer-term, institutionalized team structures, and this is where understanding team development over time is critical. Moving forward with a concept like "self-directed" or "self-managed" work teams without having established the anticipated evolution for *each* group, results in disillusioned employees and frustrated supervisors. Companies must acknowledge, understand, and communicate the anticipated evolution of newly created teams into the "self-managed" teams of the future. If they do not, they set up team programs for failure.

Acknowledging the role of supervisors in this evolution is essential. Too often supervisors are left out of the loop. It is assumed they will support teams and be involved in their implementation. Yet, it is the supervisors who often see that they have the most to lose with teams. The words "self-directed" or "self-managed" send job security alerts to even the best supervisors. Supervisors must understand what role they have in the transition to teams and what longer-term role they have with the organization. If omitted from the team definition process, supervisors may find themselves, at best, apathetic to teams and, at worst, actively sabotaging teams.

DOIN' TEAMS

Having acknowledged the evolution of teams, how does a company effectively set up teams? There are five Action Steps to defining teams:

Defining Teams
Action Steps

· Establish team purpose and performance objectives.
· Develop appropriate team structure.
· Establish team leadership.
· Define roles and accountabilities for team members.
· Establish team boundaries/authority.

---

1. Establish team purpose and performance objectives.

Teams adhere to the adage "Form follows function." Teams, for the sake of teams, do not establish a suitable "function" for teams. Teams require purpose and objectives. Today, most teams are a response to a need for improvement. The improvement can be in the form of a one-shot project for addressing particular problems or for developing a new process. Or teams may be the result of an ongoing improvement effort toward the major processes of the work flow. The team purpose could be a focus on the quality of a process, the elimination of waste and redundancy in the process, or to shorten lead times and reduce delays. Whatever, the purpose of the team should be clearly stated.

One company established teams or work cells in all its factories. A purpose statement was developed and applied to all of the more than 80 work teams: "The purpose of work teams is to improve the operational performance of the company through reducing production cycle times and inventories; building a higher-quality product; improving customer satisfaction; reducing costs; and creating employee ownership for manufacturing performance and customer satisfaction."

Effective teams have specific performance objectives. A recent McKinsey study indicates that a key factor in the success and functioning of teams is the establishment of a clear performance challenge. Such a challenge breeds more success than "team-building exercises, special incentives, or team leaders with ideal profiles."[3]

Team performance objectives flow from the team purpose. Clearly stated performance objectives support the purpose, set specific direction for the team, and allow the effectiveness and results of the team efforts to be evaluated. A team with the purpose of improving quality may have specific, measurable performance objectives that relate to the reduction of defects, cycle-time improvement, errors, scrap, and rework.

2. Develop team structure.

After developing team purpose and objectives, the actual structure of teams can be determined. There are several structures a team can take.

· *Ad hoc problem-solving teams* (often called "employee involvement teams"). One of the simplest team structures is a problem-solving team. These have been widely used with employee involvement programs. A problem is identified and a team of interested and experienced people meet to resolve the problem. Team member home reporting relationships do not change. The nature of everyday work for each team member remains the same, with team activities being handled in addition to normal duties. The life cycle is usually short—until the problem is resolved.

· *Special project teams or task forces.* This type of team is an especially clear matter of "Form follows function." The membership and structure of the team depend entirely on the purpose and objectives of the team, i.e., the nature of the project. In general, these teams function best when diverse membership brings a wide perspective to the task at hand. Not only should these teams be cross-functional in nature, but when appropriate they should represent a cross-section of different organizational levels. Depending on the nature of the project, a team may include operator-level through management-level employees.

These teams function best with no more than 8 to 10 members. The size restrictions often pose limitations on organizational representation. However, the use of "open chairs" and temporary members helps alleviate pressure to have representatives from *every* area.

A team should be empowered to bring in temporary members at various points in the project on an as-needed basis.

For companies with unions, it is imperative that the union leaders and members be involved in the planning and membership of project teams in which there is impact to the people side of the business, particularly those projects that potentially impact work rules or contract items.

· *Work teams* (often referred to as "natural work teams"; may be self-directed or self-managed teams). The purpose and objectives of work teams are to effectively perform work according to defined processes, and to continuously improve those work processes. With form following function, the structure of work teams forms around the work processes themselves. Work teams may represent *all* employees in a particular area or department, or a work team may represent a dozen or so employees responsible for a smaller *segment* of the entire work process. The lead question in determining work team structure is: "How wide do we want the circle of accountability to be; where do we want to establish linkages with other teams along the work process?" There are as many ways to structure work teams as there are ways to get the work done. Nonetheless, all effective work teams—blue-collar and white-collar—share certain common characteristics:

Characteristics of Effective Teams

• Process- or product-focused, rather than functionally focused.
• Aligned along the flow of work, i.e., the flow of work is through the team.
• Performing their work in a layout that minimizes all barriers to flow and communication, the most visible evidence of which is minimized distances between both people and equipment.
• Multifunctional, e.g., on the factory floor, formerly separate functions such as inspection, material handling, and expediting are incorporated into the work team structure.
• Structured to permit the production or processing of smaller "lot sizes" of products or services, depending on customer demand, how discrete the product or service, and the state of process improvement.
• Able to move team members around freely about the process performing different tasks, ultimately without direct supervision.
• Flexibly structured to permit the team to employ the services of shared "experts" and others who influence the team's ability to perform. For a manufacturing work cell, a typical example might be a "planner," who, though not physically resident in the cell, is a full member of the cell.
• Directly control major elements of the work flow and processes—a response to the work team's twofold purpose: to do work and improve the way that work is done.
• Include all those who significantly influence the outcome or the process or segment of the process, in one way or another, on the team—including supervisors, and employees from different departments.
• Varies in size, shape, and appearance, as form follows function—there is no magic number or description for work teams.

• *Resource or support teams* (generally a cross-functional team of technical and functional specialists). Although work team members are both the "doers" and "improvers" of the processes for which they are responsible, there are times in their improvement efforts when they need help from the "experts." In most companies, that level of expertise is confined to a few functional, technical specialists whose number is limited by frequency of use, rareness of competency, or economic expediency. In the traditional environment, these functional technical experts have resided physically apart from the processes and mentally apart from the "doers" of the process.

Today, the High Performance Enterprise wants to remove that barrier. However, there are usually not enough specialists to be included in each work team. As a work-around for this situation, and in an effort to best use the expertise of their specialists, some companies form cross-functional technical resource teams to support multiple work teams, generally with positive results. Greater improvement comes from the collective and collaborative expertise of the *process "doers"* and the *process "experts."* The "doers" have a great capacity to learn from the "experts," and to the surprise of the "experts," the reverse is also true. The experts also discover that with guidance and instruction, much of the time they've been spending on non-expert activities can appropriately be handed over to the doers. However, one industrial engineer on a technical support team had unusual insight into the "hand-off" dynamics. He said, "We forget our own learning took place over a period of years. We have made the mistake of going to employees with 'Here, do this,' without giving *them* time to learn."

The transition from individual contributor to team member is often difficult for professionals. It is dangerous to assume that just because support team members are "professionals" that they will automatically *know* their role on the team, will be effective instructors and mentors to those they are "supporting," and be willing to loosen the grip on their professional identity. It is just as critical that purpose, objectives, evolution, etc., be established before implementing these teams, as it is with any other.

Team structure takes on special meaning for support or resource teams. In some respects, the resulting arrangement resembles a traditional matrixed organization in which an individual or team has more than one boss—an operational boss and a functional boss. While the impact on reporting relationships is a big challenge, equal challenges arise from performance feedback, rewards, and career development (all of which are covered in later steps of the High P·e·r·f·o·r·m·a·n·c·e·s People Systems Process).

For the specialists, all previous reinforcement has been based on individual contribution, technical smarts, problem-solving ability, and political savvy. And not on sharing that with other professionals, much less with hourly employees; or on encouraging and coaching others in those skills. Transitioning to a support team structure is as challenging as transitioning to work teams.

A large manufacturer of electrical equipment jumped headlong into the support team concept without thinking through the impact on the individual professional. The essence of the company's direction to their professionals was the repeated admonishment to "blur the boundaries." The response from members of the newly created support teams depended on their perception of "blurring," and their conscientiousness. Some interpreted this as a requirement to learn at an expert level the other technologies represented on the support team. Others felt responsible to take on supervisory roles in addition to their engineering responsibilities. And many were upset with the perception the professional focus they had chosen and for which they'd studied was now being weakened. One engineer said, "I've worked 16 years as an engineer, and I feel like I'm now going through an identity crisis. I don't want to be a coach, I want to be an engineer." Eventually, the company took a mid-course correction to reestablish objectives, roles, and structure for their support teams, but by that time, a large percentage of the support team members was already physically and emotionally burned out. Teams of professionals, no less than factory work teams, require detailed definition to ensure effective performance.

3. Establish team leadership.

Once again, form follows function. Traditionally, for both project teams and ad hoc problem-solving teams, the team leader was selected by management on the basis of a combination of leadership skills, management experience, and in-depth experience in the subject matter of the project or problem to be solved. The leadership position was usually designated for the life cycle of the team. Today, companies use a less traditional and more open approach to the selection of team leaders. Leadership skills, or the potential of same, are still an essential criterion, but management experience and subject matter expertise are sometimes viewed as impediments rather than requirements—breakthrough thinking is difficult for those whose thinking and experience have been formed (*pre*formed) by the current operating environment.

For work teams, tradition is abandoned altogether and a new leadership role evolves over time. The evolution reflects a shift in roles and relationship between supervisor and team. A common mistake encountered in many companies is to move too quickly through this shift. The transition desired is from controller and director of work to coach and facilitator of work—a shift in team leadership that must correlate with the needs of the team as it shifts through the stages of team evolution. When the team is first formed, the role of supervisor does not change significantly—the team plans for process improvement and learns to work together. Eventually, however, as the team becomes fully implemented and enters the transition phase, the traditional role of supervisor transitions as well. By the time the team is at maturity, a less direct form of supervision is required. The supervisor should then be a facilitator and resource to the team.

Moving to this stage does not mean that team leadership is no longer required. Formal team leadership is still important— "formal" in the sense of being formalized or clearly defined. All members of the team may be involved in team leadership at different times. Some teams do this on a rotation basis; others elect team leaders for a predetermined period of time. Regardless of the approach taken, it must be formally and clearly defined to preclude confusion.

When leadership issues are unclear, direction is unclear and confusion the inevitable result. A medium-sized manufacturing company in the Midwest established a process in which "team leaders" were elected from among the employees at the end of the initial two-day training session on teams. The team leaders were meant to be, at most, "team *meeting* leaders." However, because their exact role was left unclear, some of the newly elected "team leaders" soon felt as though they were functioning as assistant supervisors (an already existing position). They felt increased pressure and stress, both symptoms of increased responsibility with no authority. The team leader position was not integrated into the company's organizational structure, resulting in a situation in which both the team leaders and supervisors were unsure of exactly how a team leader was expected to act. Eventually, management understood the issue, clarified the roles of team leader and supervisor, reviewed with all concerned the concept of team evolution and its likely progression in the company, and put the program back on track.

The words "self-directed team" imply that such teams are *leaderless*. Certainly, in the early stages of team development, we have yet to see or hear of effective leaderless teams. Mistakes are being made up front in the definition and formation of teams. Some companies, in the earnest belief they are doing the right thing, require that managers and supervisors turn over leadership to the employees as a demonstration of their commitment to self-directed, empowered teams. This is a guaranteed route to failure, because it deprives immature teams of the direction required to safely and successfully negotiate the path to maturity.

Practical Guideline

When forming work teams, do not initially remove directive leadership. The transition to self-direction occurs most smoothly when the supervisor initially retains the leadership role and has a clear mandate to develop over time a leadership system within the team.

---

4. Define roles, scope, and boundaries for team members.

Clearly, it is essential for the team leader's role to be established, but it is also vital that roles be established for team members. The purpose of this Action Step is to define the role and scope of team members in broad, useful terms—to provide a framework within which team members, supervisors, and managers have freedom to act.

Companies that stress performance standards develop more "real teams" than those companies that simply "promote" teams. Naturally, then, the role/scope/boundaries process begins with establishing the purpose and specific objectives of the team. Regardless of the type of team—work team, support team, project team, ad hoc problem-solving team—clear, measurable objectives must be established. A group of work teams, for example, might all share three primary objectives:

· Improving product or service quality by 45 percent.

· Achieving on-time delivery or response time of 98 percent.

· Reducing operating costs by 5 percent.

Every team in the group is responsible for supporting these three shared primary goals. However, each individual team of the group could have other "subobjectives" and measures specific to the way their products or processes contribute to the primary goals shared by all.

The next step is to establish the actual role/scope/boundaries within which the team will meet those objectives. The following format is helpful in organizing the decisions made about team roles/scope/boundaries. The format is similar to the one used when defining role, scope, and boundaries of JOBs. First, review the role, scope of each new JOB.

In those situations in which the JOB is the same as the team—a 100 percent overlap of the "team"—the work of defining the team is done. If there is a difference, it would be in the boundary of decision making for the team as opposed to that of the individual JOB holder.

When a team contains *more* than one JOB, the following process must be completed in its entirety. The process begins by identifying the role of the team, then developing the three elements of its scope, and finally defining the team by its boundaries:

1. *Role.* Prepare a brief statement outlining the team's part in meeting the performance standards for the products or processes for which it is accountable, and a brief explanation of how accomplishing that will support the strategic direction package of the company.

2. *Scope.*

- *Activities.* Outline how the team spends its time in supporting the objectives.
- *Major accountabilities.* List those elements and objectives specified to be within the scope of the work team, and on which the team and/or individuals have significant influence or impact.
- *Key interfaces.* Outline the routine contacts and communication links required between the work team and the other specialists or organizational entities required to support the work team in meeting its objectives.

3. *Boundaries.* Regardless of team structure, boundaries of empowerment must be established to provide direction and focus. Not only boundaries to grant permission to act, but also to identify areas that are off limits. For example, when work teams are new, personnel and policy issues may be off limits; and only as the teams mature, responsibility for a variety of personnel issues may fall within their boundaries. Whatever the beginning boundaries, they will change and expand, synchronized to the actual evolution of the team, and the growth of two-way trust between management and worker.

The following are a few of the areas in which companies acknowledge that the team's freedom to act is bounded by clear limits.

- Decision making

  "Independent" decisions—those decisions team members can make independent of external review. Normally, these decisions concern the work process itself, and are made within parameters or boundaries spelled out clearly, and in advance.

  NOTE: Often work teams assume responsibility for daily activities such as assignment of work, tracking of performance measures, and ordering supplies.

  "Chain-of-command" decisions—are within the bound-

aries of the team, but because of budgetary or oversight issues require the approval of another layer(s) of management. In an effort to enhance decision-making speed, team effectiveness, and productivity, these should be gradually moved toward the "independent" category.

Input only—not really decisions, but issues on which the team is required to provide information for decision making to take place at another level of the organization.

· *Operational restrictions*—establish the team products, processes; its freedom of activity in the process (can it draw materials, move equipment, etc.?).

· *Degree of direction*—establish where on the leader-directed/ self-directed continuum the team is and what the expected evolution is.

Why do teams work so well at one company while at another we find management has used the perceived "silver bullet" of teams to shoot itself in the foot? It's no secret—the process we've just outlined explains why teams work well.

To guarantee the creation of effective, successful teams, ensure that teams are focused by purpose on improved performance; have specific goals aligned with the operating business objectives of the company; are integrated with the initiatives undertaken; and are systematically defined by the process just developed.

WRAP-UP

· Job redesign is often the most complicated and difficult step in the entire High P·e·r·f·o·r·m·a·n·c·e·s People Systems Process. It forces a hard and often uncomfortable look at the traditional ways work has been done, and then requires the Design Team to redesign JOBs to be more in line with the new ways work will be done in the high performance operating environment.

· The work redesign effort requires breakthrough thinking. The Design Team must work diligently to get past the mind-set of "This is the way we've always done it." For the Human Resources repre-

Synopsis: Process Step 3
Redesign Work: Redefine Jobs and <u>Define Teams</u>

Objective: To maximize team effectiveness and results in meeting the business objectives, by establishing team purpose, objectives, evolution, structure, leadership, role and boundaries.

Process: **Define Teams**

· The purpose of teams must first be determined. Most teams are in place to create improvements and support the business objectives. Specific performance objectives are then established for teams that link the strategic success factors and business objectives with team accountabilities.

· Once purpose and objectives are established, the appropriate team structure is developed. There are often four different types of team structure: ad hoc problem-solving teams, project teams, support teams, and work teams.

· The evolution of teams and their leadership must then be planned. Leadership often starts with the existing supervisor.

· The roles and accountabilities for team members are developed to reflect the purpose and objectives of the team.

· Finally, the team boundaries and authority are determined.

Results: The resulting documentation prepares your company for implementing teams or provides a mid-course assessment for how well your existing teams have been structured.

sentatives on the Design Team, this can be particularly challenging. If they lack an "operational perspective," or if they operate from the traditional HR control and consistency paradigm, they may be resistant to innovative thinking regarding job redesign and team definition.

The claim to fame for some Human Resources departments has been their expertise in job evaluation. Unfortunately, the new broad job definitions do not easily fit traditional job analysis and job evaluation methodologies, nor do they require the rocket scientist approach previously used. And for both Operations and Human Resources, empowered teams and broad jobs may initially be perceived as more difficult to manage within the twin credos of control and consistency. Regardless, it is beneficial to have a variety of perspectives infused into the design process, and to test the design against a variety of opinions. Resistance is a problem only when it becomes a clear constraint to progress.

· The results from Process Step 3: Redesign Work: Redesign Jobs and Define Teams:

For Job Redesign

  · A document for each new JOB that includes:

    · Identification of the role, scope, and boundaries of each JOB.
    · A skill model identifying core, support, and operational skills.
    · JOB characteristics listing physical and mental demands, and knowledge, skills, abilities, and equipment required.

  · A simplified JOB evaluation methodology.

For Team Definition

  · A document for each identified type of team that includes:

    · Team purpose and objectives.
    · Team structure.
      The anticipated team evolution to meet the targeted organizational profile.
    · How team leadership is established and changes with team evolution.

- · The roles and accountabilities of team members.
- · Team boundaries and authority

The expectations being established for the workforce have now increased at the completion of this Process Step. Not only are people being asked to now work in teams and focus on problem solving and process improvement, they are also being asked to think and operate differently within their jobs. They are being asked to take on a broader definition of JOB. For your people to succeed at these new requirements, they must have the proper skills. The next chapter gives you a process for developing the needed skills within your organization.

References:

1. "Future Work: Impact on Direct Compensation," Thomas J. Hackett, in *Perspectives in Total Compensation*, (ˆcottsdale, AZ: American Compensation Association, August 1992).
2. This team evolution model was developed by Belgard, Fisher, and Rayner (BFR) of Beaverton, Oregon.
3. *The Wisdom of Teams*, Jon R. Katzenbach and Douglas K. Smith (Boston, MA: McKinsey and Company, 1993).

CHAPTER 10

"Hey, Coach"

Process Step 4: Redefine Roles and Scope of Supervision

THE YEAR WAS 1991. Hank Truesdale, the president and founder of a $350 million electronics firm was perplexed. He had recently spent $40,000 on the first company-wide attitude survey, and had just completed an executive summary of the results. Parts of it made sense, but to his amazement, the group most unhappy with their jobs were not production workers, clerical staff, or even the sales force. The employee group with the lowest scores for job satisfaction was his first-line supervisors.

Hank's first reaction was anger. "What the heck's wrong with them?" he fumed. In the past 18 months, the company had spent $75,000 on team leader training for all the supervisors. And not only that, he'd personally kicked off a self-directed work teams project for the production employees to get them involved in problem solving and to take more ownership for daily production schedules. The supervisors' jobs should be easier now! All they had to do was to "coach" their teams to help them meet the monthly production goals.

It just didn't make sense. Hank put in a call to Margaret Ransom, the lead consultant of the firm that had conducted the survey. The resulting 45-minute discussion was an eye-opener. He'd wanted her perspective on the low job satisfaction scores of supervisors, and he'd gotten it. Margaret told Hank her firm had been collecting survey data for 15 years from over 275 companies. The disturbing trend had started a while back—norms indicated that supervisors and middle managers were becoming increasingly the most dissatisfied group of employees for many companies, and the size or industry didn't matter.

Ransom was leading a research project in collaboration with two other survey firms. The project was still under way, but preliminary results indicated that the slowly decreasing job satisfaction was widespread and positively correlated with companies undergoing major changes. The only exception seemed to be those companies that had in advance done an exceptional job of clearly defining a new role for supervisors. One of the hypotheses being tested by her project was that supervisors bear the brunt of organizational change, are ill prepared to do so, and as a result suffer accordingly. Hank thanked Margaret for her help and asked that she share with him the final results of her project when completed.

After he hung up the phone, Hank sat there for a while and slowly conducted a mental inventory of all the organizational changes over the past two years. Back in 1989, they'd begun a series of world-class initiatives—first, setup reduction, and then on to statistical process control, work cells, and cycle-time reduction. Recently, with these programs in some stage of development, he had started the self-directed work teams project to support the changing way work was done. It was a lot! Perhaps the team leader training for supervisors was not enough. Maybe they needed some other kind of training? Or maybe something *else* was wrong? At the moment, he didn't have a clear picture of what to do. I'll bring it up at next week's staff meeting, he thought. If these people are unhappy, we'd better do something quick.

THE REACTIVE/DOER ROLE

Hank is a "composite executive." The problem he faces is shared by many top managers at companies throughout North America. Recent surveys have exposed a steady decline in job satisfaction among supervisors and managers as their roles have begun to change dramatically. Conversely, companies that have provided their supervisors with good direction and role definition tend to fare better than those who did little. In general, supervisors in companies going through change are an unhappy group. A recent *Industry Week* survey found 77.6 percent of the first-line supervisors were not enjoying their work. The major reason cited was the lack of teamwork—actions lagged behind words about teams. The same survey found 63.1 percent of middle managers unhappy and for similar reasons as first-line supervisors.[1]

Traditionally, the roles of supervisors and managers have changed infrequently. Their roles have always been linked to the "way work is done," and that has changed infrequently. Traditional roles were defined as plan, organize, coordinate, and control—translated through the job description as scheduling work, supervising, communicating, administering policies, meeting organizational performance goals, controlling budgets and expenses, and the like. Traditionally, supervisors work out an approach to get all this done, moving from activity to activity, but after a while, settling into the routine. The "routine," however, was not one that allowed them to accomplish the job as described. The proactive role of plan or organize and coordinate was replaced by a "reactive" role. True enough, the daily activities might be characterized by a lot of "fire fighting," but it's still a routine.

Supervisors in most traditional companies, in the "reactive roles," have described their job as:

- Fire fighter.

- Chief expediter.

- Meeting attender.

- Paper pusher.

They typically close the description of their role with a sad statement that goes something like this ". . . And I don't get to work with the people in the reactive role as often as I'd like to."

While they moan and groan about it, many supervisors and managers wouldn't have it any other way. The high level of stress, the constant flurry of activity, and the endless meetings pump the adrenalin and give them a sense of security. Besides, many of them got promoted into their supervisor role because of their ability to fight fires and solve problems—because of their *ability* to react . . . to make things happen . . . to *do*.

Companies often promote their best "doers" and "technicians" into the supervisory ranks. For these people, there is comfort in the reactive role. Eric Flamholtz and Yvonne Randle, authors of *The Inner Game of Management*, identify what they call the "Doer Syndrome," described as "the tendency of a person who has been promoted to a managerial role to continue to think and act as a doer rather than as a manager."[2]

Operating in a "reactive" role is a great opportunity for a "doer" to continue relying on the skills that got him promoted in the first place. The transition from doer to manager is difficult, likened to the transition from professional sports player to coach. If supervisors have Doer Syndrome they tend to:

- Tie their self-esteem to their own performance rather than that of their subordinates;

- Spend a lot of their time actually engaged in the work itself rather than the more traditional managerial activities of coordinating, planning, etc.;

- Perceive that to be a good manager, they must continue to be the best technician; as a result, they can compete with their own employees for the "title of technical expert";

- Have difficulty handling decreasing degrees of control; as doers, they had a lot of control over the results of their efforts, as supervisors or managers, the control over results is not as direct.

These tendencies to "do" have perpetuated a reactive routine that takes supervisors away from their proper roles, and makes the role of choice—by default—the reactive role.

In many companies today, "reactivity" of the supervisor's role has deepened as the "routine" becomes increasingly chaotic. Internal and external changes now include significant changes in the way work is done. Supervisors still face "fire fighting," but on top of that there is implementing new initiatives, one after the other, top management seemingly confused about direction in general. Worst of all, to accommodate the new ways of working, companies are moving to a team-based environment.

Regardless of how companies have defined the traditional roles, supervisors have always assumed the "reactive" role when the traditional role no longer reflected reality, or how work is really done. Significant changes in the way work is done have made neither the traditional nor the standard reactive roles satisfactory. The old roles are no longer valid, and a future role of coach has emerged. But what clearly does not exist are plans to transition supervisors into coaches and, in many cases, the stark lack of a solid description of what being a coach or facilitator means. In the absence of transition plans and concrete role definitions, the "reactive" role of supervisors has worsened. Supervisors are now in a "victim" role.

"We were told not to attend the team meetings," Frank said bitterly. "The teams are now *empowered*, and, therefore, we shouldn't attend their meetings unless invited. We felt like we were in no-man's-land." The people in the teams got all the attention and training. Frank and his colleagues interpreted the "guidelines" as a threat to their future. A layoff of salaried employees just six months earlier, and now the new team guidelines created a rumor that supervisor positions were being set up for elimination in the next layoff. Their concerns were unfounded. Management's intention was to encourage a rapid development of teams, but they failed to understand the role of supervisors in that effort.

The new team-based environment requires of the team many of the same "doing" kinds of things that supervisors have historically used in their "reactive" role—now those familiar tools are no longer available. How is the supervisor to "react"? For some, it's to say, "Forget it," and return to the hourly workforce. For others in the "victim" role, reaction takes the form of inadvertent or even deliberate sabotage of the new team-based environment and the strategic initiatives that support it. And others keep trying their best to "do" and to "react," and become ineffective at both.

When the future role of coach and facilitator is too amorphous, companies provide an excuse for their supervisors and managers to remain "doers" and encourage the "reactive" or "victim" role to be the predominant *de facto* role today. With companies neither understanding nor planning a transition role from today's reactive/doer role to that of coach/facilitator, supervisors will cling to the reactive role—it is the only way they know how to play the game.

Another reason supervisors and managers are uneasy with the role of coach/facilitator is job security. With good coaches and facilitators supporting effective self-directed work teams, companies need fewer supervisors and managers. And supervisors and managers know it. In addition to an unclear coaching role, they bear the very real threat of losing their job, and strengthening their role as "victim."

WINNING THE GAME

Henry Mintzberg is a leading thinker on management issues, and after years studying managers' roles, Mintzberg has concluded that "managers' effectiveness is significantly influenced by their insight into their own work. Performance depends on how well a manager understands and responds to the pressures and dilemmas of the job."[3] To provide supervisors with the necessary insight into their changing, evolving work, the High Performance Enterprise must engage in two important actions: (1) a periodic definition or redefinition of roles and scope, and (2) the development of transition plans to move supervisors into their new roles.

1. In the High Performance Enterprise, the habit of continuous change and renewal means that the way work is done will always be changing. As the nature of work continually changes, the role of supervisors will continually evolve.

High Performance Enterprises are team-based and hierarchically flat. Just as their employees' jobs will broaden, supervisors' roles and scope will be broader, with significantly greater spans of control not uncommon. In such an environment, supervisors can no longer direct the minutiae of daily work, nor can companies afford to permit them to take the "reactive" role.

Roles must be absolutely clear to permit everyone to concentrate on his or her area of responsibility. Well-defined roles are essential throughout the new organizational hierarchy to enable and support the broader scope of responsibility. Periodic redefinition of the roles of supervisors and managers permits the High Performance Enterprise to periodically realign and integrate the roles of front-line supervision with the company's strategic direction and the changing characteristics of the high performance operating environment.

Without clear role definitions and transition plans, the potential for stepping on toes and redundancy of effort is increased. This "horrible example" of role confusion occurred at a multiple facility company that had installed dozens of "self-directed" work teams. Nothing was done to involve supervisors in the process, or to work with them on their new roles with the teams. It was *assumed* the supervisors and managers would naturally "fall into line" with the teams.

Several months later, the multiple factories were in a state of anarchy. The "self-directed" teams had discovered they could call a meeting at any time, and then leave their work area *without informing the supervisor*. Teams were often found "having meetings" out by the picnic tables, smoking cigarettes during working hours. Supervisors were angry and frustrated by how the team *thing* was dumped on them. They were tired of fighting with the teams to bring order out of chaos. Many supervisors had mentally "checked out," and were just putting in time. The situation finally came back under control when management sat down with supervisors and went through a process of redefining supervisors', work teams', and managers' roles and a transition plan for achieving the new roles.

2. Since roles *will* continually evolve, supervisors expected to fulfill those roles will be continually faced with having to transition gracefully from the old role to the new. A well-developed transition plan will help maintain the commitment and loyalty of a company's supervisors and managers. They can now see how and where they fit into the company's future. Job security fears can be addressed

openly. Transition plans also identify options for those who may contribute better in a different role.

There are plenty of opportunities for supervisors to feel victimized by the changes taking place. Periodic role redefinition and effective transition plans enable the High Performance Enterprise to balance such changes with enhanced opportunities for supervisors and managers to evolve, grow, and succeed with the changes. The company benefits because the potential for stepping on toes and redundancy of effort is reduced. The supervisors benefit when their roles are continuously reintegrated with the company's initiatives and direction—they benefit because they become *successful* supervisors. And the Hank Truesdales of the world will see an upward shift in the trend of supervisor job satisfaction.

THE GAME PLAN

In the empowering context of the United States Constitution, specific responsibilities are carved out and assigned to the federal government, with all other responsibilities reserved naturally and legally for the states of the federation. Each state holds those reserved responsibilities to itself, until that state in turn legally grants partial or specific responsibilities to individual towns, cities, or counties. In this manner, the Founding Fathers sought a method for ensuring that each entity of the federation concentrated on those things it did best—and to keep them from stepping on each other's toes when they did it. With "occasional" assistance from constitutional law, this amazing approach has worked for a couple of hundred years. It has worked because the roles and scopes of the participants were clear to each other, and there has been available a legal process to continually improve the performance of the approach.

The approach used in the High P·e·r·f·o·r·m·a·n·c·e·s People Systems Process is similar to that employed in the Constitution: Process Step 3 carved out a portion of the company's total p·e·r·f·o·r·m·a·n·c·e·s—a significant portion of activities, accountabilities, interfaces, decision making, and boundaries—and granted them to teams and new broader JOBs through clearly defined roles and scopes. What was not granted to the new JOBs and teams is reserved for the rest of the company. Now the company in turn must "grant" partial and specific responsibilities to its supervisors, managers, etc.—with a similar definition of role and scope used for JOBs and teams.

Though in this chapter we concentrate on "granting" or "carving out" role and scope for supervisors, the same process should be progressively carried out up through the company's hierarchy, right to the top.

In redefining the role and scope of supervision and providing a transition plan, the Design Team follows a familiar approach, this time with six Action Steps.

Redefine Roles and Scope of Supervision
Action Steps

1. Define and describe the target roles and scope.

2. Review target role and scope against team member role and scope.

3. Develop a *realistic* contrasting profile of today's supervisor role and scope.

4. Analyze the gap between target and baseline role and scope.

5. Develop a transition plan.

6. Empower the supervisors.

DEFINING ROLES AND SCOPE OF SUPERVISION

1. Define and describe in detail the target roles and scope for supervisors as required by the high performance operating environment and reflected in the targeted organizational profile:

- Role
- Scope:

  - Major activities
  - Accountabilities
  - Key interfaces
  - Decision making, boundaries, flexibility, etc.

2. Review the targeted role and scope of supervision against the responsibilities of those reporting to the supervisors to ensure no overlap or redundancy of activities, accountabilities, interfaces, or boundaries.

3. Take an honest look at what supervisors do today, and establish a realistic contrasting descriptive baseline profile of today's roles and scope:

- Role
- Scope:

  - Major activities
  - Accountabilities
  - Key interfaces
  - Decision making, boundaries, flexibility, etc.

4. Perform an analysis of the gap between the baseline roles and scope and the targets to reveal "What's missing?" between the two contrasting profiles: what behaviors, training, tools, processes, etc. In other words, what "action items" are required to close the gap.

5. Develop a transition plan to:

   a. Move supervisors from the baseline role and scope to the target role and scope;
   b. Provide other opportunities to those supervisors who cannot transition from the baseline to target.

6. Guarantee a successful transition by ensuring that empowerment includes empowered supervisors. In a fully empowered organizational context, will they flourish in their new roles, and provide effective and successful "new" supervision?

It's hard to believe, but companies tend to forget their supervisors and managers are human. Often this group feels the least empowered to change. The eight attributes of an empowered organization are just as important in creating a context for supervisors and managers as they are for the rest of the organization:

- Build trust: address their job security concerns.

- Share information: provide ongoing business education.

- Provide new skills training: "coaching" and facilitating are not intuitive skills for most supervisors and managers.

- Support new boundaries: allow the supervisors to operate successfully within the boundaries established for their new role.

- Enforce roles and accountabilities: hold supervisors and managers accountable for the behaviors required to support the high performance operating environment, not just for the "numbers."

- Provide ongoing feedback: supervisors need feedback on their p·e·r·f·o·r·m·a·n·c·e·s against their new roles and job scope.

- Reinforce through pay and rewards: as with all employees, supervisor pay should be tied to performance; and supervisors should be part of any Performance-based Rewards program.

- Provide necessary resources: the greatest resource constraint will be time; make sure supervisors are allowed the time for all of the above, especially to gracefully transition to their new role.

The typical targeted role of supervision with which most Design Teams work is that of "supervisor as coach." The typical question they face is, what is a coach? The answer is, coaching is an evolving role, not a static definition. It looks something like this:

The Evolution of "Coaching"[4]

Early Teams	Intermediate Teams	Mature Teams
· Direct people	· Involve people	· Build trust and inspire teamwork
· Explain decisions	· Get input for decisions	· Facilitate and support team decisions
· Train individuals	· Develop performance	· Expand team capabilities
· Manage one-on-one	· Coordinate group effort	· Create team identity
· Contain conflict	· Resolve conflict	· Make the most of team differences
· React to change	· Implement change	· Foresee and influence change

---

To reinforce the change in role, many companies have changed the title from "supervisor" to "coordinator" or "coach."

Let's follow one company through the process of redefining the roles and scope of supervision. The decisions made by the company as they followed the process were theirs, were organic to their felt needs and organizational environment, and not necessarily reflective of decisions that might be made by other companies with different needs and environments.

Practical Guideline

When defining the role of supervisors, expand the Design Team membership temporarily to include supervisors from all different areas.

This particular company followed the process several levels beyond that of supervisor. A vertically integrated manufacturer of large industrial systems had implemented work cells in all its factories, all located in roughly the same geographic area. A representative team of supervisors and managers from all facilities met over a period of weeks to complete the role and scope definition process for a variety of organizational levels in Operations, from team member up through director of operations.

HOW ONE COMPANY MADE THE TRANSITION

Action Steps 1, 2, 3

As part of the move to work cells, major changes had occurred in the level of involvement of the hourly employees in the major processes for which they were responsible. Cell members took over many of the daily scheduling and administrative duties previously performed by their supervisors. The team of supervisors and managers began the redefinition of the supervisors' roles and scope by reviewing the new role and new broad JOB definitions of work cell team members to determine exactly what responsibility had been assumed by the teams.

Three additional positions were addressed before the team handled the supervisory position. Decisions regarding these positions were made on the basis of the targeted organizational profile for the company. The new role of cell leader had been targeted as a rotational position within the work cell, and was not to be part of the official hierarchy of the organization. Positions of group leader and assistant supervisor were not part of the targeted profile. Accordingly, both positions were planned for elimination within 18 months, and that decision made an "action item" for the transition plan.

The next organizational level addressed was the supervisor. The team first compared the targeted roles, major activities, accountabilities, key interfaces, and decision making (authority boundaries) for supervisors against the *same* elements for the new team definition for work cell members. Immediately, they were able to identify and eliminate areas of scope overlap and redundancy either by modifying team member scope or boundary elements or correcting the targeted roles and scope for supervisors. Then they developed a realistic profile of the supervisors' current roles and scope—a baseline profile.

After ensuring alignment and integration of the roles of team member and supervisor, the team continued the process with the positions of manufacturing manager and the director of operations. They completed the target and baseline roles and scope outline for these organizational levels, and reviewed the targeted positions from top to bottom once more for alignment and potential redundancy.

At that point, on paper at least, the four key levels below general manager were now aligned with each other, and the company's business objectives. A glance at the following summary of roles and scopes reveals that each position's place in the evolutionary scheme of things was beginning to develop. It also clearly points out that, especially for cell members and supervisors, a lot of change was required to move from the current baseline profile to the targeted profile.

One Company's Role and Scope Alignment

Work Cell Member
Target: Primary producer and improver of work. Operate as a team member; administer the cell; problem solver; monitor of cell performance; trainer; communicator of issues.

Baseline: Primary producer of work.

Supervisor
Target: Supervise—coach and facilitate—multiple teams; disciplinarian (final resolution after input from cell members). Auditor of goals and performance; motivator and facilitator of continuous improvement; trainer.

Baseline: Supervise one team; disciplinarian; director of activities; scheduler of work; motivator; chief expediter; primary information source; paper worker and tracker; fire fighter.

Manufacturing Manager
Target: Leader in development and implementation of world-class manufacturing processes; coordinator of efforts between factories; business manager; supervisor backup and support system; team player; adviser to director of operations.

Baseline: Fire fighter; referee; coordinator of daily schedules.

Director of Operations
Target: Architect of world-class manufacturing programs; visionary; planner for the future; supporter of new ideas; adviser to GM.

Baseline: Adviser to GM; leader of world-class manufacturing programs; fire fighter; referee/coordinator between factories.

Action Step 4

The shifts or evolutions in roles and scope outlined in the summary do not occur just because they exist on paper. The team acknowledged this, and once comfortable with the relationships among the various targeted positions, they moved quickly to identify, point by point,

"What's missing?" between the baseline and target for each position. Their gap analysis revealed a laundry list of "action items" for each of the position's action items. The team studied each one intensely to make sure they knew what was required.

The supervisor position required dramatic changes in expected behaviors, and also required a major shift of activities to the cell members. Among the action items were: shifting performance tracking to the cell members and giving the supervisor more of an audit, feedback, and an adjustment role in work cell performance rather than the current directive role; and shifting much of the supervisor's administrative paperwork to the cell members, and tasking the supervisor with an audit and check-off responsibility.

Other action items were developed to ensure a fully successful transition. Rather than just superficially identifying the transition as "paperwork," the specific types of paperwork were defined. The following types of paperwork responsibility were listed for the work cells:

- Purchase requisitions and ordering of supplies for work cell supplies under $500.

- Maintenance work order requisitions.

- Computer operations.
  - Database management.
  - Report generation.

The action item for "paperwork" also required that a document package for each of the paperwork items was to be developed, and training on their use provided to the work cell members. The supervisor's audit role, the kinds of feedback to be provided, and what adjustments should be made were specified in the action item for the supervisor.

Action Step 5

The team performed a reconciliation of the total list of action items. Items that were exposed during their role and scope process, but had no direct bearing on the transition, were outsourced to other management teams. They grouped items where appropriate, prioritized to ensure completion in time to meet targeted dates, and incorporated all action items into a formal transition plan. The resulting plan made it clear that the transition would not be easy, but also that if success were the goal, the transition plan required immediate implementation. The team assigned dates and accountabilities to each of the action items, with most supervisors having some responsibility for the implementation of the transition plan.

The director of operations worked with the manufacturing managers regarding the second major element of the transition plan: the transition of some supervisors into other organizational roles. The plan spanned a 24-month period. Approximately 20 percent of the 40 supervisors were identified as unlikely to easily make the transition. The plan focused on attrition to reduce the total number of supervisors. No supervisors would be replaced upon departure. The team identified two openings in the materials organization, and planned to create an in-house training department that would handle an additional three supervisors. In the end, they identified legitimate opportunities that within the two-year goal would allow all former supervisors to continue to make a contribution in a new role.

Once the transition plan was developed and approved by the general manager, the director of operations met with all supervisors in a series of general meetings. Roles were reviewed with the group. Input from supervisors resulted in further refinement and clarification of terms. After a final consensus was reached on the four sets of roles, the director discussed the details of the transition plan. It was presented in a confident, upbeat manner that communicated the company's desire to maintain every supervisor in a contributory role. It was also presented as an opportunity to make dramatic role changes, perhaps into another area of interest within Operations or the company at large.

After the general meetings, the manufacturing managers began meeting one-on-one with each supervisor to encourage their involvement in the transition plan. During the meetings, supervisors and managers acknowledged that they were relieved to have a graceful evolution into their new roles.

Action Step 6

The team had maximized the benefits of their world-class manufacturing initiatives by realigning the operations organization to support the changing work processes. And by providing clear roles and scopes to their supervisors, the company empowered its supervisors to be successful contributors in the drive to become a High Performance Enterprise.

Synopsis: Process Step 4
Redefine Roles and Scope of Supervision

Objective: Ensure that work and accountabilities of supervisors are realigned to support the various elements of the high performance operating environment.

Process: · The process is similar to that completed for JOB redesign in Process Step 3. Targeted role and scope (including boundaries) are developed for supervisory positions and are then compared with the current or baseline role and scope of supervisors.

· The targeted role is compared with the baseline role and a "gap" analysis is completed by generating a list of action items to close the gap.

· Transition plans are created to assist the supervisors in developing the skills for their new roles. The transition plan includes projected opportunities to contribute elsewhere in the organization for those supervisors not able to transition to a "coaching" role.

Results: Creating transition plans for supervisors shows commitment to their development, reduces their concerns about job security, and ensures that the work of supervisors is coordinated with that of the teams.

WRAP-UP

- "We want you to be a coach" may have been music to Vince Lombardi's ears, but there are plenty of supervisors who find that request pretty discordant. The more rapid the changes in organizations and work processes, the more frequently a company needs to modify or redefine the roles and scope of its front-line supervision. And it takes more than a liberal sprinkling of buzzwords and a little encouragement to make a successful transition to the new roles. It takes a defined process—an ongoing transition process.

- The process presented here has been used successfully in a variety of companies. However, it is not a sacred process. If your company has another format suitable for defining roles and scope, use it. This format was provided as a tool. Its real importance lies in the thought process and direction that it provides. What is important is the *content*, not the form.

- At the end of Process Step 4—Redefine Roles and Scope of Supervision—the results are:

  - Clear roles and scope for the company's supervisors, targeted for a time frame that supports the strategic direction of the company as it's carried out at the operational level.
  - A transition plan that acknowledges the gap between the targeted and baseline roles and scopes, and that organizes the resulting action items to:
    (1) move supervisors from their current roles and scope to the targeted; or
    (2) move those no longer suited for supervision to other contributory roles within the organization.

- Although the accent of this step is on front-line supervision, as illustrated, the process has application across the broad range of positions from cell member to the top of the organization. The empowered context requires roles and scope for everyone.

References:

1. *Industry Week*, November 2, 1992.
2. *The Inner Game of Management*, Eric Flamholtz and Yvonne Randle (New York: American Management Association, 1987).
3. "The Manager's Job: Folklore and Fact," Henry Mintzberg, *Harvard Business Review*, March–April 1990.
4. The information on evolution of coaching came from Zenger-Miller, Inc., and their *The Challenge of Team Leadership* materials. This information was slightly modified for our purposes.

CHAPTER 11

It Worked for the Navajos, but . . .

Process Step 5: Design a Skills Development Process

"THOUGH THE MORNING sun beat down hotly, warming the young boy's back and the ground around him, Burning Star noticed it not. His attention was focused on the voice of the old man seated in front of him. Bear That Sings did not notice the sun either. He was focused deep within himself, calling forth the point-by-point details of building great ceremonial fires. The right kinds of wood . . . the structure designed to send the flames high into the air . . . and the tinder placed just so to ensure a quick start to the fire.

"As the description unfolded, Burning Star took in each thought and stored it carefully in its right place, so that he could call forth the exact details when Bear That Sings would ask him to repeat it— which he would do countless times during the next few weeks. But it did not cross his mind to be worried. All his short life he had been trained to listen, to learn, and to remember. Listen, learn, remember. It was his role in the tribe—he was to be the one who remembers. He was to be the bearer of the history and the ways of the people."

Early Native Americans had no written language. For them, the "oral history" approach was the only way to pass on skills and history from generation to generation. It was not a haphazard approach. Individuals were chosen at very young ages to take on the role of "oral historian." They were trained to listen, to learn, and to remember.

The oral history tradition lives on. Adopted by business, oral history skills development is a training methodology used by count-less companies around the world. New employees learn how to do their jobs from current employees. Employees new to a certain position or new to the company are paired up with a "buddy," a more experienced employee, to learn the new skills. From the number of companies that train this way, one would think it to be the most efficient and effective way of accomplishing skills training. But is it?

No, it is not. The "buddies" and "new hires" are not like Bear That Sings and Burning Star, trained since youth to listen, learn, and remember. Along with the skills new employees learn, they also learn all the shortcuts and bad habits that have been developed over the years by the experienced employees. The basic skills get passed on, year after year, and so do the bad habits.

The scary question is, are the *correct* basic skills being passed along? And is it only a few bad habits that get passed along? Have you ever played the game where a person starts a certain story around a circle of people by whispering it to the person next to him, who in turn whispers it to the next person, and so on, all the way around the circle? By the time it comes back around to the initiator, each person's variation has made the original story generally unrecogniz-able, and usually pretty outrageous.

But because manufacturing and service are not games, passing on an "unrecognizable" skill is not "pretty outrageous"—doing so cre-ates process variation. The saving grace for most traditional com-panies has been that workers do not move from position to position, that processes are repetitious, and that ample quality inspections take place. This keeps variation within "acceptable" levels. There are two problems with this scenario:

1. "Employees working repetitiously" is becoming a poor foun-dation for building an informal skills training program. Repetition is out . . . flexibility is in. The requirement for flexible production from flexible processes supported by flexible workers is becoming more than a "nice to have" feature—it's becoming a competitive mandate for survival and growth as the High Performance Enter-prises both in the Far East and in the West increasingly use flex-ibility as a weapon.

2. Formerly "acceptable" levels of variation are not good enough for a competitive position today. Process variation caused by marginally trained workers performing in poorly documented processes is a quick route out of business.

Skills may be defined across the entire organization in the High P·e·r·f·o·r·m·a·n·c·e·s People Systems Process, for hourlies, non-exempts, professionals, and managers, as well. Though the focus of this chapter is on operator-level skills, and not the technical or professional levels, the skills development issues are similar. Developing a "white-collar" skills model is similar to the one we will develop for the basic JOB—the differences lie in how the skills are defined, and how current "white-collar" certification includes a greater provision for experience than demonstrated skill competency. The most striking shared element among operator, professional, and managerial skill development is a company mind-set that clings to clearly outmoded concepts and practices.

The questionable nature of the oral history skills development is so obvious—especially today, with quality, flexibility, and throughput-time so critical—that its continued use is truly amazing. Why would any company want to continue this dated tradition? Well . . . because a more formalized approach to skills training has its own challenges; otherwise, there would not be the reliance on the oral history method. Companies balk at a formalized skills training program because:

FIVE GOOD (?) REASONS NOT TO FORMALIZE SKILLS TRAINING

· The benefits of a formal skills training program may not appear to outweigh the costs or challenges of implementing one—it's an expense on today's income statement; not an investment on tomorrow's balance sheet.

· Many companies are trying to operate with just enough employees to get the work done—100 percent optimal capacity—leaving no "capacity" or time or funds available for training.

· Taking experienced employees from the more critical operations or positions to allow others to cross-train can negatively impact productivity—it could hurt *today's* production.

· With limited resources, the documentation required to formalize skills training appears overwhelming, and its maintenance, burdensome.

· And a formal skills training may require extra training personnel that organizations cannot "afford."

On the whole, these are impressive reasons not to implement a formal skills development program. All appear to be legitimate challenges, especially in these times of lean and mean manufacturing and downsized, right-sized organizations. Are there options between oral history training and a formal skills training program? Maybe, maybe not. Let's broaden our view of the situation for a moment and review some startling estimates and statistics. [1]

AN OVERSUPPLY OF THE UNDERSKILLED

· In general, work is becoming increasingly complex due to information requirements, technological advancements, and empowerment. In general, the labor supply is becoming increasingly less skilled. In the United States, in particular, education is failing to deliver. Unless dramatic changes are made almost immediately, companies will no longer be able to rely on the educational system to provide workers with basic skills. Companies must be prepared to ensure that the required skills are present in their workforces.

· By the year 2000, the U.S. workplace will require the most skilled and educated workforce of any economic system in history. With that in mind, the following statistics are alarming:

· By the end of the '80s, only 39.2 percent of 17-year-olds could read well enough to understand and explain complicated information, and only 4.9 percent could synthesize and learn from such materials.

· Only 51.1 percent of the 17-year-olds could correctly perform moderately complex mathematical procedures, and only 6.4 percent could perform multistep problem solving and algebra.

· In science, only 41.4 percent could analyze scientific data and only 7.5 percent could integrate specialized scientific information.

· Not only are those currently in our school systems not adequately prepared for the mental challenges of the High Performance Enterprise, but the adult generations preceding them are even less prepared for the changes ahead. The reeducation challenge is overwhelming.

· Eighty percent of applicants screened by Motorola failed an entry-level test that required nothing more than seventh-grade English and fifth-grade math.

All of this adds up to a serious picture: it is going to be difficult for companies to find good new employees; the oral history method of training is ineffective in preparing new hires *and* incumbents with the skills required by their broad JOB; and flexibility is becoming an increasingly powerful competitive weapon.

There are few options available to companies in this situation. Whichever option is selected, the answer is going to be, "Pay me now . . . or pay me later!" And, to some companies, paying later may be either too late, or impossible. In the end, most companies will have little choice but to acknowledge the requirement for skilled workers, and the necessity for an approach to make that happen. For companies determined to be competitive, and convinced that flexibility is an essential ingredient in the high performance work environment, the appropriate option is a formalized skills development process with its combination of definition, training, and certification.

FROM EXPENSE TO INVESTMENT

Fortunately, there are significant benefits that encourage companies to overcome the initial challenges to an effective skills development process—benefits other than raw survival. Companies that have replaced their oral history skills training with a defined skills development process enjoy positive results quickly.

Siemens owns a factory in Newport News, Virginia, where several years ago they wanted to build a new automobile fuel injector. The workforce, however, was accustomed to years of routine assembly work. They did not have the skills needed to run complex new machine tools, or to handle the new ways of organizing their work. Rather than move the product elsewhere, Siemens worked with a local community college to develop an in-house course on world-class manufacturing. It emphasized the case for change and the need for learning new skills. The results have been outstanding. The part is produced to tolerances greater than what the machine tools manufacturer said was possible, and sales of the fuel injector have risen 40 percent a year for three years. For the employees during this time, the benefit has been a higher increase in wages and a doubling in the number of jobs available.[2]

Allstate Insurance Company has also invested heavily in a skills training effort that details the thought process and decision points required for each operation. Their initial results showed productivity increased 75 percent and quality improved 90 percent, with estimated savings of $35 million a year.[3]

For both Siemens and Allstate, the immediate benefit was improved performance. An improvement that came not just from the training itself, but from all the elements involved in a skills development process. With skills development, improved performance and other benefits flow from:

Improved process control results in a higher-quality product or service. For the High Performance Enterprise, it goes like this: define the process . . . control the process . . . improve the process. A formalized skills development process takes the same approach: work procedures, standards, and tools are documented; they are updated through a formal change-control process; and they become the basis for establishing the skills required.

Work instructions define the process and visually assist operators as they move from product to product, or process to process. They run the gamut from basic flow charts to simple diagrams and drawings to the sophisticated computer-generated instructions used by

Toshiba at their Ome facility. Engineering drawings and blueprints and the like are generally not as useful unless "cleaned up" or in other ways made easier to use.

For your company, this may be the first experience with process documentation. Good "shortcuts" are formally incorporated into the process providing all employees with an opportunity to share in process improvement. Bad habits and inappropriate shortcuts are identified and eliminated. Further process improvements are routinely fed back into new work instructions through the documentation system. Defect rates invariably decline and, just as surely, quality improves. Everyone learns each new operation the same way, using the same documentation. People who have already learned an operation have a ready reference source as an occasional process check.

Increased flexibility is a key characteristic of the high performance operating environment and is a major competitive strategy for the '90s. To achieve flexibility in the workforce, workers must be able to proficiently perform a variety of tasks, correctly apply multiple skills, and be able to use those skills when called upon. There is no flexibility if a supervisor cannot call upon a "skilled worker" at any time to perform tasks and utilize skills for which he's been trained. Therefore, skills are not only acquired, they are also maintained. To make sure this happens, an effective skills development process always contains a formalized skills training and certification program.

The benefit of developed, certified, and maintained flexibility is improved performance in the form of *increased productivity*. Companies bring new employees up-to-speed faster. They produce high-quality products or services sooner, because there is less process variation. In organizations that honor "bumping rights," the domino effect of flexible worker movement is less disruptive to productivity than in the traditional environment. Flexible workers move up and down the process easily in response to kanban signals or other directions to relieve bottlenecks or satisfy varying customer requirements. Routine absences and vacations no longer have the potential to so significantly impact production or services—volume may drop, but the process does not stop dead just because a critical skill is "out." An inventory of skills is available—listing qualified or certified employees by skill—to enable teams and supervisors to respond quickly and effectively to unplanned requirements.

With skills development, improved performance and other benefits flow from:

- Improved process control,
- Increased flexibility,
- Increased productivity,
- Job enrichment,
- Relationship building with customers, vendors, and regulatory agencies,
- The increased employability of the people.

The *company's relationships* with its customers, vendors, and stakeholders in general *are enhanced* by effective skills development. How? Obviously, through the timely delivery of higher-quality products, but also because of a visible demonstration of quality. Companies use skills certification programs to demonstrate to customers or regulatory agencies that their processes are under control. The Tellabs sales force brings customers out onto the manufacturing floor to demonstrate the quality of their production process. The product-specific color-coded work instructions at each operation, and the ease and confidence with which Tellabs' electronic associates move up and down the process, are powerful quality statements.

Job enrichment or, more accurately, *JOB enrichment* occurs when formalized skills development "stretches" the depth and breadth of an individual's skills. In the High Performance Enterprise, with JOBs more broadly defined, people have the opportunity to learn additional skills without changing JOBs. Such opportunities were not necessarily welcome in the traditional environment where the "sink or swim" mentality of informal training programs intimidated people and left them reluctant to try new things. When skills development provides formalized, documented training, and allows for adequate practice time, the "user-friendly" learning environment encourages broad participation. People feel better about their work when they're on top of their skills, when they know their ability to contribute is expandable, and under their control. A Canadian union official described well the benefit of formal cross-training opportunities when he said, "You just feel a lot more valuable to the team."

Increased employability is a benefit to both company and the well-skilled employee. In today's uncertain times, guaranteeing job security to employees is becoming more and more difficult. Companies continue to eliminate jobs, and new jobs are not created at the same rate. A. Gary Shilling, an economic forecaster, predicts that the U.S. unemployment rate will be stuck above 9 percent at the year 2000. In California, where aerospace represents 20 percent of manufacturing jobs, many workers are losing their jobs as a result of the peace dividend. Yet only 15 percent of those workers have skills that are easily transferable. For many people, decent-paying jobs will become more and more scarce.[4] The type of skills acquired through a formalized skills training and certification process are skills for life.

One way people may ensure a more secure future is to increase the depth and breadth of their skills. This includes conceptual skills like problem solving and teamwork, as well as the technical and operational skills. A division of a *Fortune* 50 company began a "workforce upgrade" program in 1987. For two years, employees spent time learning additional manufacturing skills, and many attended in-house math and reading classes sponsored by the company and the local junior college.

When the company decided to close this facility in 1990 and consolidate its products with another division, 800 hourly workers were faced with no employment in the company. Worse yet, the city in which this division was located had recently been hard hit by major layoffs from other large companies. However, the company was able to place every single employee who wanted to continue working in a job with other companies. The community was well aware of the division's upgrade program, and came seeking those 800 employees. The outplacement program coordinator said that companies calling in for names of possible candidates were willing to hold positions open just to find trained, multiskilled workers of the caliber available among the division's former employees. For these employees, enhanced employability was a form of "alternative" job security.

Despite the growing awareness among companies of the imperative for a highly skilled and flexible workforce, and the benefits of a skills development process, relatively few companies are taking concrete action to develop such processes. A recent study by the National Association of Manufacturers indicated only 5 to 7 percent of the study's participants had made significant changes to their training programs. A 1992 *Fortune* article entitled "The Job Drought" speculated on the lack of progress toward formalized skills training:

> Why do firms that contemplate creating a "high performance" work organization—one that combines high skill levels, high productivity, and relatively high wages—so often give up before they start? One reason is that there's no consensus, even within industries, about how best to do this.[5]

THE MECHANICS OF SKILLS DEVELOPMENT

There may not be a consensus, but the following approach works well. Here the Design Team concentrates on designing a general process for skills development and a certification model, or master template, but not all of the detailed development for each and every skill in each and every JOB. When the design is complete, the Design Team normally hands off the development work to the company's training department or to a skills training and certification documentation project task force. Using the skills certification model as a template, one of these groups will complete the development work.

Designing a skills development process for your organization involves much more than simply setting up skills training. In fact, when actual skills training takes place, it's almost anticlimactic. To demonstrate this, we'll begin with a few of the questions that require answering *before* skills training takes place, and even before the Design Team can hand off its skills development "framework" to the skills documentation project team:

A Dozen Pithy Questions

1. How will training opportunities be made available?

2. How will a manager or supervisor know the employee is now competent in a certain skill?

3. What will be done to ensure that employees maintain their skills?

4. Are all the skills to be given equal credit or recognition?

5. How are the differences among skills accounted for?

6. Who will be conducting the skills training?

7. Who will evaluate competency and grant certifications?

8. How will skills documentation be maintained and updated?

9. Is it possible for an employee to lose a skills certification?

10. Is there a minimum or maximum number of mandatory skills required?

11. What happens when a skill becomes obsolete?

12. Is there a predescribed sequence of skills training to follow?

If the Design Team is not able to answer these questions at the completion of this Process Step, you can be sure of two things:

1. *Someone* in the company will ask these questions.

2. Eventually, someone in the company *must answer* each one fully.

To complete its design of a skills development process, and answer all those questions, the Design Team is going to enlist the help of outside experts from the operator level and human resource training and compensation specialists. Operators will help wrestle with the attributes of different skills, and the HR specialists will contribute with their knowledge and experience to the formalization of parts of the process. As one Design Team member described this Process Step, "Defining the certifications took forever because of the level of detail. Yet, we now think about things in a completely different way than before."

The seven Action Steps in this Process Step require the Design Team to:

1. Assess current training programs, methods, and resources;

2. Identify and organize JOB skills;

3. Develop a certification process;

4. Build a certification model (for each JOB);

5. Create and manage opportunities for certification;

6. Develop training resources;

7. Address design issues/establish administrative guidelines.

1. Assess current training programs, methods, and resources.

The Design Team begins with the decision not to reinvent the wheel, nor to fall prey to the not-invented-here mind-set. They should beg, borrow, or steal from what already exists, from what already works. The starting point for designing a skills development program is taking stock of current skills training programs inside the company and outside at other companies, including examples of existing on-the-job training (OJT) procedures and any documentation or training aids used. Cover all areas of the company, because it is likely that approaches will differ from department to department. It's not unusual to find a jewel of a training program operating somewhere in the company—successfully operating, unbeknown to the company in general.

Companies in pharmaceuticals and the food industry regulated by the federal Food and Drug Administration may already have some type of job or skills certification program in place. These can provide a great framework on which to build.

The Design Team needs information regarding existing or already planned classroom instruction, either being developed in-house or purchased off-the-shelf. It is not unusual for major training programs to be under development without widespread organizational awareness. If something is found, does it fit, can it be adapted, or is it a possible framework for the skills development process? Lists of on-going skills training are used as input during the development of the certification process and model.

Finally, an inventory of current training resources (if there are any) should be taken. For larger companies, the inventory should document the number of the training staff and skills, their position in the organization, their charter and objectives, the financial resources available for training, and the long-range training plan. Small to medium-sized companies may not have a training department, much less all these items in place. However, smaller companies may have employees who take on training responsibilities in addition to their "regular" job. Regardless of the situation, an inventory of what is available should be completed. This will be used as input later on as the Design Team works to develop necessary resources to support this design.

2. Identify and organize JOB skills.

In Process Step 3, when the Design Team redesigned jobs and created new broad JOBs, they developed a skill model for each JOB similar to the following:

Skills Model for Job Content and Required Training

Knowledge Transfer Only
- *Core skills*—those skills that are common across all the JOBs, e.g., safety and housekeeping, teamwork, etc.
- *Support skills*—those skills that are JOB-specific and represent peripheral effort in the overall execution of the JOB, e.g., material handling, inspection, etc. NOTE: Some support skills require more training, practice, and evaluation.

Knowledge Transfer, Training, Practice, and Evaluation
- *Operational skills*—those skills that represent the majority of JOB content, that reflect the "work" being done, e.g., machine operation, setup, or preventive maintenance on multiple machines.
- *Technical skills*—for some JOBs, these are the highly technical skills that require a base knowledge of operational skills, but represent specialized aspects of the "work" being done, e.g., major machine repair, the use of highly specialized technical test equipment, etc.

In the model, skills are grouped according to the training process required: (A) a simple knowledge transfer; or (B) knowledge transfer plus hands-on instruction, on-the-job practice, and an evaluation. Core skills such as teamwork, an understanding of world-class principles, and safety, and some support skills, require a simple knowledge transfer before the participant can begin utilizing those skills. The training typically occurs in a more traditional learning environment, where information is presented in a lecture or demonstration format, normally off-the-job, in a classroom or meeting room. Once the training is delivered, it is assumed the participant has received or acquired the skill. Unless the knowledge content changes, this is normally a "one-shot" training experience.

Other skills require a hands-on approach with more interaction on the part of the participant to acquire the skill. Usually these skills require knowledge transfer, a degree of hands-on instruction, a practice period, and an evaluation to determine the competency level. Typically, skills contained in the operational and technical content of the new JOB definitions fit into this category. For example, machine operation and setup skills, testing skills, product specific assembly skills, frequently require an extended period of instruction and practice followed by an evaluation.

Once the skills are identified and organized by the types of training required for each JOB, the Design Team more or less sets aside the knowledge-only skills and focuses on the skills requiring hands-on training, normally the *operational* and *technical* skills identified in each JOB skills summary.

3. Develop a certification process.

A certification program is a means for formally acknowledging that a person has met defined minimum requirements and been able to demonstrate a minimum level of proficiency for a specific *operational* skill. It is a quantifiable, objective means for recognizing and rewarding skill acquisition and utilization. Why is it necessary? A certification program is a necessary management tool if skills standards, once achieved, are to be maintained, and when consistency of treatment is important. It is also necessary because most companies plan to link some type of financial reward to the acquisition of skills.

What are the steps an individual must complete to gain certification? The process will vary from company to company, and perhaps within a company vary from department to department, but it should not vary among groups of similar skills or among the skills within a JOB. Given the different nature of skills, manufacturing may require different steps than engineering, but within manufacturing, the steps should be the same. This consistency of treatment is especially important when certification becomes a factor in performance or pay.

To obtain the benefits of a skills training program, and to avoid criticisms of unfairness and favoritism, the Design Team will create a comprehensive certification process. The certification process also ensures the company a greater return on its training investment. The certification process requires demonstrated competencies in those skills that are deemed critical for producing a high-quality product or service to meet its customer requirements.

The Design Team will include at least the following nine steps in a typical certification process, for any area of the company.

A Comprehensive Certification Procedure

1. *Initiating a certification* defines the procedure for applying for an opportunity—an opening—to train for and eventually become certified in a particular skill or group of skills.

2. *Verification of minimum qualifications* is applicable in those cases where specific prerequisites have been identified for certain skills.

3. All certification processes include the *actual training or instruction.* In most cases, it will be on-the-job training (OJT) conducted by another employee certified as a trainer, and focused on a checklist of organized skill elements to ensure accurate and thorough training on the skill.

4. *On-the-job application or "practice time"* takes place concurrently with the instruction, but extends beyond the actual training time. Practice time allows the trainee to acquire the experience of applying the skill under a variety of circumstances—part of learning

the skill is learning to know how to respond when things are not going right.

CAUTION!

The Design Team may be inclined to talk itself into unrealistically short training and practice times, based on "superstar" performance: "Well, a *good* new hire should be able to . . ."

Practice time serves as an opportunity to practice for a period of time, as "payback" to the company for its training investment, and as a device for controlling demand for training and the movement of people.

5. The *evaluation of competency* can take several forms, depending on the skills to be tested and the company's preferences. Some companies use written tests. Most, however, use an observation checklist.

6. Some companies require as a part of the certification process that the employee be able to demonstrate his or her ability to use the skill documentation to instruct another employee in that skill. *Demonstration of ability to instruct* is an innovative way to involve employees in developing needed skills, and to develop internal training resources.

7. A system must be established for *recording and tracking certifications*. The details of tracking and recording are normally handled during Process Step 9—Plan for Implementation, and Implement.

8. Recertification is an essential part of a certification process. The tracking data base should include a mechanism for flagging the expiration date of an employee's certification and providing ample *notice of recertification*.

9. *Recertification* is a formal process for ensuring that an individual who has been certified, but not actively engaged in a skill, has maintained the skill. The recertification process often consists of a reduced practice time followed by an evaluation.

When developing a skills model for technical or support JOBs, a different "certification" process will be included the same way operator skills are "certified." Technical or professional-level skills tend to focus on the knowledge of specific processes, products, technologies, or some combination of the three. They are more difficult to observe and "certify." The expansion of these technical skills is, therefore, often managed through a matrix developed to specifically meet the technical needs of the organization.

4. Build a certification model.

At this point, in addition to accumulating a pile of information about actual skill training practices inside and outside the company, the Design Team has accomplished the following:

- Prepared a skills model for each new JOB that outlines core, support, operational, and technical skills for each JOB;

- Completed a basic design for the certification process.

Now they need to combine skill summaries of JOBs and specific elements of the certification process into a skills certification model for each JOB. The skill certification model is a way to organize the critical elements of JOB skills and the certification process in a format useful for supervisors, employees, and those administering the skills development process. The Design Team will first build a certification model for each JOB. Then, if needed, additional models for supervisors, engineers, or other positions will be created for jobs where the company will require skills certification. The certification model identifies categories of skills and key certification requirements such as practice time. The model helps organize different skills according to level of difficulty by weighting broad categories or levels of skills.

Beginning with the first JOB, the Design Team studies the various skills summarized for the JOB with an eye toward identifying critical differences among the various skills. Then they move to establish groups or categories of skills based on critical differences, such as the length of practice time involved, the difficulty of mastering the skill, its importance to the company, the experience required, and other factors the Design Team decides are critical to the creation of a flexible, high performance workforce. The categorizing of the different skills is always an interesting and "invigorating" discussion. Members of the Design Team and those they may have brought in to aid in the discussion tend to differ on the difficulty of one skill over another.

The Design Team for a major consumer products company created three categories or levels of skills for a new broad JOB consisting of all the employees once part of shipping, receiving, and distribution. The critical factor was the practice time involved because it reflected the relative difficulty of the skills and their relative importance to the company based on the "payback" implied in the practice time.

For more conservative environments, or those accustomed to job evaluation slottings, a point-factor methodology can be modified to rate each skill against a few critical factors such as the nature of the skill and its relative difficulty. In the end, the results should be similar, in that there will be several different categories or levels of skills.

After the skills are categorized, they are weighted. Weighting is a way to highlight differences by creating ratios among the categories. A company with three different levels of skills weighted the lowest a "1," the middle category a "3," and the top level a "6," with the inference that it required roughly six times more effort to achieve proficiency in the top-level skills than it did in the lowest level. The weightings developed are important in that they are later used in translating the number of current certifications held by an individual into a p·e·r·f·o·r·m·a·n·c·e·s flexibility rating.

With the skills put into categories and weighted, a matrix is created and filled in with the critical certification elements selected by the Design Team. For its matrix, the consumer products Design Team selected "prerequisites, practice time, recertification period, and recertification practice time" as the critical certification elements for their model.

5. Create and manage opportunities for certification.

When it comes to "opportunities for certification," there are three critical questions:

1. How many certifications are to be made available?

2. When are certifications available?

3. Who gets to apply for available certifications?

A skills training and certification process is developed to support the business, not to provide ongoing, random training for employees. Companies have no obligation to provide training in all skills, at any time, to all employees. The answers to the first two questions are based on *business* need, and only management can provide those answers.

Because the presence or lack of opportunity to certify may impact an employee's growth or income, it is important to remove any opportunity for employees to feel victimized by the certification system. In answering the first two questions, managers must be careful that the restrictions they create are only on the *numbers* of people certified, not actual individuals. The logic behind the numbers must be shared with employees.

A Honeywell ammunition plant in Joliet, Illinois, was one of the first defense contractors to use skill-based pay, in the mid-'80s. The first design implemented had numerous problems. The design and documentation were somewhat informal. There were numerous inconsistencies in dealing with issues like training opportunities, job rotation, and evaluation procedures. This caused trouble when business slowed, and management was forced to lay off about half of the workforce. The layoffs were partly determined by the number of skill points an employee had accumulated at that time. Because the skill points had been earned in inconsistent ways across the teams, and the arbitrary sequence of training opportunities employees had received influenced how fast they had been able to earn points, employees naturally resented the skill-based pay skill point system.[6]

It's ironic, but initially some managers are worried about motivating their employees to learn additional skills. However, once monetary reward is linked to skills certification, managers are faced with the opposite problem—the demotivating impact of balancing limited certification opportunities with the employees' desire for certification. Companies need a well-conceived certification process with clear guidelines and reasonable practice times. And, as we will discuss later, a compensation plan that avoids putting *all* the employees' eggs in the skill basket.

Pragmatically, the three certification questions about how many, when, and who gets to apply must be answered more than once: first, at a macro-level by management, and next at the individual level. In most cases, the individual level for the first two questions should be addressed by department management, with input from supervisors and teams. For those companies with self-directed work teams (or moving in that direction), all three individual-level questions may be turned over to the teams themselves.

Who gets to apply for available certifications? This third question is always answered best at the work team or employee level. Employees and teams of employees are creative, and operate out of a sense of internal fairness when working on the third question. Work teams develop effective opportunity systems as simple as picking two names out of a hat for the two opportunities available. Or the "key tag" FIFO system that allowed each employee three key tags to place on plastic pegs in queue for the specific certifications they desired—when a position opened up, the next key tag in line was moved to that peg. In union environments, where seniority rights are often the decision maker, the most senior employees tend to get first choice of opportunities.

CAUTION!

The most common challenges to an "opportunity system" approach to certifications do not come from the employees. They come from supervision and management.

- Supervisors are reluctant to move their "best" people out of critical positions to allow others to train.
- Management fears the potential productivity impact of employee movement during skills development and certification.
- Companies believe in RONA, but they don't believe in ROTI (return on training investment).

---

6. Develop training resources.

Few companies today have the resources to significantly add to a training department, or to build a new training department to support skills development. Where limited resources are the order of the day, an innovative form of peer training makes sense. Supported by detailed skills documentation and their own certification, employees themselves make excellent skills instructors. Many already filled that role under the old informal "buddy" system. Now, with consistent materials and processes, employees can take the role of Bear That Sings and do a truly great job of passing on their skills.

A simple way to build a cadre of employee-trainers is to make the "ability to instruct others" a part of the skills certification process. This means that as a person completes the certification, he or she would then demonstrate to the certifier the use of the training materials, and the fundamental techniques for training that skill. When the certification is complete, the company gains both a skill user and skill trainer.

Some companies include a brief "train the trainer" course as a support skill for all employees. The course provides helpful hints on how to be an effective skills instructor, and in this way, the company includes training as part of everyone's job.

7. Address design issues and decisions/establish administrative guidelines.

We've covered the nuts and bolts of the skills development process, the *generic* aspects of the process. Here, at the end, it is appropriate to address the *specific* aspects of the process—the *company*-specific aspects. Just as we began with a list of questions to be answered by the Design Team in their design, we finish with another list. This time, the answers will not be generic, but rather must flow from the way *your* company does business, from its operating principles, and from how the skills development process supports its business objectives. The answers to these questions will shape your skills development process as much as the way your Design Team completes its job. The common company-specific issues that require attention with a skills certification program are:

TEN GUARANTEED QUESTIONS FROM EMPLOYEES ABOUT CERTIFICATION

1. *Is participation in skills development and certification voluntary or mandatory?* Many companies start out hoping to make these programs voluntary. But "voluntary" sends a mixed message. When among other requirements, the case for change clearly establishes the need for a flexible workforce as a primary tool for achieving the company's business objectives, "voluntary" or "optional" do not apply. To allow some employees opportunity to opt out of an essential program is unfair to them, their co-workers, and the company.

2. *Is there a minimum/maximum number of certifications an individual can earn in a year?* Often the reluctance to participate is driven by fear. Employees may fear failure at new skills, the evaluation portion of the certification process, or they may just fear change of any kind. Based on the case for change, firmly establish the program as mandatory. Then, set minimum requirements of at least one further skill certification in addition to the certification they should be able to attain from their current position or job. Maximum certifications are limited by business needs and budgetary and resource availability.

3. *Who owns the skills development process, especially the certification process?* While wrapping up the design of the certification process, the Design Team should discuss "ownership" for the process, especially the certification process. A frequent reaction from managers is that the tracking and maintenance of the system will be an administrative nightmare. Automating the tracking eliminates that nightmare, but the only way to avoid burying supervisors and the training department is to give ownership for the certification process to the employees. The employees should be responsible for initiating, following, and completing the process. Some companies have designed their administrative forms in a way that employees can easily manage the process. When the certification process is complete, signatures and all, the employee submits the paperwork for input into the training and certification data base.

4. *How and who will maintain and update certification materials?* A tough question for every company, because "how and who" gener-

ally means the company is going to have to spend some money. In this case, maintaining certification materials should be folded into an existing company system such as documentation control, engineering control, or an SOP system.

5. *How is skill obsolescence to be handled?* Probably as companies handle most obsolescence . . . reluctantly. There is hardly a piece of equipment, a process, a technology, a policy, or procedure with which companies deal that does not have its own obsolescence built in from the beginning. Because skills do become obsolete, the certification program should provide for a trade-in program. When a skill is declared obsolete, certified employees are given a defined period of time within which to certify for designated alternative skills. They normally receive priority in the queue for certification opportunities.

The problem built into most traditional people programs is that by the time they're designed, developed, and implemented, they're already on their way to obsolescence. On the other hand, new high performance programs are born with built-in renewal because the last design step is a commitment to continuous improvement.

6. *How are noncertified employees, e.g., temporaries, to be handled?* Would you let a noncertified brain surgeon inside your head? What about a noncertified employee in your assembly line? Perhaps a little more leeway in the latter instance? It can, however, be just as deadly to your products. Companies with flexible employees move experienced people to difficult operations, and then backfill easier positions with quickly trained *and* certified temporary employees.

7. *What are the consequences of certification/recertification failure?* The answer lies in your culture. And it will be right and fair for everyone, *including* the company. Assuming that the company no longer supports an environment of entitlement, repeated failure *will* have an impact at least on future earnings. Depending on the culture, the impact may range from a smaller percentage increase to a reduction in pay.

8. *Is there an appeal process, and what is it?* All High P·e·r·-f·o·r·m·a·n·c·e·s People Systems projects have standing committees to handle continuous improvement. Part of their responsibility is often handling some of the employee or labor relations issues that may occur when a person feels unjustly denied a certification.

9. *Is there a minimum commitment to the number of training hours, classes, certifications?* Probably, but a better question would be, "What's the *right* number of training hours, classes, certifications?" Forty hours per year is a typical minimum.

10. *Is there to be peer or team involvement in the certification process?* Yes, and no. Because certifications may have positive and negative financial consequences, it is unwise to ask peers to take on the role of certifier. For sure, teams and peers should be the certified

---

Synopsis: Process Step 5
Design a Skills Development Process

Objective: A formalized skills training and certification process is designed to improve process control by eliminating variability of how work is done; to increase the flexibility of the workforce; to enrich the jobs and employability of the people; to increase productivity; and to enhance customer relations.

Process: • The Design Team begins by assessing current internal training programs. The intent is to build off of what already exists if possible.
• The skills model that was developed for each new JOB is then organized and further developed.
• A certification process is developed that outlines the certification procedure. In most cases, the procedure will include initial instruction, a practice time, demonstration of the ability to train others, and competency evaluation. A recertification procedure is included.
• For each new JOB, a certification model is then developed that integrates the skills model and certification process.
• The Design Team then begins discussions on how opportunities for certification will be managed.
• The required training resources are identified.
• Finally, the Design Team addresses a host of administrative and policy issues surrounding training and certification.

Results: At the conclusion of this Process Step, a skills training and certification model and process will be identified for each new JOB. These results serve as a framework for the detailed development of each skills training and certification documentation.

instructors, but those who actually conduct and sign off the evaluation should be in a position of authority.

WRAP-UP

- The results from Process Step 5: Design a Skills Development Process are:
  - Skills/training models for the company's new JOBs;
  - A defined certification process, certification models, and administrative guidelines—a framework or template into which the documentation of individual skills can be organized.

- When the Design Team reaches Process Step 8, the "development step" of the High P·e·r·f·o·r·m·a·n·c·e·s People Systems Process, the remaining unanswered questions, such as how to handle the rotational opportunities for certifications, will require answering.

References:

1. "The Nation's Report Card" and "System Failure," *Wall Street Journal,* March 31, 1989.
2. *Fortune,* August 24, 1992.
3. *Business Week,* September 21, 1992.
4. *Fortune,* August 24, 1992.
5. *Fortune,* August 24, 1992.
6. *Compensation and Benefits Review,* March–April 1991.

CHAPTER 12

"Differing" with Deming

Process Step 6: Design a P·e·r·f·o·r·m·a·n·c·e·s Feedback System

"DR. DEMING SAYS performance reviews are one of the seven deadly diseases. How do you justify a performance review process in light of his principles?" Good question. Inevitably, during our private classes, public seminars, and during consultation, when the topic turns to performance management, we get this question.

The answer is, *no one* can justify the traditional, subjective, ill-prepared, individual contributor–based, ranked, and forced distribution performance reviews customarily practiced by the majority of companies. Clearly, those reviews do not work.

We believe that traditional performance reviews have failed their user companies because they *are* ill conceived: they are poorly focused on narrow objectives seldom linked to the real objectives of the company; typically fragmented goals bring about suboptimized performances; they pit person against person; and as Deming has so rightly insisted, they create fear.

Yet, a *type* of performance management system is an essential tool for the High Performance Enterprise—a system that provides feedback to ensure that the p·e·r·f·o·r·m·a·n·c·e·s of the company are aligned with the company's business objectives. Not a traditional annual performance review approach, but a P·e·r·f·o·r·m·a·n·c·e·s Feedback System. A system that corrects the deficiencies of the old performance appraisal, and replaces them with a tool that supports the kind of environment called for by Deming . . . the kind of environment found in the High Performance Enterprise.

Before we outline the P·e·r·f·o·r·m·a·n·c·e·s Feedback System, let's examine the traditional performance appraisal approach and learn why it no longer serves those striving to become High Performance Enterprises.

It is not too strong a statement to say, "In this global economy, the future of growth and productivity lies in a team-based High Performance Enterprise." This thought is echoed by most business thinkers and doers. Potential role models are the world-class Japanese companies where *teamwork* is not only a business imperative, but also a way of life—a cultural attribute. "Teams"—the word rolls off our tongues easily and comfortably. Doesn't the Western world also have a cultural tradition of teams and teamwork? After all, we have great traditions of team sports, teamwork in the military services. Yes we do, but in spite of this team tradition, particularly in the United States, the roots are in *individualism*, not in teams and teamwork. Even our mythical heroes—Superman and Wonder Woman—are individuals.

The reward system in professional athletics, the favorite macho team analogy, seldom reinforces *real* teamwork. The individual athlete, with his megabucks contract, gets positive or negative feedback based on his individual contribution—seldom on the p·e·r·f·o·r·m·a·n·c·e·s of the team as a whole. Only rarely, in Super Bowls and World Series, is there a *team* payoff.

So . . . back to our original statement: "In this global economy, the future of growth and productivity lies in a *team-based* High Performance Enterprise." If this is a true statement (it is), and our roots lie in individualism (they do), then companies in the Western cultures have a "long way to go" to achieve the team-based high performance operating environment essential for world-class competitiveness.

How do companies respond to the challenge of the ". . . long way to go"? There seem to be two extremes—two vastly different responses to a team-based environment: (1) "Forget it! We can't/don't want to/

couldn't be like them" (the Japanese); or (2) "Let's *do* teams!" For the sake of our future growth and prosperity, a reasonable response would be closer to the latter than the former, something like:

"The *cooperative* effort of a team-based work environment is truly an effective way to increase productivity and performance. Let's take the best aspects of the team-based world-class approach, learn what it has to offer, and develop a team-based approach of our own—one that acknowledges our roots, builds on our strengths, and ensures that we evolve quickly, but gracefully, along that '. . . long way to go!' "

In American companies, the roots of individualism are reflected in the way companies provide performance feedback. The traditional individual annual performance appraisal is a classic example. Some companies benefit from this performance management tool, but these companies are deprived of the *full* potential benefit by the limitations inherent in the traditional approach. Parenthetically, not *all* companies have even this limited traditional practice. Many companies do not provide any sort of feedback to their employees, much less the ineffective feedback of an individual annual performance appraisal.

Exactly what's wrong with the traditional annual review? Why hasn't it worked well in the traditional environment, much less been a useful tool in the new high performance operating environment?

THE PERFORMANCE PREDICAMENT

· How can an individual be appraised when, in most cases, the process in which he or she works dictates most of the performance? People do not work on their own—*people work in processes*. In the traditional company, most processes are poorly defined, or have been passed on by an ineffective oral history approach. When they are defined, it is usually in arcane engineerese that is totally useless to the folks doing the work. And to make matters worse, the traditional operating environment provides an employee little opportunity to change the process once they eventually learn how poor it is.

Evaluating individuals in the traditional environment is equivalent to putting them in a baseball game in which they are brought up to bat every time with two strikes already against them; forced to face Nolan Ryan; have one arm tied behind their back; and then criticized when they fail to get a hit every time. (The only thing worse is the kind of game in which companies ignore the employee entirely, ignore the effort they expend, and the fear they face in regularly going to bat under such conditions.)

· The individual seldom receives proper training to do the work. This issue picks up where our first issue left off. Not only does the individual work in a lousy process, but is forced to do so with inadequate training (generally from an ineffective oral history approach). For most workers, this is the third strike . . . and they're *out*. Actually they drop out—they leave the game, they lose interest, they work the "system" rather than work the process, and they ultimately get drawn into the "entitlement game" instead. They work for "pay for time spent," rather than effort extended, or the satisfaction of a job well done.

· Supervisors are supposed to be the judges: neither do they do a good job of it; nor do they have good tools to use. The reactive/doer supervisors are busily caught up in doing, fire fighting, meeting, and other activities that pull them away from observing their people in action. And the annual appraisal system is a poor tool for providing useful feedback. With poor tools, the supervisor is inclined to avoid feedback that may raise a conflict and thereby permit performance problems go on unattended.

· Goals and objectives vary from department to department, and encourage the suboptimization of performance in one department in order that another might succeed. The traditional annual performance review system is a system at war with itself. There is little linkage between an individual's performance factors and the business objectives of the company. One area's goals may lead to playing an angle of the system to promote its own success, to the detriment of another area.

In some companies, a performance review consists of meeting a given piece rate or quota of production units. This particular approach does provide plenty of feedback, but all of the wrong kind. It promotes quantity over quality, produces inventory rather than sales, and satisfies the "system" rather than the customer.

· The traditional appraisal approaches do not provide useful feedback. The traditional approaches attempt to judge employees working in processes that encourage failure rather than success—only Superman and Wonder Woman stand out because they beat the system. Feedback from such an environment is useless to the average employee.

Feedback in the system is a joke when employees know that there is no linkage between what the written goals and objectives demand and what the actual job requires. This leads to an informal "real" system, and workers working the "system" rather than working on the process.

Feedback from a supervisor who really does not know what's going on is equally useless, and a not-very-funny joke. This is feedback that breeds disrespect and distrust for management that cannot see the unfairness of such a system.

Finally, in many companies, employees receive little or no formal feedback at all. Except for the immediate "kick the dog" burst of angry disappointment when things go wrong with the system.

· In spite of the negatives of the traditional feedback systems, the limited feedback has been one of the few positive reinforcers and "teachers" for the traditional company. In spite of this limited benefit, there is no current justification for continuing the traditional performance management approaches—they don't work. Is there an approach that does work? What's different about it, and why does it work?

LEVERAGING P·E·R·F·O·R·M·A·N·C·E·S

The traditional approach to performance management does not work. To gain some perspective on the importance and potential impact of an effective P·e·r·f·o·r·m·a·n·c·e·s Feedback System, let's step back and review a few of the Design Team's accomplishments so far:

· From the company's mission, vision, strategic success factors, operational business objectives, and tactical initiatives, the Design Team created a targeted organization profile and a Migration Strategy to move the company toward becoming a High Performance Enterprise (a Migration Strategy that uses the 10-Step People Systems Process as a framework).

• They established flexibility boundaries within which skilled workers might move without barriers, and then redesigned work into new broad JOBs that encourage flexibility, require workers with specifically identified skills, and encourage a team-based approach to work.

• Then the Design Team established the evolutionary growth of teams and defined teams according to the needs of the company—defined teams by their purpose, objectives, roles, and scope. And then defined how supervisors could evolve along with teams.

• With broad JOBs requiring multiskilled workers, the Design Team designed a skills development process to guarantee an appropriately skilled workforce. This process provides a framework for individual growth in the broad JOB/team-based environment by requiring: that processes and skills be defined, documented, and maintained; a process for certification; and offering a skills certification model to establish a clear path for growth and improvement.

In the few steps already taken, the Design Team has conceptually moved a long way from its starting point. One of these days, the company and its employees are going to be asked to organizationally move along the same route toward the operating environment described in the targeted organizational profile. How is the Design Team to ensure that every one in the company travels the same route? What process can they put in place to provide employees signposts that they are still on the correct path?

The *purpose* of a P·e·r·f·o·r·m·a·n·c·e·s Feedback System is to establish, for teams and individuals, realistic goals aligned directly to the company's business objectives; to provide ongoing, regular feedback relative to performance against goals; and in this way, to establish continuous improvement and renewal as a way of life in the company.

The P·e·r·f·o·r·m·a·n·c·e·s Feedback System is based on three principles:

1. The performance of a company is really tens of thousands of daily p·e·r·f·o·r·m·a·n·c·e·s—countless individual activities, deci-

sions, and transactions taking place at every level and in every process across the company. The *performance* of a company cannot be likened to a one-ton boulder—it's more like a ton of thousands of tiny pebbles mounded together in one place. Both the boulder and the mound of pebbles have the same mass, but each occupies a different amount of space, responds differently to the same applied force, and requires a totally different process for effectively moving it about.

In an empowered operating environment, one that is hierarchically flatter, managers and supervisors do not have to provide minute-by-minute direction to control the company's p·e·r·f·o·r·-m·a·n·c·e·s—everyone in the company understands the direction and expectation for his/her contribution to the business objectives of the organization.

At the Abbott Laboratories facility in Ashland, Ohio, the Banbury machine department was always over budget. It had been for years. And for years, Charlie and the guys on the machine were visited by management who told them the Banbury machine department was theirs, that they knew the process, and could make it better. But Charlie and the guys were never given the clear accountability or freedom to act to make the changes. A couple of years ago, under a joint union-management—sponsored program, the Banbury team was empowered, and actually given the financial information for their department. They prepared a new budget, it was approved, and ever since, Charlie and the guys have improved their performance, to the point they have been formally recognized by their outside customers as producers of especially high-quality products and as a supplier with extraordinary customer responsiveness. The Banbury team has taken responsibility for its p·e·r·f·o·r·m·a·n·c·e·s, and now performance has improved.

2. It is a fact that performance *feedback* leads to improvement. This is not new information. It may be new in a formal sense—in the sense that behavioral science is relatively new, and studies on the impact of feedback are new. In *Managing for the Future*, Peter Drucker establishes three new skills required for personal effectiveness. The third skill is that of building learning into the system. He goes on to say:

One of the great puzzles of history has always been the sixteenth century. By 1560 Europe was dominated by two institutions which 25 years earlier did not even exist: the north by the Calvinist church and to the south by the Jesuit order. Both came into being in 1535, and by the seventh decade of the century they had become dominant institutions. Most of their members worked by themselves, in considerable danger and under great pressure. What was their secret? With the benefit of modern learning theory, we can begin to see what happened. Calvin and Loyola applied the most important principle in learning: that of feedback. . . . As Loyola and Calvin discovered, feedback is the primary key to learning. Crucially, since no one is productive by putting weaknesses to work, feedback identifies the strengths. Learners need to know their strengths in order to find out where to improve.[1]

The High Performance Enterprise is a changing organization. A changing organization is a learning organization. Learning takes place at every level and for every individual in the organization. For that learning to be effective, for change to take place as planned, feedback is essential.

The Japanese manufacturing techniques of JIT, Kaizen, and TQC were conceived from and grew upon basic principles of which *feedback* is one. Whether it is referred to as the PDCA Cycle (Plan-Do-Check-Action), or Deming Cycle, or Shewhart Cycle, this fundamental tool relies on "check," observing the results (feedback), as the input and stimulus for the improving "action." This concept was presented to the Japanese by Dr. Deming over 40 *years ago*.

The importance of feedback is well documented by years of research. In *Workplace 2000*, the authors report on a survey conducted by *The National Productivity Review* on 27 studies regarding the use of objective performance feedback. The studies indicated performance improvements ranging from 6 percent to 125 percent, with half of the 27 studies reporting improvements of 53 percent or better. The survey cited effects of the performance feedback that led to improvement:

- With no feedback, employees tended to assume they performed well, when in fact the opposite might be true.

- Employees wanted to know how they were doing. They liked to keep track of their progress.

- Whether positive or negative feedback was provided, management and employee relations improved when performance feedback was provided.

- The process of measuring conveyed the message that the area of performance being measured must be important. What gets measured, gets done.

- Feedback had a positive impact on performance because it was instructional.[2]

3. To make changing and learning a positive experience, a *system* is required to provide feedback to the individuals and teams whose efforts make up the company's p·e·r·f·o·r·m·a·n·c·e·s. Moving the one-ton boulder of performance is a lot easier than moving a ton of thousands of pebbles. A boulder can be moved with a lever and fulcrum. Try that with a ton of thousands of pebbles! The system we will develop in this chapter provides companies with a way of focusing, aligning, and integrating the tens of thousands of activities, decisions, and transactions through a systematic approach to establishing goals and objectives, and then providing feedback, providing "instruction" for the learning organization and its employees. The system applies a cohesive energy to the pebbles to mold them into a solid body that responds to the lever and fulcrum of strategic direction.

There's the story about the old cowboy at the dude ranch trying to teach city slickers how to rope a calf. He began the lesson by saying, "Okay. This mornin', I'm gonna learn ya how to rope a calf."

One of his pupils piped up smartly, "You mean *teach* us, don't you?"

"Nope! I mean *learn* ya. I ain't gonna *teach* you nothing. I ain't got time. I'm just gonna show you how to do it. You're gonna do it, and I'm gonna tell ya if you're doing it right. You're gonna haf' to *learn* yourself!"

In the High Performance Enterprise, management must create an environment in which all employees at every level can "learn" themselves to get better at what they do—can receive the feedback they need to perform as expected. That is the purpose of a P·e·r·f·o·r·-m·a·n·c·e·s Feedback System. The features and benefits of such a system are:

PROFITS OF P·E·R·F·O·R·M·A·N·C·E·S

• It acknowledges that *performance* is really *p·e·r·f·o·r·-m·a·n·c·e·s*. In other words, it acknowledges that managing *performance* really means managing *p·e·r·f·o·r·m·a·n·c·e·s*, which is possible only when those that perform the tens of thousands of activities, decisions, and transactions have ownership for their p·e·r·-f·o·r·m·a·n·c·e·s, when they are empowered to join in achieving performance.

• It creates shared goals and objectives to directly link p·e·r·-f·o·r·m·a·n·c·e·s to the company's business objectives. The system provides a direct link between an individual's daily work and elements of the business strategy. When companies translate vision into action, key strategic success factors and specific business objectives are established. These are now translated into performance factors for teams and individuals.

• It requires balanced performances from teams and individuals. As the High Performance Enterprise moves from an individual-based environment to one that is team-based, both teams and individuals must evolve. The feedback system involves weighting the performance of teams and individuals according to where they are in that evolution, and the performance expected at that point.

• It provides feedback on team and individual contribution. Performance feedback and recognition are provided for both the team and the individual team member. This gives companies moving to a team-based environment a feedback tool to use with teams. Employees still receive feedback on their individual performance, but also receive feedback as a member of a team responsible for meeting specific goals.

· The system eliminates subjectivity in evaluation by measuring quantitative operational performance and observable individual behaviors. As a result, supervisors are more comfortable using the tool. The data provide them a platform on which to stand while delivering the feedback.

· It involves teams actively in tracking and evaluating their performance as individuals and as a team. The process is a joint effort between the supervisor and the team. The team is actively involved in collecting and monitoring their own performance data. This eliminates surprises and makes them participants in the process rather than victims of the process.

· It modifies the supervisor's role: less of a judge, and more of a communicator and coach—the data speak for themselves. Because performance factors are quantitative operational performance and observable individual behaviors, the supervisor becomes a feedback communicator.

· It fosters a mind-set of continuous improvement. Annually reviewing the weights of performance factors reinforces continuous improvement efforts, and ensures alignment of team and individual performance factors with the changing needs of the company.

The P·e·r·f·o·r·m·a·n·c·e·s Feedback System provides focus, alignment, integration, and system to move the tens of thousands of daily p·e·r·f·o·r·m·a·n·c·e·s in the same strategic direction.

THE P·E·R·F·O·R·M·A·N·C·E·S PROCESS

The design of the P·e·r·f·o·r·m·a·n·c·e·s Feedback System is completed by the Design Team and augmented, if necessary, by supervisors and/or employees who understand the basis for the new JOBs. Their input will be an essential reality grounding for the process. This is another of the Process Steps in which the Design Team will complete its design work and hand off the detailed development to others. Where the scope of the project is limited to a few JOBs, the Design Team should complete *all* steps of the design and development in their entirety, except for the inevitable "tweaking" that will take place later by those actually involved in the JOBs. This approach is particularly effective when there is a high degree of similarity in the work throughout the organization.

If, on the other hand, the scope of the project includes many new JOBs, the Design Team should first complete the entire design framework for the feedback system. This step includes the design framework for subfactors, metrics, performance measures, and rating scales. Then, the Design Team should turn over the actual development of detailed subfactors, metrics, performance measures, and rating scales for each of the JOBs to a separate project task team. The Design Team often waits until the development phase of the project to turn the development of details over to project task teams. Regardless of exactly how the final development unfolds, the design of the P·e·r·f·o·r·m·a·n·c·e·s Feedback System consists of eight Action Steps.

Designing a P·e·r·f·o·r·m·a·n·c·e·s Feedback System
Action Steps

1. Establish major performance factors for teams and individuals.
2. Develop team performance subfactors and data anchored rating scales.
3. Develop individual measures and behaviorally anchored rating scales.
4. Link skills with an individual flexibility factor.
5. Develop factor weightings.
6. Create an employee development section.
7. Develop guidelines for feedback.
8. Prepare the p·e·r·f·o·r·m·a·n·c·e·s feedback tool.

---

1. Establish major performance factors for teams and individuals.

The purpose of a P·e·r·f·o·r·m·a·n·c·e·s Feedback System is to establish, for teams and individuals, realistic goals aligned directly to the company's business objectives and supportive of its targeted organizational profile; to provide ongoing, regular feedback relative to performance against goals; and in this way to establish continuous improvement and renewal as a way of life in the company.

Much earlier, the leadership of the company developed a mission and vision for the company. Then, through a process of translation, they put vision into action in the form of broad strategic success factors and specific measurable business objectives. Finally, certain initiatives were selected as a framework for taking action. The Design Team followed by developing a profile of a high performance operating environment in which to take action—the targeted organizational profile.

Now, much later, the Design Team must complete another translation. This time the Design Team must translate the strategic success factors and operational business objectives for the company into major performance factors that reflect the daily work of teams. And, then, translate the individual behaviors expressed in the targeted profile into major performance factors for individuals.

If improved quality or a 50 percent reduction in through-put time are broad strategic success factors, then the daily work of every team must also focus on those same factors. The major performance factors should be shared by all teams. This provides a common purpose for all teams, and precludes fragmentation and suboptimization.

If self-directed teamwork and regular use of problem-solving tools describe the targeted work environment, then the daily work of individuals must also focus on those same behaviors, translated into and expressed as performance factors in the feedback system.

As with teams, all individuals should share common major performance factors. Avoid attitudinal factors like commitment, attitude, loyalty, and dependability. Attitudes are manifested by behaviors—describe the behaviors expected of employees working in the high performance operating environment—behaviors that support characteristics of the targeted organizational profile.

The chief criterion for all performance factors is that they express performance over which teams and individuals have significant influence. Sometimes, the issue of significant influence is a hurdle for the Design Team. Managers and supervisors are reluctant to hold employees accountable for things over which either teams or individuals do not have 100 percent control. In the real world, few people have 100 percent control over every aspect their jobs. Consequently, do not set 100 percent control as a criterion for establishing performance factors. Look for performance factors on which teams or individuals have *significant* influence—for those things on which they directly impact results.

In the traditional annual appraisal, it might not have been fair to establish performance factors over which employees had only *significant influence*. Why? Because if they had 85 percent control of the factor, they were unlikely to have the tools or environment to either be able to document that fact, or to positively impact the other 15 percent.

In the High Performance Enterprise, however, the situation is different. For example, on-time schedule completion for employees on a production line is always influenced by the availability of materials. Yet, meeting the schedule is also significantly influenced by how well the team works together, and by how well they work with their internal suppliers to get the job done. Employees *can* be held accountable for schedule even if they only have 85 percent control. Why? They have at their disposal the problem-solving tools and commitment to continuous improvement to document the materials problems, to provide suggestions for resolving them, and the data to support changes in the production processes for which they are responsible—they are empowered to take action. They *can* significantly influence on-time schedule completion, both as teams and as individual members of teams.

Design Teams will also select performance factors for teams that do not necessarily flow directly from the strategic success factors and business objectives. For some companies, safety is an important consideration, though it is unlikely to be a strategic success factor. Team factors, therefore, may flow from strategic success factors, business objectives, the targeted profile, and other company requirements.

Limit the number of major performance factors to six to eight. Too many performance factors will produce an unwieldy feedback system. Rather than have too many, group similar factors, or consider their use as subfactors as outlined in the next step of designing a feedback system. A typical set of performance factors might look like this:

Typical Performance Factors

Team Factors
- Quality
- Schedule/delivery/customer service
- Costs

Individual Factors
- Teamwork
- Problem solving
- Work habits
- Flexibility

In this first Action Step of designing a P·e·r·f·o·r·m·a·n·c·e·s Feedback System, the Design Team worked on performance factors for teams and individuals. In the next Action Step, the Design Team will focus on taking each of the performance factors for *teams*, and designing additional levels of measurable detail for each factor; and, then, in the Action Step after that, focus on *individual* performance factors and their behavioral detail.

2. *Develop team performance subfactors and data anchored rating scales.*

Just as each broad strategic success factor led to the development of specific, measurable business objectives, each major team performance factor will lead to specific, measurable performance subfactors. Though all teams share the major performance factors, how each team acts out its daily work will be different. Now the job for the Design Team is to tailor the major team performance factors to the specific work of each team or JOB. The Design Team must develop quantitative performance subfactors that define how each team or each JOB will contribute differently to the business objectives of the company.

Quantitative performance subfactors can differ for each major JOB, because each JOB impacts work differently. Regardless of the differences, each performance subfactor for each team must be aligned with and contribute to its major performance factor. Team members must be able to look at a specific performance subfactor and say, "Yes, if we accomplish this, our team will be contributing directly to the business objectives of the company." For example, the contribution of a production team to quality performance might be reflected in performance subfactors such as its yields, its scrap rates, and the number of defects or rejected products it produces—three different subfactors for quality. For a claims processing team, its contribution to quality performance might be reflected in performance subfactors such as its paperwork error rates, the accuracy of information provided to claimants, and the number of follow-up calls made by customers regarding faulty claims—three different subfactors for quality.

Each quantitative team performance subfactor should be developed to the degree of detail necessary so that what is being measured and how it is being measured are clear to team members. The following format should be completed to describe each performance subfactor:

- Operational definition: what activity or result is to be measured.

- Metrics: specifically, *how* it is to be measured.

- Source: from where is the measurement obtained?

- Measurement frequency: how often it is measured.

- Rating measurement: the measurement applied to the performance rating scale.

Taking two examples of quality performance subfactors for a wood products production team, the defined subfactors might look like this:

Major Performance Factor: Quality

Performance Subfactors:

1. *Defects*

- *Operational definition:* flaws in workmanship that require repair or rework prior to release for shipment (visible cracks, chips, missing hardware, etc.).
- *Metric:* number of defects per thousand units produced.
- *Measurement frequency:* daily.
- *Source:* daily quality inspection report.
- *Rating measurement:* a three-month rolling average defect rate.

2. *Scrap*

- *Operational definition:* units that contain flaws in workmanship or material that cannot be repaired and are therefore unsuitable for shipment.
- *Metric:* number of units scrapped per thousand units produced.
- *Measurement frequency:* daily.
- *Source:* team daily scrap report.
- *Rating measurement:* a three-month rolling average scrap rate.

Once fully developed, the team performance subfactors will provide significant feedback to each team. At this point, however, the feedback is only data—a lot of data. It is not yet information. Ultimately the performance feedback will be incorporated in an overall performance "rating"—useful information for the teams. To make that process easier, the Design Team will develop a type of shorthand to convert the actual performance measurement for each subfactor into a simple rating. Simple ratings for each subfactor can then be accumulated, weighted, and consolidated into a rating of overall performance.

To establish simple ratings for quantitative team performance subfactors, the Design Team will use a device referred to as a data anchored rating scale, or DARS. They might select an odd number, a five-point rating scale, in which the 1, 3, and 5 would be *anchored* by "unacceptable," "expected," and "exceeding expectations" data points, respectively. Here is an example of how a quantitative team subfactor might look.

Sample Team Performance Subfactor

Major performance factor: Quality
Performance subfactor: Defects

- Operational Definition: Flaws in workmanship that require repair or rework prior to release for shipment (visible cracks, missing hardware, etc.).

- Metric: Number of defects per thousand units produced.

- Measurement Frequency: Daily.

- Source: Daily quality inspection report.

- Rating Measurement: A three-month rolling average defect rate.

Rating Scale: Defect Rate

1	2	3	4	5
1/1,000		.5/1,000		.2/1,000

---

3. Develop individual measures and behaviorally anchored rating scales.

In the previous step, the Design Team began with major performance factors for *teams*, and developed for each, quantitative subfactors and a data anchored rating scale. This created a quantitative approach for linking each specific team's performance with the company's business objectives.

In this step, the Design Team will take a similar approach for each major performance factor for individuals—an approach that will lead through observable behaviors to "measures" on a behaviorally anchored rating scale (BARS) for each major performance factor. Rather than develop detailed performance subfactors, as they did for each team major performance factor, the Design Team will develop detailed behavioral measures for each individual major performance factor.

Teams > major performance factors > subfactors > DARS. Individuals > major performance factors > behavioral measures > BARS.

The objective for the Design Team in this step will be to complete the following outline for each of the individual major performance factors.

Major Performance Factor

- *Operational definition:* what performance is to be measured?

- *Metric:* the specific observable behaviors that describe performance.

- *Source:* from where is the measurement obtained?

- *Measurement frequency:* every three months.

- *Rating measurement:* a behaviorially anchored rating scale (BARS) based on observable behaviors.

When the Design Team has completed the outline, the finished product for each individual major performance factor will resemble the following example.

Sample Individual Performance Factor

The individual performance factor in this example is *teamwork*.

Teamwork

- *Operational definition:* the ability and willingness to participate and contribute to the success of the team.

- Metric: performance and behaviors as defined.

- Measurement frequency: determined by team.

- Source: team records, peer input, team meetings.

- Rating measurement: a three-month rolling average.

Rating scale: Teamwork

1	2	3	4	5
Has verbal warning for absenteeism.		Has no verbal warnings YTD for absenteeism.		Rarely absent.
Habitually tardy or leaves early.		Seldom tardy and/or leaves early.		Rarely tardy or leaves early.
Seldom volunteers for overtime.		Often volunteers for overtime.		Always willing to take on different assignments.
Unwilling to perform different assignments.		Generally will take on a variety of assignments.		Actively participates in team meetings.
Seldom participates in team meetings.		Generally participates in team meetings.		Always easy to get along with.
Quarrelsome, causes friction.		Generally easy to get along with.		Helps reduce tension in conflict situations.

---

4. Link skills with an individual flexibility factor.

Flexibility is singled out for special attention in the P·e·r·f·o·r·-m·a·n·c·e·s Feedback System because of its importance to the High Performance Enterprise. Companies include a flexibility factor as a way of linking skill acquisition and utilization to their feedback and reinforcement systems. Most companies will include a "flexibility" factor, but to each company, flexibility will look different.

For some companies, the flexibility factor will reflect the individual's skill level as indicated by the number of current certifications held. Or, in a more technical skill development program, the flexibility factor may represent progress within a documented skills framework in which the employee must apply increasingly greater technical expertise to multiple products or processes.

Regardless of how it is defined, to ensure consistency with other ratings, the flexibility factor must be translated into the same 5-point rating scale as other performance factors. Each organization will develop its own algorithm for making the translation, because of the differences in how "flexibility" will be defined. Some companies use the skill weighting factors to develop "points" for each skill. The total number of points is then translated into the 5-point rating scale by anchoring exceptional performance at "5," and backing into the other ratings. For example:

Accrued points		Rating
0– 25 points	=	1.0 –1.75
26– 50 points	=	1.76–2.75
51– 75 points	=	2.76–3.75
76–100 points	=	3.76–4.50
100 + points	=	4.51–5.00

Other companies translate certification points into "proficiency levels" created by linking expected proficiency levels to time or experience. One company established a multiyear period during which an average employee was expected to accumulate a specific number of certification points. For each year of the period, a "minimum" and "maximum" expectation for certified skill acquisition anchored the 1-to-5 scale, with the balance distributed across the rating scale.

5. Develop factor weightings.

Up to this point, the Design Team has selected and defined six to eight team and individual major performance factors, supported by a variety of subfactors and observable behaviors. If the team has done a good job, this group of "factors" should represent the performance expected of employees as individuals and members of teams. With consistent rating scales for each "factor," the Design Team has created a framework for compiling the six to eight ratings into one consolidated overall rating. Only a few questions remain: Are each of the "factors" as important to the company as the others? Are there "factors" that are more important than others? Is there a specific factor that, because of its importance in furthering a certain initiative, will ensure achieving the company's single most critical business objective?

If the Design Team believes that all six to eight factors support the company's objectives equally well, a simple average of the ratings of the six to eight performance factors will generate a suitable overall performance rating. If, however, they wish to emphasize certain performance factors over others to better align the "factors" with the relative importance of current business objectives, then *weightings* are a good tool.

The purpose of using a weighting system is to arrive at a single, numeric performance rating that reflects not only individual and team performance, but also the relative importance of the various major performance factors. Team subfactors are generally not weighted, but, rather, their ratings are compiled to produce a single rating for the major performance factor of which they are a part.

Some companies, rather than analyze and weight each of the six to eight major performance factors, make a macro-level decision first, i.e., team factors as a whole receive a weighting and individual factors as a whole receive a weighting. Then, each of the major performance factors within team factors and individual factors can be weighted by using the overall weighting amount designated for both team and individual factors.

For most organizations, the decision to first assign macro-weights to the two categories of team and individual performance factors is more important than it might seem. Remember, that eventually the overall performance rating will have a significant impact on individual pay increases. Perhaps for the first time in many companies, this means that an individual's pay increases are affected by the performance of his or her team members. The more weight given to the team performance factors, the more impact the performance of the team has on an individual's pay increases. Especially for companies just moving to a team environment, it is prudent to be sensitive to this impact when establishing macro-factor weights—perhaps beginning with an opening overall team weight of no more than 25 to 40 percent. The rationale is twofold:

1. For most companies and their employees, the concept of tying one's pay to team performance is radical. The mere fact that even a portion of one's pay is tied to team performance is enough to get someone's attention. The benefits of reinforcing the team environment can still be gained without the individual contributor feeling as though their efforts got "lost" in "the team thing."

2. Flexibility is an individual performance factor with a positive impact on team performance. By allowing room to weight flexibility more heavily, the organization may emphasize flexibility while the benefits from increased cross-training are high.

Taking the macro-level approach first, and then weighting each major performance factor from its available pool, companies have developed a picture that often looks like this (see facing page).

Here the individual's performance will account for 70 percent of his or her potential pay increase, a large portion of that being the number of current skill certifications he or she holds. The team performance will impact 30 percent of the potential pay increase—

Performance Factor Weightings

Team Factors	*Individual Factors*
• Quality (10%)	• Teamwork (15%)
• Schedule/delivery/customer service (10%)	• Problem solving (10%)
• Costs (10%)	• Work habits (15%)
	• Flexibility (30%)
Total team weight = 30%	Total individual weight = 70%

---

large enough to capture attention but not overwhelm the intent. As the company acquires experience with teams and team performance, the weights can be shifted for a greater emphasis on team performance.

6. Create an employee development section.

One of the more unpalatable characteristics of the traditional performance review process was its resemblance to an "autopsy." It looked at "dead" issues—most reviews were based solely on past performance—and there was little attention given to the developmental needs of the "living" employee.

The P·e·r·f·o·r·m·a·n·c·e·s Feedback System requires a section that creates a development plan for the "living" employee based on need, skill deficiency, interest, etc. It provides the employee with realistic expectations about his or her future progress in the organization.

In practice, this establishes an individual "continuous improvement" process for the P·e·r·f·o·r·m·a·n·c·e·s Feedback System. The mind-set of the High Performance Enterprise demands continuous improvement in all processes, in performance to goals, and in management processes. Naturally, each employee must also engage in a process of continuous improvement. The sting can be taken out of potentially negative feedback about skill deficiency when the feedback is part of an organization-wide continuous improvement mind-set, and when that feedback is backed up with an action plan for growth and improvement. The end result is that over time the employee develops a rich skills portfolio that is his or her job security of the future. The concept of developing a skills portfolio is discussed in more detail in the next chapter.

7. Develop guidelines for feedback.

All previous work by the Design Team on the P·e·r·f·o·r·m·a·n·c·e·s Feedback System has been prelude to the main act of the system: the actual feedback for teams and individuals. To calibrate the expectations of supervisor and employee alike, the Design Team must prepare guidelines to ensure that both form and content of the feedback are aligned with the original purpose of the system.

The purpose of a P·e·r·f·o·r·m·a·n·c·e·s Feedback System is to establish for teams and individuals realistic goals aligned directly to the company's business objectives and supportive of its targeted organizational profile; to provide ongoing, regular feedback relative to performance against goals; and in this way to establish continuous improvement and renewal as a way of life in the company.

The deliberate nature of the highly structured feedback system design dictates that the company is just as deliberate and structured in actually providing the feedback. To ensure this, the Design Team will develop a set of guidelines for feedback, and a tool to assist those involved in that process. Exactly what these two items look like will depend on the particular design that results from the People Systems project, and on the operating environment of the specific company.

MANAGING P·E·R·F·O·R·M·A·N·C·E·S

· Guidelines should clearly document the following processes:

  · Administering the feedback process—general guidelines;
  · Tracking, monitoring, and documenting the measurements called for in the outline for each major performance factor and its subfactors;

- Developing and continuously improving a feedback "tool" for use by the feedback communicator;
- Preparing (filling out) the feedback "tool"—preparing the ratings, computing the overall performance rating, and filling in the "blanks";
- Completing a feedback checklist—a job for the feedback communicator (pilots do it . . . and flying a plane is a lot easier than providing effective feedback);
- Administering pay practices relative to performance ratings;
- Training both supervisors and employees, and calibrating expectations regarding how the feedback system will function.

ENSURING FEEDBACK

Two kinds of feedback are anticipated:

- *Ongoing feedback* that results from: (A) the teams' involvement in tracking and monitoring their own performance; (B) the "visible" nature of quality in the High Performance Enterprise; and (C) from periodic monthly or quarterly updates by supervisors and team members.
- *Annual formal feedback* synchronized with changes in pay. In a sense, this session should be anticlimactic. Most of the feedback given during the year should provide an ongoing sense of the "process," with the "results" anticipated based on how the "process" has gone.

Companies must determine whether the annual formal feedback is to be in a general focal point review for all teams and individuals, or an anniversary/service date review. The experience of most companies in a team environment is that focal point reviews have more advantages than service date reviews. The advantages are that team feedback is now consistent among all team members, and budgets are easier to manage and control. The perceived disadvantage of a focal point review is the volume of reviews for the supervisors to conduct at one time. However, because supervisors now are communicating data prepared with the aid of an effective feedback tool, those using such an approach do not feel overwhelmed at review time.

Peer performance review is always a question for companies moving to become High Performance Enterprises. How much should there be? For each company, this will be an "it depends" kind of answer. In some companies, a degree of peer review tends to occur as a natural part of team problem-solving efforts. Teams willingly take an active role in correcting performance problems, particularly when everyone on the team is held accountable for the same goals—teams want a say in individual performance ratings of team members.

The degree to which they are given a say depends on the maturity of the team. For most new teams, it may be appropriate to allow anonymous completion of a performance appraisal work sheet on the individual factors for their co-workers, with these work sheets submitted to the supervisor as input only. At this stage, the supervisor has jurisdiction of final individual performance ratings. Among mature, self-directed teams, peer ratings become an integral team activity, especially as such teams take on more of the administrative roles of the supervisor.

8. Prepare the p·e·r·f·o·r·m·a·n·c·e·s feedback tool.

The guidelines for the P·e·r·f·o·r·m·a·n·c·e·s Feedback System require development of a feedback "tool" for use by the feedback communicator. The "tool" envisioned is more of a Swiss Army knife than a hammer—it's a package of documents, checklists, and work sheets. The Design Team will develop the feedback tool based on the design of the feedback system and requirements for the feedback system spelled out in the company's guidelines. Most feedback tools include at least the following features:

· A copy of the guidelines for the P·e·r·f·o·r·m·a·n·c·e·s Feedback System.

· Instructions and documentation package for the feedback communicator:

- · Data collection: ratings from individual measures and team factors and subfactors;
- · Computing the overall evaluation;
- · Completing the employee development plan—specifically, what is the plan—scope, schedule, and resources;
- · Completing the rating work sheet, i.e., filling in the blanks with ratings, feedback, and development plans.

· A peer review work sheet, if this activity is included.

A TESTIMONIAL

How well does this P·e·r·f·o·r·m·a·n·c·e·s Feedback System work? you might be thinking. Here is a small illustration. One company broadened the concept of "team" to include all three shifts when considering accountability for the team performance factors. After the first review period, where pay was distributed based on team and individual p·e·r·f·o·r·m·a·n·c·e·s, the team performance factors were pretty good, except for one major factor—safety and housekeeping. It appears that the second shift had a habit of being sloppy with the housekeeping requirements. As you can imagine, the people on the first and third shifts immediately cried "foul." It was not fair in their minds that the second shift pulled their rating down. However, second shift housekeeping immediately improved and has remained good through the next round of reviews.

WRAP-UP

· Designing and developing a P·e·r·f·o·r·m·a·n·c·e·s Feedback System is a significant undertaking—the payoff is equally significant. This system establishes a network of linkages from the thousands of daily activities, decisions, and transactions that make up a company's p·e·r·f·o·r·m·a·n·c·e·s back to the business objectives of the company. It provides focus, alignment, integration, and system at the point of feedback—a crucial point in reinventing the people side of the

Synopsis: Process Step 6
Design P·e·r·f·o·r·m·a·n·c·e·s Feedback System

Objective: The P·e·r·f·o·r·m·a·n·c·e·s Feedback System is an approach to ensuring the alignment of team and individual p·e·r·f·o·r·m·a·n·c·e·s with the business objectives.

Process: Major performance factors, that directly reflect strategic success factors, business objectives, and target organizational profile are developed for teams and individuals, e.g., quality and teamwork.
· Subfactors are developed for each team major performance factor that contributes to achievement of the performance factor. For example, subfactors for quality may include scrap, defects, error rates, etc.
· Individual performance factors are then developed.
· The skills certification process is linked into the P·e·r·f·o·r·m·a·n·c·e·s Feedback System through an individual flexibility rating.
· The different performance factors are weighted to emphasize those areas in need of extra effort and performance. These are modified annually to reflect changing needs of the business.
· A section for mapping out individual development needs is established.
· A tool containing all the p·e·r·f·o·r·m·a·n·c·e·s elements is developed for use by supervisors and employees.
· The approaches for providing ongoing feedback are developed.

Results: A comprehensive framework for a P·e·r·f·o·r·m·a·n·c·e·s Feedback System that establishes realistic goals for teams and individuals that are directly linked to the company's business objectives and supportive of its targeted organizational profile.

business. Reinventing involves change . . . change requires learning
. . . and feedback is a primary learning principle.

• To take full advantage of this approach, the team performance
factors should be "visible." Teams are responsible for tracking, posting, and monitoring their own performance. A standard format for
displaying performance data at the work location should be adopted
for all the teams (trend data are particularly useful for visually tracking and displaying progress). This facilitates a shared awareness of
performance and eliminates "surprises" for teams and individuals.

• This feedback system is a continuous improvement tool for
teams, individuals, and supervisors. All participants now share the
responsibility, opportunities, and a "hard" process to improve their
performance, to be active participants in the process of improvement. For the company, this system is a tool to keep performance
efforts aligned with current business objectives. Annual review of
performance factors and weightings ensures a regular, ongoing re-
alignment of performance expectations and business objectives.

• The *results* from this process step are:

  · A comprehensive design, or framework, for a P·e·r·f·o·r·-
    m·a·n·c·e·s Feedback System for establishing realistic goals for
    teams and individuals—goals aligned directly to the com-
    pany's business objectives and supportive of its targeted orga-
    nizational profile.
  · A defined process for providing ongoing and measurable feed-
    back relative to performance against goals.
  · A system that establishes continuous improvement and re-
    newal as a way of life in the company.

References:

1. *Managing for the Future*, Peter F. Drucker (New York: Truman Talley
   Books/Dutton, 1992).
2. *National Productivity Review*, Winter 1982–1983.

CHAPTER 13

"New" Compensation

Process Step 7: Design *NewComp*: Strategy-based Pay and Performance-based Rewards Systems

HAVE YOU HEARD the story about the company that established a policy to daily flush thousands of dollars down their toilets? If you haven't, you may not have to look too far. Perhaps just outside your office door. The traditional pay and reward policies of most companies were originally designed to control an organization's most significant cost factor—its payroll. However, because these traditional systems are not linked to the business objectives of the company, this money really pays for little more than time spent at work. *Traditional pay and reward systems waste money.* Even the "new" pay-for-performance programs of the '80s have been largely ineffective, because they were unidimensional, and not aligned with the direction of the company. The sucking sound you just heard was another day's worth of payroll dollars down the drain for tens of thousands of companies around the world.

The conventional wisdom on compensation theory is that compensation systems flow from compensation policy, which flows from the mission of the company. Current compensation practice does not make this happen—because it cannot.

Compensation

We use the terms "pay" and "reward" in their common operational reference, rather than from a technical compensation viewpoint.

"Pay" is *base* pay, the *fixed* pay rate that a person makes per hour, week, biweekly, semimonthly, or monthly; the rate used as the basis to calculate pay premiums such as overtime and shift differentials. "Reward" is *variable* pay distributed apart from base pay. Generally, rewards are programs designed specifically to reinforce selected business objectives. Gainsharing and team incentives are typical examples.

The fact of the matter is that classic approaches to base pay establish no real linkage with the company's mission or with the strategy of the company. Traditional compensation theory and practice simply don't include a process for establishing the linkage between pay and strategy.

Compensation theory and practice do a slightly better job of linking rewards and strategy. Because reward programs, such as gainsharing or team incentives, focus on "improvement in the numbers," there is greater likelihood that these programs be aligned with the mission of the company. Too frequently, however, traditional rewards programs are add-ons—stuck on top of other programs. They lack proper focus, alignment, and integration with the strategic direction of the company and once begun, seldom are subject to "continuous improvement" as the direction of the company inevitably changes.

For most of the years following World War II, the area of compensation theory and practice experienced little significant change, perhaps because companies changed little. Most of the excitement in the field was generated by responses to legal issues, by the latest statistical tools for plotting linear regression, and by new point-factor job evaluation approaches that permitted a microscopic analysis of jobs (which, by the way, permitted companies to even more narrowly define jobs, and thus more easily proliferate new jobs).

The period of little change was supported by a reluctance on the part of Human Resources and other operational departments to change compensation systems: (1) the process was too painful for HR and its operational colleagues—"Wow! Now that we have the new pay system in place, I don't ever want to do this kind of thing again!"; (2) continuous improvement was not an operational mandate— "Does anyone remember why we structured the program that way back in '72? We haven't had that kind of job around here for 10 years!"

The postwar period of "little change" ended in the '80s. It ended because everything else was changing, and at an unprecedented rate. Though change across a broad front of corporate activities is now the order of the day for most functional departments, it appears that compensation will be among the last activities to be brought into alignment with the world-class strategies of the High Performance Enterprise. But it *will* happen.

It *will* happen, and *soon*. A phenomenon known as the "compensation crunch" is a dilemma that becomes a driving force for change in companies seeking to become High Performance Enterprises. If your company is moving toward the high performance operating environment, you will have no choice whether or not to respond to this force. There will be a response, either by design, or by default. While you cannot choose whether or not to respond, you may choose *how* to respond. That is what *NewComp* is about, designing and developing new compensation solutions for the new requirements of the High Performance Enterprise. *NewComp* is an approach to compensation that challenges the conventional wisdom of compensation by focusing on a process rather than a type of pay or reward.

THE "COMPENSATION CRUNCH"

What is this "compensation *crunch*" that forces change? Basically, the company's traditional compensation systems are caught between two powerful, inexorable opposing forces: (1) the necessity to change how individuals are paid in an environment of broad JOBs performed by flexible workers; (2) and the necessity to create new compensation systems for teams in the team-based environment of the future, as the companies move away from the individual-based environment of yesterday.

Figure 13a
THE COMPENSATION CRUNCH

THE "ROCK"

Traditional compensation systems are caught between the proverbial "rock and a hard place," with the "rock" being the *need to change how individuals are paid*. The emotional nature of pay and its relative complexity make it difficult for companies to *want* to change pay. Often, however, it is too late for companies to have any choice in the matter. New initiatives promoting broader JOBs and more flexible workers are already putting the crunch on the company's current compensation systems. Here's how manufacturers moving to work cells or implementing JIT feel the compensation crunch:

· The traditional manufacturing environment, pictured in figure 13b, is organized functionally. Workers perform work only on a portion of the product, and have no "ownership" for the entire product. In functional organizations, jobs within each functional area tend to be similar, with pay differentiation coming as workers move from level to level within the "silo" of similar, but increasingly more difficult, jobs. Workers with certain pay rates don't do the work of those with a different pay rate.

A traditional compensation system built on "job-worth hierarchy" works well in the traditional service or manufacturing operation with its narrowly defined, hierarchical job environment—as long as workers don't move around a lot, especially as long as they don't

Figure 13b
THE COMPENSATION COLLISION

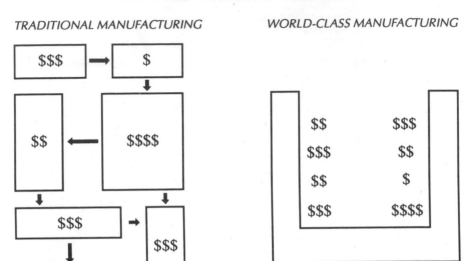

move back and forth from level to level. The fact is, however, that companies are employing initiatives that require employee movement. Then comes the "crunch."

Typically, when a company takes on "world-class initiatives" such as work cells, work processes are restructured more like the rudimentary depiction on the right of figure 13b. In this work environment, workers with different "functional skills" come together in a single work cell. To maximize the benefits of work cells, generally *all* the work on a certain product or product family may be performed by any of the members of the work cell. Members of the cell share "ownership" for the product. Workers are required to leave their narrow bands of work, and move up and down the process, from "job" to "job"—jobs of varying pay and skill levels. Workers with different pay rates are now working side by side, and move from position to position where the pay levels are different. When this happens, two questions inevitably arise: (1) When lower-paid people do the work of a higher-paid job, do they get the higher pay?; or (2) When higher-paid people work in a lower-paid job, do they take a pay reduction? *CRUNCH!!*

· The crunch worsens when companies encounter these questions and when they avoid addressing the changes that need to be made. (Especially when they don't quite know what to do—so, they do nothing.) *That* approach just doesn't work. Thirty years ago, one of the authors worked part-time at Atomic Liquor Stores (true name). When things were not moving quickly enough, the owner, Max Grossman, would shout, "Hey, you! Do zumzing, even if it's wrong! Do zumzing!" More often than not, when things were not moving quickly enough, supervisors and employees "do zumzing" to resolve their problems, only sometimes "zumzing" is a work-around—work-arounds that are seldom ideal, and often set unwelcome precedents for the rest of the organization.

A large manufacturer on the West Coast felt this crunch. They'd begun a work cells pilot in a large department handling rework for a variety of products—a department located down the street from the main plant. Encouraged by "team training" and a facilitating department manager, employees took eagerly to cross-training and were soon skilled in grinding, welding, inspection, etc. And they soon began asking the crunch questions.

The department manager went to the Compensation Department and was told the organization was not ready to change the compensation system for them alone. Neither the manager nor his employees were satisfied with that answer. Though he periodically returned to the Compensation Department, the answer remained the same. Finally, the department manager did "zumzing." As employees became fully trained, he and his supervisors eventually promoted most employees into the higher-paying levels of the higher-skilled jobs. Work teams were happy—supervisors heard few complaints. Later, however, a costly precedent for similar "work-around" treatment had been set among the employees at the main plant. When the remainder of the plant began converting to work cells a year later, their "zumzing" turned out to be wrong. *CRUNCH!!*

THE "HARD PLACE"

The "compensation crunch" is a clear dilemma—it catches companies between "a rock and a hard place." The "rock" was how to compensate individuals—the "hard place" is how to compensate teams. With traditional compensation incapable of handling the changing role of the individual, companies also find themselves on unsure footing when it comes to compensating teams.

· Companies that have implemented teams, talk about the importance of teamwork, and parade their "showcase teams" to visiting groups still focus reinforcement entirely on the individual. And after a while, the "showcase teams" begin to lose interest, their "spiel" begins to sound hollow to themselves, and the company drifts slowly back to a dependence on Superman and Wonder Woman. *CRUNCH!!*

· There is no strong published consensus among most leading compensation thinkers about how to compensate teams. They focus on this "type" of pay, or that "type" of pay and its suitability for use with teams in *this* situation, but definitely not in *that* situation. Companies are confused.

· Companies eager to promote teamwork maintain *individual* suggestion programs and recognize team accomplishment with pizzas and individual accomplishment with cash bonuses; and wonder why employees view the whole teamwork "thing" with skepticism—and continue to work the system as individuals, because that's the way the system *really* works. *CRUNCH!!*

Caught in the compensation crunch, most companies react just as one would expect: they look for a compensation answer. "We're doing teams, and we're having a compensation problem. Can you guys come in and help with a new compensation system?" Sure we could, but it would be like taking jalapeño peppers out of the diet of someone with severe stomach ulcers. Taking away the jalapeño would still leave the root problem unsolved. *Yes*, the compensation crunch hurts, and *yes* the compensation system is part of the problem, but the real problem lies elsewhere—as does the solution. The real problem is a flawed view of compensation as an end in itself, rather than as an integral part of the strategic direction of the company.

Traditional compensation has had as its purpose to "attract, motivate, and retain human assets" for the company. This sounds good on paper, but falls short of the company's real needs. Historically, traditional compensation has done a good job of controlling and administering the "attracting and retaining" function, done a poor job in "motivating," and today fails to ensure a return on the company's human assets.

Before acquiring any asset, most companies require a formal justification based on the calculated return on that asset—there is always a linkage between the cost of acquiring an asset and the improvement or cost savings to be generated by it. Does "attract, motivate, and retain human assets" create a link between the acquisition cost and expected improved performance? No, it does not. In spite of its formulas, point-factor evaluations, and penchant for statistical presentation, traditional compensation theory and practice reflect a "soft-issues" mind-set. It does little to improve the performance of its user companies. It falls short because it does not provide the focus, alignment, integration, and system (or process) required to reinvent the people side of the company, and to guarantee a return on the company's human assets.

The High Performance Enterprise needs a *new compensation* approach, one that can reinvent the people side of the company. "Attracting, motivating, and retaining human assets" are still important goals for any company's compensation system, but they are not the primary goals. But, more importantly, in the High Performance Enterprise, pay and rewards are an integral part of the business strategy. *NewComp*—"new" compensation for the High Performance Enterprise—has as its purpose reinforcing the p·e·r·f·o·r·m·a·n·c·e·s that make up the *performance* of the company.

NEWCOMP: COMPENSATION FOR THE HIGH PERFORMANCE ENTERPRISE

NewComp represents a non-traditional approach to compensation. A powerful multi-step process, *NewComp* produces a reinforcement system that anchors the linkage from the case for change, through the business strategy and objectives, to the p·e·r·f·o·r·m·a·n·c·e·s of the individual and team. Its two major components are Strategy-based Pay, a method for reshaping base pay to ensure a return on human assets; and Performance-based Rewards, which reinforce shared business goals among *all* members of the organization. No longer a non-value-added element of an entitlement system, compensation becomes an integral component of the Strategic Process. With *NewComp*, the High Performance Enterprise is likely to have multiple types of different pay and reward plans residing within the same general employee categories, such as hourly, nonexempt, or exempt employees.

NewComp is neither a type of pay, nor is it a type of reward. It's not pay-for-performance, or broad banding, or gainsharing, or any other type of pay or reward. *NewComp* is a *process* for designing compensation systems that align pay and reward with the business objectives of the company, with the strategic direction of the company. After working through the *NewComp* process, a company will select a type, or types, of Strategy-based Pay and Performance-based Rewards to reinforce the p·e·r·f·o·r·m·a·n·c·e·s that make up the *performance* of the company.

How does *NewComp* differ from traditional compensation? Here are a few of the ways:

NewComp	Traditional Compensation
· The focus is on *process* to produce desired results.	· The focus is on types of pay and reward plans—results.
· Builds from the inside out; origins lie in the mission and vision.	· Are add-on programs built from the outside in?
· Focuses on the broader "external" picture of the business strategy.	· Focus is turned inward, on compensation as an end in itself; a focus on hierarchy and job evaluation.
· Consistency is in the alignment, focus, and integration of multiple pay and reward plans with the business strategy.	· Consistency is among the pay and reward plans for major categories of employees, such as hourly or nonexempts, regardless of the business strategy.

If you didn't just open this book for the first time directly to this chapter, you are already familiar with six-sevenths of *NewComp*. *NewComp* is not a *type* of compensation—it is not compensation for the sake of compensation. It is a *process* that builds directly and systematically on the business objectives and the requirements of the high performance operating environment of the company. It produces compensation that is focused, aligned, and integrated with the objectives and requirements of the company. Yet, *NewComp* acknowledges a company's uniqueness because it is a defined process that yields a tailored product.

Essentially, *NewComp* takes the output of Process Steps 1 through 6 of the High P·e·r·f·o·r·m·a·n·c·e·s People Systems, and in Process Step 7 employs two specific approaches for turning that output into pay and rewards for the High Performance Enterprise: Strategy-based Pay and Performance-based Rewards. Strategy-based Pay results in a base pay system that reinforces new broad JOBs, skills training and certification, and p·e·r·f·o·r·m·a·n·c·e·s feedback. Performance-based Rewards is a rewards system that reinforces and encourages performance improvement by sharing the benefits of improved performance.

STRATEGY-BASED PAY

Strategy-based Pay is a process designed to produce a base pay program tailored to the inputs from Process Steps 1 through 6. This is the most technical Process Step in the entire project—it requires the assistance of the company's compensation experts. The Design Team will not usually include the technical expertise to develop a logically, emotionally, and legally defensible base pay system. One of two approaches is possible: the Design Team can add experts from the company's compensation or human resources function and proceed with the Strategy-based Pay Process; or the Design Team can hand off this pay process to a subgroup especially called together for this purpose, e.g., a Pay Task Force. The latter is recommended.

How the Pay Task Force is staffed will depend on the type of internal compensation resources available. It is recommended that two to three Design Team members be included in the Pay Task Force. For larger corporations, with significant compensation staffs, the internal expert resources should be available to work the Strategy-based Pay Process.

Smaller companies may not have compensation specialists. The expertise likely available will reside with the person who administers the current compensation system. While their knowledge can be helpful, it is unlikely they've had the opportunity to actually design and implement new compensation systems. In such cases, expertise from outside the company may be required.

To ensure the success of this handoff, the Design Team will provide the Pay Task Force with a thorough briefing on the High P·e·r·f·o·r·m·a·n·c·e·s People Systems Process to date as a framework within which the Pay Task Force is to work, and a list of objectives for the task force. The focus of the objectives will be that the task force builds on the work already done by the Design Team, particularly in areas of broad JOBs, skills development, and performance. Typical objectives will be similar to the following, and require the task force to ensure that:

PAY TASK FORCE OBJECTIVES

- The Strategy-based Pay design supports and maintains the integrity of Process Steps 1 through 6 of the High P·e·r·f·o·r·m·a·n·c·e·s People Systems design.

- The design reinforces individual and team performance as outlined in the P·e·r·f·o·r·m·a·n·c·e·s Feedback System.

- The design reinforces flexibility.

- The pay design stays within annual salary budget.

- The task force looks for any "hidden" money that may be available to fund the design.

- The task force utilizes the concept of broad bands for optimal growth within the newly created JOBs.

- A translation factor is developed that allows people to easily move, without penalty, from the Strategy-based Pay design to other pay systems within the company.

- Base pay growth for "overpaid" employees is slowed until their skill level reaches their pay level.

The Pay Task Force and the Design Team will agree on a basic statement of scope, schedule, and resources, with key milestones spelled out by the task force, and regular progress reporting established. The following is a high-level overview of the Strategy-based Pay Process to be followed by the Pay Task Force. The work of the Pay Task Force will be incorporated into the People Systems design later in Process Step 8.

Strategy-based Pay
Action Steps

1. Review business objectives, team and individual performance objectives.

2. Review current compensation strategy and total compensation package.

3. Determine ability to pay.

4. Review internal and external equity positions.

5. Establish a new JOB grade structure.

6. Design pay distribution and guidelines.

7. Model career progression.

---

1. Review business objectives, team and individual performance objectives.

To ensure the support of strategy through base pay delivery, the Pay Task Force begins with a brief review of the business objectives, team and individual performance objectives. The key to linking the pay distribution to these objectives is by tying pay to actual performance ratings developed in the previous step of the People Systems Process—developing a performance management system. The performance factors and subfactors are direct translations of the business objectives. That actual linkage can then be accomplished through several different pay distribution structures.

2. Review current compensation strategy and total compensation package.

With input from the Human Resources Department, the Pay Task Force reviews the current, official compensation strategy and the total compensation package that reflects their desired position relative to the external labor market. The total compensation package provides another view of the organization's competitiveness with the labor markets. The review of the total compensation package is used as data when comparing the organization's position to the external labor market.

3. Determine ability to pay.

The next step for the Pay Task Force is to determine the company's ability to pay. They start with understanding the amount of money already set aside annually for increases. A source of "extra" dollars can be monies that are budgeted for promotions or monies used for step increases.

There are several Strategy-based Pay designs that will help maintain a budget. They range from a strict performance distribution budget to other structures that require a higher degree of coordination and management, but can be done.

CAUTION!

Strategy-based Pay can present a real challenge to those compensation specialists who are charged with managing rigid point-factor job evaluation programs. The compensation specialist may be faced with career issues similar to those of the first-line supervisor—the way work is changing lessens the technical importance of their areas of expertise. One company moving from 145 jobs to 7 met the greatest resistances from the woman who maintained the job evaluation system. In essence, her area of technical expertise was being eliminated.

4. Review internal and external equity positions.

"Equity" is a term used by compensation specialists to reflect the monetary value of jobs relative to each other within an organization (internal equity) and relative to similar jobs outside the organization found in the relevant labor market (external equity). The determination of internal and external equity provides important data to assign pay rates or ranges to the pay or labor grade structure.

Practical Guideline

When reviewing your new JOB against jobs in a traditional job survey, return to the list of old jobs and identify the representative low-, medium-, and high-skilled jobs within each new JOB. Pull those out and benchmark them against the low-, medium-, and high-skilled jobs within benchmarked job families in the salary survey. This will help anchor the spread of the new grade structure.

---

5. Establish a new JOB grade structure.

Much of the work completed in Process Step 3: Redesign Work and all of the work completed to this point in this chapter are now used to develop a new grade structure. The Pay Task Force uses the results of the job evaluation completed earlier as input into a new grade or broad band structure. A structure is developed with pay rates or ranges appropriately assigned.

6. Design pay distribution and guidelines.

Now that the Pay Task Force has developed a new grade or band structure and assigned pay rates or ranges to the structure, the team must wrestle with how pay is to be distributed to individuals in these new JOBs. The task force begins by establishing objectives for the pay distribution plan. These objectives may include items like:

- Reinforce team and individual performance.

- Reinforce skill acquisition and maintenance.

- Maintain the annual salary budget.

- Manage the individual's progression within a broad band so that those good performers whose pay is below the market accelerate at a faster rate than those good performers who are well above the market.

- Minimize base pay increases to those employees whose base rate exceeds the current market by 30 percent.

The Pay Task Force may modify the grade or band structure created earlier to help control the progression of highly paid but minimally skilled employees. There are numerous approaches to take.

Regardless of the final structure developed by the Pay Task Force, guidelines for progression must be established. The nature of the structure will dictate many of the guidelines. Guidelines regarding promotional opportunities must also be established. Placement in the new structure for new hires must be established. Addressing the issue of a large portion of the population being overpaid relative to the new skill requirements is part of the process for establishing guidelines.

While the Pay Task Force is completing its assignments, the Design Team will continue to work on the remaining Action Step of Strategy-based Pay, "Model Career Progression." The Design Team will incorporate the work of the task force when they finalize the design blueprint in the Process Step 8 of the High P·e·r·f·o·r-·m·a·n·c·e·s People System.

7. Model career progression.

A difficult hurdle for "new" alternative pay systems and broad JOB structures is the perceived and real loss of traditional career advancement opportunities. Regardless of the nature of the workforce, whether blue- or white-collar, this is an important issue. It is perhaps a larger issue for white-collar groups than others because of the strong characteristic professional identity of these groups. This problem results not only from new pay and JOB designs, but also from years of downsizing and rightsizing. And as more companies create an empowered operating environment, more organizations will eliminate layers in order to facilitate decision making and communication. Flatter organizations, whether by design or downsizing, represent fewer opportunities for upward or vertical ascents.

Today's career advancement concerns are a result of traditional operating environments built on a mind-set that says recognition for performance comes primarily in the form of pay and promotions. During the expansive growth period after World War II, as companies grew and new companies came into existence, people advanced rapidly to fill the gaps at all levels. Then, as the growth slowed, people still continued to advance because traditional compensation systems did not change. Companies continued to use guidelines regarding the number of people supervised, years of experience, etc. As a result, managers continued to create layers, and promote people into them as the primary means of reinforcing individual contribution.

The typical promotion mind-set with its time-in-grade upward movement mentality reinforces a multitiered management structure. As one Design Team member at a large U.S. corporation put it, "If you aren't promoted every two years here, something is wrong with you. Of course, it's not so much that the real content of the job changes, just the title." To change this situation, the promotion mind-set must change, and then the traditional reinforcement systems must also change.

There are no magic potions or silver bullets to address the promo-tion mind-set. Changing the mind-set requires a combination com-mitment from the top management to change *and* education of employees about the realities of the workplace of the 1990s and beyond. Top management will have to break the very promotion mind-set that put them at the top. For this to occur, top managers must believe they have the support of a strong new People Systems, and a compelling case for change.

The education of people about their careers will begin when they clearly understand that a shift in paradigms is under way: from the promotion mind-set to a developing-my-skills-portfolio mind-set. A skills portfolio is the key to maintaining career viability—inside and outside your company. Not skills in the sense of training received, but rather a portfolio of jobs held and in which successful perfor-mance is validated.

Scores of business articles in the '90s have pointed to the need for people with a broad range of skills—the generalist is in, the spe-cialist is on the way out. "A narrow focus on a single specialty doesn't do much for your employability quotient. The more tasks you've performed and the more problems you've solved, the greater your chances of getting another job. So don't get stuck doing the same thing year in, year out. You shouldn't just keep getting to be a better and better accountant. You need a diversity of skills in your career portfolio. The more you have, the more marketable you are."[1] This quote from a *Business Week* article on career sur-vival echoes the foundation for the career reeducation process. Staying in the current up-the-ladder mode seldom provides the variety of experiences necessary to enrich your skills portfolio—taking advantage of opportunities available in new broad JOBs will.

Once top management makes the commitment to change para-digms, and people are educated about the value of a skills portfolio, then additional preparations can be made to help people make the mental transition. Test the Strategy-based Pay design to illustrate parallel progression under both the current and new pay systems. The Design Team should be able to demonstrate that people will not lose ground financially under the new system.

> If promotional increases have been a routine occurrence, those monies are often factored into the pay distribution pool available to plan participants.

For the Design Team to determine the approach to career progression that is appropriate for their company, they must begin by assessing the current career culture within the organization. Next, the team embellishes the targeted organizational profile with the elements of a new skills portfolio career progression model. The P·e·r·f·o·r·m·a·n·c·e·s Feedback System is a primary tool to guiding the development of a skills portfolio. Top management must endorse the new paradigm and then agree to support it through their actions. A "re-education" package is then developed for those affected.

The Design Team works with Human Resources to reinforce the development of skills portfolios, modifying current policies inhibiting lateral movement and developing new policies to support a skills portfolio approach. Finally, a proposal is developed for new, meaningful recognition programs to support the employee's becoming a worker-with-portfolio. Recognition programs for outstanding performance must be developed and given status similar to what promotion recognition received in the past. Naming outstanding performers to project leader positions is one such approach. A resurrection of mentor programs using the most skilled and experienced employees is another option. This is a People Systems area that will continue to undergo change throughout the 1990s. The challenge of creating innovative and satisfying new career progressions is just beginning.

PERFORMANCE-BASED REWARDS

An effective rewards plan is a critical element in reinforcing the high performance operating environment. The design, development, and implementation of a reward system should be planned for a later phase of the High P·e·r·f·o·r·m·a·n·c·e·s People Systems project. Performance-based Rewards require improved performance to fund a payout to participants. Improvement will be much more likely *after* the implementation of new broader JOBs, a skills development process with its skills training and certification, an effective P·e·r·f·o·r·m·a·n·c·e·s Feedback System, and new base pay programs from Strategy-based Pay. These programs are the driving force for creating the high performance operating environment, an environment much better suited to a Performance-based Rewards program than the traditional operating environment.

It is not our intention to provide a full exposition of Performance-based Rewards strategy. However, the basic Action Steps are covered. In *NewComp*, Performance-based Rewards are a form of *variable* compensation focused on reinforcing improvement of shared and common goals among members of a major organizational unit. They are based on the premise that to create a true sense of ownership for results, there is nothing like sharing in the results. Performance-based Rewards programs focus on an area of improvement, and acknowledge the organization's desire to share a portion of the benefits of improvement with those who contributed to the gain. The names of these types of programs—gainsharing, goal sharing, and results sharing—reflect their two-step nature: improve performance, and then share in the results of the improvement. In all of its variants, the basic concept is *improve*, and then *share in the improvement*. The general characteristics of a Performance-based Rewards strategy are:

CHARACTERISTICS OF PERFORMANCE-BASED REWARDS

· Improved performance is sought in specific areas. This is not general improvement—it's improvement focused on singled-out, critical aspects of business performance, that in turn may significantly affect overall performance. Generally, improvement is sought against an historical standard, as in gainsharing. However, in similar programs such as goal sharing, improvement may be focused on "expected results," which may, in fact, reflect breakthrough performance with no historical basis.

· Most of these programs are self-funding, i.e., no gain, no sharing! In most cases, the gain on a specific measure will fund the pool for that measure. However, the Design Team may elect to use funds generated by one measure to fund a pool for a completely different measure.

• Performance-based Rewards may be used for select groups such as teams or departments. However, current conventional wisdom suggests that broader participation—and a broad-based sharing of benefits—produces a deeper improvement effort.

• Performance-based Rewards programs will not work without *significant employee involvement*. Successful company programs involve employees up front in design and development. Performance-based Rewards are a natural reinforcer for the empowered environment and benefit from the same factors as empowerment—especially trust, information sharing, and education, clear roles and accountabilities, and freedom to act. Information sharing, for example, is an essential ingredient because employees with a stake in the results will take an intense interest in those results, how they are reported, what positively or negatively impacted the results, etc.

• These rewards tend to be group-oriented as opposed to individually oriented like base pay; and are kept distinct from other compensation elements. Payouts are generally made by separate check, and even on different days to differentiate the "variable" nature of the reward from that of "fixed" pay.

• Performance-based Rewards will work with large or small numbers of people, but work better when they are facility or site-specific. When multiple locations or separate organizational entities are involved, variation in specific business objectives, operating environments, and specificity of measures increases. And it becomes more difficult to tightly equate "my performance" with "those results"— the more direct the line of sight between business objectives and daily activity, the more effective the program.

More and more, these programs include employees beyond the production floor. White-collar areas and management are being brought into rewards programs to broaden even more the shared responsibility for improved performance. It makes especially good sense in the flattened organization, where employees, supervisors, and managers can more clearly see the linkage between their actions and the performance of the company.

· Performance-based Rewards programs tend to focus on improvement over a medium- to long-term duration, rather than a focus on resolving an immediate problem or obtaining a quick-hit improvement.

CHALLENGES TO REWARDS

Though gaining in popularity, Performance-based Rewards designs come with their own set of challenges. The Design Team should be aware of the challenges, and take them into account when assessing the appropriateness of a Performance-based Rewards program for their organization. We have already alluded to the challenge of "timing." The readiness of the workforce and the status of other improvement efforts may suggest an initial focus on putting into place fundamental changes in the company's people systems—in essence, creating a high performance operating environment in which the expectation of improvement is more realistic, and the likelihood of "sharing a gain" is greater. Other typical challenges to the design and implementation of Performance-based Rewards are:

MORE CHALLENGES TO REWARDS

· Implementation requires a commitment of resources, actually two types of resources. Obviously, with a commitment to a Performance-based Reward, management should be prepared to provide the "resources" to enable the workforce to improve: tools, technical support, time to resolve problems, and people, to name a few. Also, administering Performance-based Rewards takes time and effort—providing such resources necessarily reflects management's commitment to the rewards program.

· The company's operating environment impacts success. Once again, we face a situation in which the characteristics of the operating environment have a significant impact on the success or failure of this type of program. Implementing a rewards program is an absolute waste of everyone's time when there is little trust between company and employee, when roles are unclear, when information is hoarded, or when employees have little real freedom to act to make change. A rewards program in this environment will create a self-fulfilling prophecy of no payout and ultimately broaden the gulf of distrust as the rewards program becomes another failed program-of-the-month.

· What gets measured, gets improved—Performance-based Rewards programs are "measure-based" rewards programs. There must be broad agreement among employees that the measures are accurate, defensible, and understandable. This does not necessarily mean a direct one-to-one relationship of a specific improvement to its measurement. Exactly where in the P&L is the category "customer satisfaction"? In most cases where improvement cannot be directly measured, the Design Team may select indirect measures of "improved customer satisfaction" such as "warranty costs" or "defects at final inspection."

· Communication requirements greatly increase. It has been said before, but it warrants saying once again, information sharing is an empowering factor! Employees will first require a thorough understanding of the case for change to provide a context in which to couch their role in the improvement process. Then, once the program is under way, the company must be prepared to share information on a regular basis regarding results, impacts, changes, suggestions, and how improving performance affects the company's response to the real drivers of change.

· An essential tenet of *NewComp* is that, as with all aspects of the High Performance Enterprise, compensation must be subject to continuous improvement and renewal. A Performance-based Rewards program stuck at a point in the past will ultimately lose its effectiveness, because it ultimately loses its relevance. Team and individual performance factors will periodically change to remain consistent with the company's business objectives. In the same way, the design of Performance-based Rewards programs must provide for the flexibility to refocus employee effort on performance improvement that supports the company's strategic direction and vision into action reflected in its business objectives.

· The nuts and bolts of "sharing gains" with employees is accomplished by way of formulas for calculating funding pools and determining an individual's distribution. Working with formula-dependent rewards programs requires special effort by the Design Team. They must ensure that whether it is in a standard action such as capturing gains, or in the recognition of nonstandard exceptions, the formulas are as simple as possible, and known and understood by all employees.

· Some of the classic gainsharing plans, such as Rucker, Scanlon, and Improshare, run into difficulty because their basic formulas are so simple that "performance" is affected by fluctuations in product mix, market, technology, or decisions regarding capital investment. The Design Team will need plenty of creativity and a thorough knowledge of the idiosyncrasies of the company's business to create a design little affected by factors such as these.

· A fundamental element of *NewComp* and a real challenge to the Design Team will be to establish a clear linkage between individual effort and overall results. "My performance today, in my JOB, will impact tomorrow's results." A clear line of sight from an employee's daily activities to the business objectives of the company.

THE REWARDS PROCESS

If a Performance-based Rewards strategy was delayed until after the implementation of the company's High P·e·r·f·o·r·m·a·n·c·e·s People Systems design project, the Design Team for the rewards program may be a different group than the original—forming a Rewards Design Team. This is generally the case, with the possible exception of a member or two from the original Design Team for the sake of continuity. It is important that the Steering Committee/Design Team project approach continues to be followed when designing and implementing a Performance-based Rewards strategy.

The Rewards Design Team will follow five major Action Steps to complete a Performance-based Rewards strategy. Like Strategy-based Pay, the rewards design begins after the completion of Process Step 6: P·e·r·f·o·r·m·a·n·c·e·s Feedback System. A brief review of the five major Action Steps follows.

Design and Implementation of a Performance-based Rewards Strategy
Action Steps

1. Educate the Design Team on Performance-based Rewards.

2. Design the reward strategy as part of the High P·e·r·f·o·r·m·a·n·c·e·s People Systems Process.

3. Develop and test the rewards strategy.

4. Implement the rewards strategy.

5. Continuously improve the rewards strategy.

---

1. Educate the Design Team.

Education in two areas is required: on the business itself, and then on Performance-based Rewards strategies.

a. The Rewards Design Team must develop a thorough understanding of the strategic direction and high performance operating environment as did the original design team. Additionally, the Rewards Design Team must be educated in many of the business performance measures and about the business in general. Often, a Rewards Design Team will be required to increase their knowledge of financial data and information.

b. There is not enough room in this book to cover adequately more than basic principles and practices of Performance-based Rewards. Plenty of information is available in public literature, especially on the more traditional Performance-based Rewards programs, such as Rucker, Scanlon, and Improshare. This is an appropriate place for practitioners and consultants from outside the company to be brought in to give the Design Team a jump-start in designing and developing a Performance-based Rewards strategy.

2. Design the rewards strategy as part of the High P·e·r·f·o·r·m·a·n·c·e·s People Systems Process.

When the Rewards Design Team has a clear picture of the High P·e·r·f·o·r·m·a·n·c·e·s People Systems Process and the role of *New-Comp* (and a Performance-based Rewards strategy) in reinventing the people side of the company, they may begin the design process. There is no cast-in-concrete process for designing a Performance-based Rewards strategy—it truly requires an "it depends" approach. The Rewards Design Team develops the design by answering a series of questions in great detail.

QUESTIONS FOR DESIGNING A PERFORMANCE-BASED REWARDS STRATEGY

a. What are the improvements desired? Based on the company's strategic direction and vision-into-action package, in exactly what factors is significant improvement required?

b. What initiatives are planned to achieve the improved performance? How will the initiatives improve performance?

c. How will the improved performance be measured for each factor, and when, by whom, and under what conditions?

d. What individual behaviors contribute to improved performance for each identified factor?

e. On which factors will the improvement and reward strategy focus?

f. What is the process for tracking each measure? How will it be tracked? By whom? At what periodicity? Will employees be involved in the tracking?

g. What does performance improvement have to look like to generate a payout? What are the funding formulas?

h. How will payouts be distributed? Who participates? How often? This is where the Design Team determines the distribution formulas.

i. What special considerations must be made?

These are not all of the questions that might be asked, but they are core questions that should lead the Design Team on its way to a process for designing an appropriate Performance-based Rewards strategy.

3. Develop and test the rewards strategy.

Once the design is complete, the Rewards Design Team must spend some time developing the different measures, tracking systems, documentation, etc., integral to the design. The team also tests the design prior to implementation to ensure that the rewards program operates as intended. Included among other major activities of the Performance-based Rewards design are:

DEVELOPMENT WRAP-UP ACTIVITIES

- Develop and document procedures for tracking and measuring the performance factors;
- Establish *baselines* where necessary;
- Develop any required support systems (e.g., training, performance tracking, communication);
- Develop an information-sharing system;
- Establish and fill the position of "plan administrator," more than likely only a part-time job;
- Establish a "continuous improvement" committee of which the plan administrator is a member;
- Establish the process for monitoring and reviewing the effectiveness of the reward design by the continuous improvement committee, including periodic review of performance targets;
- Test the design using financial modeling:
  Project out two to three years;
  Conduct "What if?" analyses;
  Off-line, run parallel to the current plan if applicable (this will provide important comparability information for both employees and management).

4. Implement the rewards strategy.

When the design and development are complete, and the design tested satisfactorily, the Rewards Design Team is ready to implement the Performance-based Rewards program. (Detailed implementation planning and action for People Systems are covered in the next chapter.)

5. Continuously improve the rewards strategy.

Once implementation occurs, the Continuous Improvement Committee takes over from the Rewards Design Team. Ideally, some of the Design Team members stay on to provide continuity. (This process is discussed in the next two chapters.) It is important that the entire design of a Performance-based Rewards strategy stay updated and current with your business. Business needs and strategies change so rapidly that if the formulas and measures of the rewards system are not modified accordingly, there is a real danger of soon having a rewards strategy that is counterproductive to your business.

One large manufacturer finds itself in that very uncomfortable position with its Performance-based Rewards program. Seven years ago, their primary performance measures were costs. They implemented a gainsharing program that paid out cash when employees beat the standards for number of units produced per labor hour. Seven years ago, this strategy helped the company and its employees really focus on getting more units out the door—yesterday's definition of productivity. Two years ago, the company initiated several "world-class initiatives" to better meet customer delivery requirements. The primary manufacturing initiative was JIT.

During the JIT pilot stage, the company discovered that the gainsharing program was beginning to have a negative effect on its JIT pilot efforts. The pilot team spent time in training, and working on "solving" production problems. Nonpilot employees perceived that the "nonproductive" time spent in training and team meetings negatively impacted the organization's "productivity" rewards—and ultimately their pocketbooks—payouts were averaging 18 percent of *every* employee's annual pay. There was great reluctance to change the rewards program and its easy payouts. Eventually, the rewards program remained, and JIT went by the wayside.

If this company had established "continuous improvement" as a key element of their rewards strategy from the onset, they may have avoided the resulting situation. Continuous improvement is an important major element in *NewComp*: it helps wipe out the virus of entitlement.

THE *NEWCOMP* PAYOFF

The *NewComp* People Systems Process approach looks for a return on the company's human assets. Its focus is not on compensation as an end in itself, but rather on compensation as a tool for reinforcing the business objectives of the company.

A composite of recent compensation studies reveals a list of design elements that enhance the success of alternative "new" compensation systems. Programs with these characteristics are successful. As you read through this list, you will recognize the design characteristics of the *NewComp* process:

- A clear vision of the organization's strategy and culture;
- A reward strategy installed proactively toward strategic objectives rather than reactively to business conditions;
- A design clearly tied to business priorities;
- A high degree of involvement from all levels of management;
- A defined notion of intended results of the programs;
- Employee involvement in the design and implementation;
- An ongoing evaluation and monitoring against intended results;
- Program flexibility through continuous improvement.[2]

The *NewComp* process is based on these design characteristics. Applied to a variety of organizational situations, it will produce pay and reward systems that ensure a return on the company's human assets. And complete the reinventing of the people side of the business by linking the company's "backbone."

Synopsis: Process Step 7
Design *NewComp*

Objective: Improve the return on human assets by reinforcing p·e·r·-f·o·r·m·a·n·c·e·s through a base pay program aligned with the business objectives and by sharing improvement gains through Performance-based Rewards.

Process: Strategy-based Pay
     · The Design Team begins by reviewing business objectives, team and individual performance objectives to set the stage for *NewComp*.
     · The Design Team usually hands off the technical compensation design to a Pay Task Force composed of the company's Compensation Department representatives and two to three members of the Design Team.
     · The Pay Task Force: reviews the current compensation strategy of the company and its total compensation package; determines the company's ability to pay; reviews the new JOB design against other internal jobs and the external labor market; develops a new JOB grade structure and develops the guidelines for administering pay. Meantime, the Design Team has continued to work on a career progression program for those in the new JOBs.

     Performance-based Rewards
     · After implementing Strategy-based Pay, a Design Team will begin a project to design a Performance-based Rewards program (if appropriate to reinforce specific performance improvements).
     · The design process begins with educating the Design Team on various approaches to Performance-based Rewards.
     · A Performance-based Rewards program is then designed, developed, and tested.
     · After the testing is complete and final modifications are made, the rewards program is implemented and turned over to a continuous improvement committee to keep the program updated to business needs.

Results: Compensation systems that pay-for-performance—that provide a return on the company's human assets.

WRAP-UP

· Pay and rewards are emotional. Universal adulation and acceptance of new compensation systems are as likely as total harmony in a barroom discussion of politics or religion. *NewComp* systems are not designed to make everyone happy. They are designed in response to a genuine case for change and with employees' satisfaction in mind—there is hardly anything more motivating than working in a JOB where your contribution makes a difference, and where you are successful because the process supports you.

· This is an "it depends" kind of process—naturally so! Every company is in some sense unique—*NewComp* acknowledges uniqueness because it's an "open" process that yields a tailored product. Yet, every company is in some sense the same—*NewComp* provides the structure of a defined process to align pay and reward with the objectives of the business—a requirement shared by all companies.

· "Taking pay away" is a controversial topic. It always comes up at some point in the design process. Given the current culture of entitlement—away from which most companies want to move—the gain of taking pay away is not worth the pain. Yet, this is a question particular to each company's culture, and each must balance the risk with the perceived benefits.

· "Pay at risk" is another issue. For most companies, the "risk" is against future earnings. This is often a more palatable approach for companies to take, especially in a Performance-based Rewards design. Some companies have used Performance-based Rewards as an effective way to "offset" continually increasing fixed costs to pay and benefits by tying future increases to the gains from improved performance. This minimizes the guarantee of the ever-increasing nature of future earnings.

· Results from the *NewComp* Process Step of the High P·e·r·-f·o·r·m·a·n·c·e·s People System Process:

· A Strategy-based Pay base pay program incorporating:

  · A process for designing a base pay system that reinforces skill acquisition, team performance, and individual contribution.

- A base pay system directly linked to the business objectives of the company.
- A design that takes into consideration traditional compensation data such as market data, budgets, etc.
- More flexibility provided in broad grade ranges or bands.
- A framework provided for establishing concrete lateral career progression.

- Performance-based Rewards strategy incorporating:

  - An organizational rewards systems linked directly to business objectives representing financial and/or operational measures.
  - Process questions to lead the design team through the design.
  - Guidelines for developing and testing the design.
  - Guidelines for implementing and continuously improving the design.

References:

1. *Business Week*, October 7, 1991.
2. From the following three studies: *Rewards and Renewal: America's Search for Competitive Advantage Through Alternative Pay Strategies*, Marc J. Wallace (American Compensation Association, 1990); *Strategic Pay*, Edward Lawler (San Francisco: Jossey-Bass, Inc., 1990); and *Capitalizing on Human Assets*, Jerry L. McAdams and Elizabeth J. Hawk (American Compensation Association, 1992).

CHAPTER 14

On Your Mark, Get Set, Go!

Process Step 8: Prepare Blueprint and Develop Major Design Components
Process Step 9: Plan for Successful Implementation and Implement

THE BLUEPRINT: PROCESS STEP 8

The couple stood atop a small boulder, looking out over the sloping, wooded lot. "I can see it now," she said. "The house'll be split level, out of natural stone, with a great view of the valley. Three bedrooms, three baths . . . a nice-sized family room with a fireplace . . . a deck wrapping around the front and back . . . oh, yes! and a *large* kitchen and adjacent dining area."

"Yeah, and a workshop on the ground floor, with the garage out of the way on that side of the lot . . . a *big* garage with enough room for me to work on the Thunderbird," he said.

This is where the Design Team was months ago when they began their design efforts. Standing in front of a blank drawing board . . . some rough ideas . . . just broad, conceptual views. And what next? For the couple it was to contact an architect, agree on the basic elements of the design, and let the architect put together a blueprint so a contractor could be hired to make the house a reality. For the Design Team, it was basically the same process, except in their case, the Design Team is *also* the architect—and the general contractor, too.

On the Design Team, you've been through seven Process Steps. You've completed various components of the High P·e·r·f·o·r··m·a·n·c·e·s People Systems design including *NewComp*, and now it's time to put together a multipurpose blueprint to be used to make the design a reality. The blueprint will be used by two different groups, for two different purposes. First, the blueprint will be used by the Design Team, or by a designated Project Implementation Team (a special Project Task Team), to plan the implementation, and then implement the design.

And, second, the Design Team earlier may have handed off to certain Project Task Teams the responsibility to complete the detailed development of specific components of the design, such as JOBs, skills certification, and the performance factors of the design. Each task team would have received a design "framework" specific for its task. This was done in order to allow the Design Team to continue with its design work concurrently with the detailed development work. The "frameworks" handed off were actually pieces of the blueprint that in Process Step 8 must now be consolidated into a completed blueprint.

Each Design Team approaches the format of its blueprint differently. Most teams document the design and use three-ring binders to facilitate updating the design documentation, and as a place to collect all detailed development work from the various Project Task Teams. The form may vary, but the content should be such that it serves as a reference for those teams charged with development activities, planning for implementation, and ongoing management and continuous improvement of the new People Systems. The blueprint also may become the document submitted to the Steering Committee for formal approval of the People Systems design. The following is a list of the specific components to be placed in the blueprint, including source information about the project itself.

Blueprint Content Outline

Overview
- Case for change
- Mission and vision statements
- Success factors
- Business objectives
- Major initiatives
- Results of readiness assessment

Design Process
- Steering Committee
- Design Team
- Project leader
- Consultant
- 10-Step Process methodology

Glossary of Terms and Concepts

Organizational Profiles

Flexibility Maps

Job Definitions and Summaries

Team Definition

Supervisor's Role and Scope

Skills Development Process
- Certification process
- Certification models
- Administrative guidelines

P·e·r·f·o·r·m·a·n·c·e·s Feedback System
- Team factors, subfactors, measures, scale, etc.
- Individual factors, measures, scale, etc.
- Factor weightings
- Tools

NewComp: Strategy-based Pay (and Performance-based Rewards)

DEVELOP MAJOR DESIGN COMPONENTS

There are typically three major components of the new People Systems design handed off to Project Task Teams for additional development work before implementation is feasible. The first is final documentation of each JOB; the second is the detailed instructional and evaluation documentation for each skill certification; and the third is the specific performance subfactors and measures for different JOBs.

JOB Documentation

In Process Step 3: Redesign Work, the Design Team may have handed off the development of a few final details requiring technical assistance from the Human Resources professionals, including pulling together a formal JOB documentation package (which may require formal legal review). In the High Performance Enterprise, JOB documentation is a summary of the scope, activities, mental and physical requirements, major skills, accountabilities, decision-making boundaries, and required experience or qualifications. Generally, what remains is the mental and physical requirements and legal documentation. JOB documentation provides guidance to employees and supervisors, and provides the company with descriptions for use in conjunction with national and local employment laws.

Skills Documentation

In Process Step 5: Design a Skills Development Process, the Design Team may have handed off the development of individual skills training and certification documentation to a Project Task Team (frequently composed of training department personnel). They will use the skills and certification framework developed by the Design Team. When there are numerous skills, this project represents a major undertaking.

CAUTION!

When embarking on the development of skills training and evaluation documentation, make sure the required level of detail is spelled out clearly in advance. One company hired outside contractors to develop their documentation. The contractors took a typical detailed task analysis approach resulting in a 25-page skills training document—for loading a truck.

When faced with significant skills training documentation, some companies have chosen not to delay the entire new People Systems implementation while awaiting completion of the training and certification documentation. There are two ways to continue implementation without having completed skills documentation.

The first approach is to reduce the weighting of the flexibility performance factor to reflect the number of skill certifications actually available at the time of implementation. For example, if at implementation time, only 25 percent of the skills certifications are completed, in a design in which the original flexibility performance factor was weighted at 40 percent, and these developed skills certifications are widely distributed across the organization, then reduce the weighting on the flexibility factor to a 10 percent weight, until all skills are developed fully.

Another approach to moving the implementation forward without the completion of the skills training and certification documentation is to delay completion of the skills certification portion of the design until a "Phase II" of the High P·e·r·f·o·r·m·a·n·c·e·s People Systems project. In this manner, an organization can implement the new JOB design, a new P·e·r·f·o·r·m·a·n·c·e·s Feedback System, and new Strategy-based Pay *without* having the skills certification and training program ready to go. This allows your company to proceed in creating a new mind-set about flexibility and broader JOBs, and begin to provide concrete team performance feedback. When the skills training and certification portion is completed, the flexibility factor can then be added as an individual performance factor.

Performance Subfactors and Measures

In Process Step 6: Design a P·e·r·f·o·r·m·a·n·c·e·s Feedback System, the Design Team may have handed off to a Project Task Team the development of specific team performance subfactors. As discussed in the chapter on p·e·r·f·o·r·m·a·n·c·e·s feedback, it is unlikely that a major team performance factor like "quality" will look the same for every JOB, or every team. Specific subfactors must be developed to reflect the contribution or impact that people in a particular JOB or team have on a major team performance factor. (In most cases, individual performance factors like teamwork do not vary from JOB to JOB.)

At the time of the handoff, the Design Team determined if separate Project Task Teams were required for each major JOB, or for each major performance factor, or for each facility. Once Task Teams of employees and supervisors were established, they were assigned the task of developing the subfactors according to the format designed in Process Step 6, i.e., for each subfactor the Project Task Team develops operational definitions, metrics, measurement frequency, performance period, and also recommends the actual data anchors for each subfactor (DARS).

The work of the project teams is submitted to the Design Team or a designated management group for final review and approval of each performance factor and subfactors for each JOB.

When the Design Team has collected all of the development work from the various Project Task Teams and completed its review of these materials to ensure compliance with the "frameworks" provided, the Design Team completes preparation of the design blueprint. This marks the *end* of the design and development stage of the High P·e·r·f·o·r·m·a·n·c·e·s People Systems Process, and the beginning of making the design a reality.

Synopsis: Process Step 8
Prepare Blueprint and Develop Major Design Components

Objective: To finalize the design documentation through the creation of a blueprint and complete the development of major components of the design.

Process: · The Design Team identifies Project Task Teams to work on those major components of the design that require *significant development*. Most often these will be JOB documentation; skills training and certification documentation; and completion of subfactors for major team performance factors.

· A blueprint that documents a detailed framework of the People Systems design is completed to be used as a reference during development and implementation, and for final design approval.

Results: The project will be ready to begin the implementation process.

PLANNING FOR IMPLEMENTATION: PROCESS STEP 9

It was late afternoon, Thursday. The sun was just sinking behind the hills outside Judy's window. Her spirits, and those of her colleague Tom, were sinking faster than the sun. They had just left a searing 75-minute meeting (whipping?) in the office of the vice-president of operations. Jim, the VP, was extremely unhappy with how the day had gone, and Judy and Tom knew that Jim held them at least partially responsible.

As she and Tom talked, they found themselves conducting a post-mortem of the day's events and, afterward, kicking themselves in the backsides for what had happened. Jim was right, they had not really anticipated the employees' concerns about the changes represented in the new program. There wasn't a single concern raised that couldn't have been answered *pro*actively. Instead, everything from here on out was going to be a big *reaction*.

It was supposed to be a day of celebration. They were kicking off the BEAT program (Brixco Employees Achieve Together). BEAT was a new People Systems program that broadened job definitions, established teams, defined a skills certification program, and included a team and individual performance feedback system. Compensation was also being changed to reinforce the new design. Those high-performing teams and employees had the potential to make more than the annual 3 percent increase. The Design Team felt that employees would welcome the changes. Besides, these changes were critical to ensuring the survivability of Brixco—flat earnings the past two years and a loss this year had stockholders concerned.

All morning, communication sessions had taken place in the cafeteria, with free coffee and donuts for employees during the sessions. Jim, as VP, had conducted all four of the meetings. The air of celebration hadn't lasted long. First, there were questions asked that Jim couldn't answer. And, then, to a couple of the questions, Jim had responded in a way that made Design Team members roll their eyes. The design was not intended to do what Jim had implied.

After the meetings, the Design Team had been a little angry—it was unrealistic for the employees to expect Jim and the Design Team to have *all* the answers. It was a rough morning. But Judy, Tom, and the other Design Team members were totally unprepared for what occurred *after* the communication sessions.

A group of employees got together over lunch to discuss their concerns about what they'd heard in the communication sessions. The most senior employees were the most upset, and they got everybody else riled up. They felt they had the most to lose, and that their years of loyalty were not being taken into account by the new BEAT program. Already, comments were being made—this was a program where Brixco could "beat" its employees, rather than beat the competition, as was originally intended. After lunch, 32 of these employees marched to Jim's office, and waited for him to return from lunch.

Imagine Jim's surprise when he entered his office. He looked around for an empty conference room, quickly found one, and asked the employees to join him. For the next half hour Jim tried to respond to their concerns and defend BEAT. He soon realized he did not know the program in the detail necessary to answer their questions. Finally, he gave up trying to defend the program and spent the next hour and a half just listening and taking notes. At the end of the meeting, Jim assured the employees that Brixco would not proceed with the BEAT program until their questions were answered—in effect, BEAT was on hold.

He returned to his office, summarized his notes, and summoned Judy and Tom, the co-leaders of the Design Team. While he was waiting for their arrival, Jim realized that he was at least partly to blame for the mess. He had really pushed the Design Team to implement BEAT as soon as possible, especially at the end. But they should have told him they needed more time to prepare for the implementation. The Design Team had put their heart and soul into this effort, with many of the team members putting in a lot of extra hours. Everyone was so excited (and relieved) when the design had been completed that there was a strong push to roll the program out immediately.

After Judy and Tom got settled, Jim reviewed his experience with them. As Jim summarized his notes, they couldn't believe what he reported:

- Employees did not understand *why* Brixco was putting in the BEAT program. To them, it appeared to be an effort on Brixco's part to get people to do more for less.

- Their perception was that they would have to certify in jobs they had held for the past 7 to 10 years. The more senior employees were especially upset.

- The higher-paid employees were concerned that they might lose money, and they were unhappy with the fact that employees with only a few years' seniority would be able to advance their pay at a faster rate than had been possible in the past.

- Teams had been tried several times before at Brixco and were never fully implemented. Employees were now concerned that the BEAT teams would also fizzle, which might impact the employee's pay through team performance ratings.

- Employees complained that their supervisors seldom let them move about and cross-train in other positions because the work load was too high. Now that skills training and certification would be required, and was part of their expected performance, the employees were concerned that supervisors would continue to refuse to let them move to cross-train. The employees also wanted to know *who* would be doing the skills certifications and *how* they would be conducted. And what happened to an employee if he or she failed a certification or a recertification?

- Employees wanted to know the longer-term effect of BEAT on pay and opportunities for advancement.

Judy and Tom were stunned. It was no wonder Jim couldn't respond. Judy and Tom, as co-leaders of the Design Team, did not know how to respond to some of the issues and concerns either. The Design Team had not tried to figure out what would happen to long-term employees' pay, nor had they looked at the issue of providing opportunities for skills training and certification. The Design Team had not taken the time to determine what the various consequences were to the people who failed to certify, or what the impact was on career advancement. Those were all details the Design Team thought would get worked out *after* BEAT was implemented.

Boy, did the Design Team ever have egg on its face. Jim had promised nothing would be implemented until all these concerns were answered. That would take several more weeks of meetings and work among different departments. How discouraging! To put all the effort into a really solid design, and then have the program "recalled" on launch day was extraordinarily frustrating.

The Brixco story is a composite of the experiences of several companies. These experiences are not uncommon. They can be avoided, but only if companies are willing to curb their bias toward action. It is critical to take the time to work out the details.

WHY PLAN?

A solid, detailed design or "blueprint" of the new High P·e·r·f·o·r·m·a·n·c·e·s People Systems is a major determinant in successful planning and implementation. Regardless of how well-crafted and detailed the blueprint, a fragmented, incomplete, ill-planned implementation will almost certainly guarantee postponement, rework, or even complete failure. On the other hand, if the design is not quite perfect, a well-planned, well-thought-out implementation will provide enough strength to carry the design into implementation and through its first iteration of continuous improvement.

The better-planned the implementation, the less emotional the response will be to the changes precipitated by the new design. The base of most emotional responses is fear. People fear the unknown, especially when they fear it will have an impact on them personally, but are not sure what that impact is. Having answers to the detailed "What happens to me?" questions will impart confidence to participants affected by the new People Systems. They may not always like the answer, but at least there *is* an answer.

It is not only employees who "fear" the change inherent in a new People Systems, but managers at all levels as well. It is important during the planning stage to make sure all senior managers are on board with the design and implementation plan. A senior manager who waffles when asked a tough or uncomfortable question weakens the implementation. Having tested the design prior to its approval should instill confidence among management, a confidence that later will help during the actual implementation. Testing permits management to see how the program is to be managed, that it is within budget, and to preview the projected impact on individuals.

The implementation planning process offers an opportunity for more people to be involved in the final touches and details of the design. The broader-based the involvement in the design, the more ownership people will have for the results of the design. Asking more senior, and perhaps more threatened, employees for input goes a long way in reinforcing their value to the organization, generating useful responses for tweaking the design, and planning for implementation.

EIGHT BASIC PLANNING ACTIVITIES

For most companies, there are eight major categories of activities in planning for a successful implementation. There could be others, depending on the individual circumstances of your company. This information applies primarily to companies implementing new People Systems that include *NewComp* with Strategy-based Pay and/ or a Performance-based Rewards program. The categories of planning activities are based on the assumption there is a detailed design document—a blueprint—available to guide implementation planning.

The Design Team may work simultaneously on these eight planning activities with several different Project Task Teams, or Project Implementation Teams, staffed by employees and representative specialists when required. For example, the team modifying policies and procedures should include Human Resources staff members.

When the High P·e·r·f·o·r·m·a·n·c·e·s People Systems are being implemented in multiple facilities, establish an implementation team at each facility composed of a cross-section of managers, supervisors, and employees. (This assumes the involvement of each facility earlier in the design process, particularly when defining JOBs and skills certification requirements.) Charge each team with planning, implementation, and maintaining the integrity of the design blueprint for their facility. Provide each team with a copy of the blueprint and an implementation checklist to complete as they prepare for implementation.

Implementation Checklist

- Scope.
  - List all the areas and employee groups to be included in the implementation.
  - Specify design components to be implemented.
- Design integrity.
  - Identify any part of design that is being modified by the facility and rationale for modification.
- Documentation.
  - JOB summaries.
  - Skills training and certification documentation.
  - Performance subfactors documentation.
  - Identification of an update process for certification documentation.
- Policies and procedures modified (list all applicable, and their modifications).
- Describe cutover guidelines for incumbents.
- Risk assessment.
  - Describe any potential risks.
  - Describe what is being done to minimize the risks.
- Training.
  - Supervisors trained on new P·e·r·f·o·r·m·a·n·c·e·s Feedback System.
  - Supervisors trained on new People Systems design.
  - Support departments (Payroll and Human Resources) trained on new procedures.
- Administrative support systems in place.
  - HRIS modified.
  - Training, tracking, notification, and update system on-line.
- Communication strategy.
  - Schedule.
  - Process.
  - Communication materials completed.

1. Test the design.

The focus of testing the new People Systems design will be in determining the financial impact of the new Strategy-based Pay program on both the company and individuals covered by the program. Most companies test by using an electronic spreadsheet to perform "What if?" analyses to forecast an individual person's progression, over time, in the new pay system compared with the current pay system; and then to forecast the total impact on the company. The testing ensures that over time: (1) the pay of top performers is progressing at a rate faster than that of mediocre or poor performers; (2) that the budget is being maintained; and, (3) there is no potentially adverse impact on any particular group of employees.

The test format and formulas will depend on the particular design of the Strategy-based Pay Systems. When testing reveals future trends not in agreement with the intent of the design, the Design Team or Project Task Team must move the design back in line with the intent of the design. Assuming the test results show trends that support the intent of the design, the Design Team can use the results as part of the final approval package to senior management. Representative trends can be extracted to use as "case studies" for communicating to management and employees examples of how the design will impact representative employees.

In addition to this quantitative testing, the Design Team should also perform qualitative testing to validate the focus, alignment, and integration of the design with the targeted organizational profile and Migration Strategy presented earlier to the Steering Committee.

2. Develop skills certification opportunities.

Methods must be developed to ensure the fair and consistent availability of certification opportunities for employees, based on the skills certification framework developed in Process Step 5: Design a Skills Development Process. As certifications increasingly impact people's pay, the more critical the perceived *fairness* of this system.

To ensure fairness, let employees or teams have a hand in working out their own rotational or opportunity systems. For some companies, this means the employees may recommend an approach. For others, it means employees can create their own guidelines within the parameters of the certification process, once they understand how business decisions establish the number of certifications available at any one time. Depending on the nature of the certifications and practice times, one system may work for an entire facility. In other situations, it may be more practical to have a system for each major area, team, or shift.

When setting up opportunity systems, consider the impact of flexibility boundaries. For example, it does not work well to have three different teams within the same flexibility boundary set up three different rules for granting certification opportunities. This would make the transfer or movement of employees from one area or team to another difficult or cumbersome.

For some environments, the guidelines may be simple and straightforward. In plants where seniority is a major cultural element, seniority may be the deciding factor for who has first opportunity. Some environments allow employees to make two or three choices, and have them take the first opportunity available. Other environments leave it entirely to chance. One company's third shift literally draws names out of a hat when certification opportunities become available.

3. Anticipate employee relations issues.

The Design Team, in planning the implementation, must anticipate the employees' questions, concerns, and issues. At the beginning of the design process the Design Team was asked to "set aside" their concerns about incumbent employees, and use a "generic" new hire employee to help them think through the design. Now it's time to bring those nagging concerns back into the process. (The Design Team should have kept a list of concerns regarding incumbents.) And now is the time to involve those who have the "pulse" of the organization—viz., supervisors and HR or labor relations specialists—in resolving incumbent issues.

Most concerns voiced by employees are universal, regardless of the industry, employee group, or company. With changes such as these, there are many common concerns or issues raised. It helps to organize them and resolve them under the major components of the design, e.g., job design, skills certification, performance, and pay. Here are some common issues and concerns organized by major design components:

JOB Design

- Loss of "identity" for some employees (especially white-collar).

- Fear of losing special or senior status for those in the most specialized jobs.

- The requirement for additional cognitive and physical skills.

- More emphasis on math, reading, and communication skills.

Skills Training and Certification

- Certification may resurrect a "fear of testing."

- Employee concern because they have to "reprove" their skills.

- A shift in status as more technical or senior employees are asked to learn "lower-level" skills; others are allowed to learn the higher-status skills.

P·e·r·f·o·r·m·a·n·c·e·s Feedback System

- In a team environment, peer pressure can be stressful.

- Teams and movement because of flexibility requirements can disrupt long-established social networks.

- The individual is not as prominent as the team.

Strategy-based Pay

- Pay is directly linked to concrete performance and skills criteria.

- Individual pay may be impacted by *team* performance.

- In pay plans linked to increasing one's skills, individuals have more control or choice over their earnings.
- There is often a loss of entitlement.

Performance-based Rewards

- Pay may be "at risk."
- Results can be perceived as out of the employee's control.
- When different groups in the same organization have different reward distribution pools, there can be ill feelings when one group gets a payout and another does not.

Advancement Opportunities

- Perceived reduction in advancement opportunities.
- Fewer title and level distinctions.
- Lateral movement may not be perceived as positively as upward movement.
- Culture still supports traditional "get-ahead" tactics.

Listing specific different concerns, questions, issues, and such provides opportunities for the Design Team to use the information as a checklist against the design; to make sure the design addresses or answers each question or concern; and to build responses to the specific concerns, issues, and questions into the communication strategy.

The answers to all these questions may not be positive or "happy." However, avoiding the tough issues undermines the credibility of the program, and those involved in the design of the new People Systems. In the end, the answers will make sense to most employees if the Design Team did a good job of aligning and integrating the design with the company's compelling case for change, its strategic direction, and required high performance operating environment.

Another major group of concerns are those raised by the "What's in it for me?" question. The team working on planning and implementation should list these concerns. The central theme of most answers to this type of question will be that the new People Systems support the business strategy and address the drivers of change, and furthers the creation of a high performance operating environment. In the end, however, each question will have its own slightly different, very personal answer, such as:

- "These changes are hard to take, but in the end, the company will be better off, and I'll have improved job security."

- "Everything I read says job security's going to be hard to get from most companies. The additional skills training I'm getting will make me more valuable in the labor market—it'll increase my employability through a richer skills portfolio. That's a kind of alternative job security."

- "At least under this new pay system, if my team and I bust our humps, we can directly affect our earnings more than under the other old system."

4. Modify policies and procedures to support the design.

With new People Systems, modifications are required in the company's policies and procedures, employee handbooks, and union contracts. The areas most commonly affected by the new design are:

1. *Recruiting and staffing guidelines.* A high performance operating environment is a different work environment for most people. The ongoing learning and utilization of skills require a different mind-set. The expansion of narrow jobs to broad JOBs often requires more cognitive, math, and reading skills than previously. Analytical skills are more important to support the continuous improvement environment. Cooperation is now as important as individual achievement. These all point to the requirement for an improved employment screening process with different filters, increased testing, and team interviewing.

Companies are moving to basic reading and math tests as part of the overall screening process. Widening the interview circle is an increasing trend. Some companies involve the work team in the interview process. The team provides input to the supervisor, who makes the final decision. In other companies, self-directed teams often do their own hiring. The company's recruiting staff must get up to speed on the design, and develop the additional screening and interviewing processes necessary to select potential employees that best fit the high performance operating environment.

2. *Assignment of temporary employees.* In the traditional work environment, temporary employees have a negative impact on quality. To maintain the improvement in work quality generated by a skills certification program, a company must be thoughtful about the utilization and placement of temporary employees. With a skilled and flexible workforce, a company can often move regular employees to the more difficult operations or JOBs, and backfill entry-level work with temporaries. Then, before temporaries are allowed to work, they should receive core and support skills training, and should be certified in the area in which they are to work.

3. *Pay practices.* Over the years, most companies have grown "pay warts" on their pay practices. Pay warts are those little circumstantial pay increases that soon become part of the entitlement fungus. Temporary pay, training pay, and alternate pay are among the most common "pay warts." *Temporary pay* is often awarded when an employee of a lower-graded or -paying job works in a higher-graded or -paying job for two hours or more. *Training pay* is additional pay an employee might receive for "training" another employee. *Alternate pay* is a premium paid to an employee when he or she is the designated alternate team or group leader. In the High Performance Enterprise, most pay warts are eliminated because those circumstantial duties or tasks become part of everyone's JOB. Broad JOBs do away with the entitlement mind-set of "If I do any additional work, I deserve additional pay."

Each pay wart must be reviewed independently and the impact of its loss on an individual's pay assessed. Depending on the degree to which it has become part of an individual's *regular* pay, some companies still eliminate these practices, but then "buy out" affected individuals accordingly.

4. *Job posting or bidding systems.* An internal job bidding system can be a great consumer of a company's administrative resources. These programs are originally designed to provide employees the opportunity to advance their careers by bidding on jobs posted within the organization. Normally, employees are supposed to compete via an interview process similar to one used for external job candidates.

The idea is commendable, but many such systems have led to employee cynicism and frustration. Too often employees rightly perceive that the selection has already been made, and they are just going through the motions of an interview.

In other systems, elaborate bumping practices accompany the movement of each internal employee to a job vacancy. In some companies, if the employee does not demonstrate the ability to perform the new job in a predetermined time frame, or disqualifies herself, she can move back to her old job. This causes a retro-bumping of her replacement to his old job, and so on, and so forth. All of this adds up to significant non-value-added internal movement of employees.

A major benefit of the 10-Step Process is that job-posting activities are greatly reduced because there are fewer JOBs, and fewer, simpler bands or grade levels. Most internal movement is now within the JOB. Once most of the non-value-added activity is eliminated, a review of current practices is suggested.

5. *Union contract.* The ability of a company to negotiate changes in the contract regarding a new job classification system or pay system will depend on the level of involvement of the union in developing the design in the first place. Some company-union teams have been successful at making significant change by working on specific People Systems programs under a letter of agreement to meet outside the collective bargaining agreement. This provided an opportunity for both company and union to exercise breakthrough thinking in a neutral venue. In some cases, the new program was included in the next contract. In other cases, there were provisions

in the existing contract for a joint job evaluation committee that approved the changes through mechanisms built into the previous contract.

5. Establish cut-over guidelines for incumbents.

Seldom do companies have the luxury of wiping the slate clean and implementing a new People Systems design in a new facility or greenfield situation. A more typical and more critical challenge is to transform the mind-sets held by incumbents and build on their existing skills. Most pay systems designed and developed in the *NewComp* process are geared to develop broad skills over several years. This may be easier on the new hire than on the incumbent. Incumbent employees may have spent years performing in narrowly defined areas of the work process, perhaps not to the current desired skill level, or with as much flexibility. There are plenty of challenges for both groups—new hires and incumbents. However, special practices are needed to handle the transition of an incumbent workforce from an old system to the new. Here are two such practices.

TESTING OUT

At implementation, it is important to acknowledge the level of experience and expertise already resident in the organization. Companies do not normally force experienced machine operators to now "practice" their skills for a period of weeks or months. Companies do, however, want to ensure that the employee with years on the same machine *is* operating the machine properly. A typical process for this is called "testing out," often little more than having the employee demonstrate competency for the particular skill(s). (No extended practice time or instruction is required.)

It is important to put specific guidelines around testing out procedures. For example, companies may only allow employees to test out of the operational skill(s) that represent their current work or position (not any position they have held over their tenure with the company). Companies often set a time period during which testing out can occur. After that time, employees must complete the normal certification process.

If the case for change is well established, and the "What's in it for me?" questions answered fully, testing out is a palatable alternative for the incumbent. Testing out can be presented as a way of completing final validation of the documented training and certification process. The employee is then more a participant in the process than a "victim" of the process.

GRANDFATHERING

As a result of the test data, the Design Team may determine that there is a group of employees that should be "grandfathered" from certain policies or guidelines. In the case of skills certification, grandfathering is the practice of exempting from new policies certain employees who have technically already demonstrated specific skills over a period years. This may be a group of long-service employees whose pay is high, but who can perform only one or a very few operational skills. Grandfathering should never exempt anyone from meeting the minimum requirements established. However, it often provides more flexibility and support to these individuals in how they meet the new minimum requirements.

At one company, during the transition to a new pay system, employees were tied to a specific pay level based on the number of skills they held. During implementation, a group of 15 assemblers was identified as having a pay level out of line, on the high side, with their "new" assigned pay/skill level. Rather than exempting these employees from increasing their skill level, a formula was developed that tied their current pay rate to the requirement of acquiring a prescribed number of additional operational skills certifications over a certain period of time. For example, if their current pay level exceeded the proper skill pay level by $1.50 per hour, they had 18 months to acquire two additional certifications. If their current pay exceeded their proper skill pay level by $3.00 per hour, they were given three years to increase their skill level by three certifications.

In the meantime, their current pay level was frozen. They were, however, given first priority for any certification opportunities. If they were unable to complete the required number of certifications, in the appropriate time frame, their pay would be reduced to a more appropriate level. After that point, pay increases would be based on performance and current skill/pay policies.

IMPLEMENTATION APPROACH

A major decision that impacts cut-over guidelines is *how* the company decides to implement the new People Systems. There are three basic approaches: pilot, rollout, flash-cut. Each has its place, its pros and cons.

Pilot

Because of the magnitude of change that new People Systems represent, often a company's first inclination is to pilot the system. This is a reaction to the required change in culture, and is natural in companies with a traditional operating environment. Here are a few questions to ask about pilots:

- Are there pilots of other initiatives already going on? Pilots are more feasible when they are integrated with the pilot of another operational initiative, such as teams.

- How is the general workforce responding to employees in the existing pilot groups? If there is jealousy or perceived special treatment, piloting the new People Systems with these same groups will likely exacerbate the situation.

- How long should the new People Systems pilot last? And how will the Design Team know if the pilot is successful? There is sometimes a tendency to pilot to the point of draining the spirit and value from a program. Set reasonable "trigger points" in advance to make the decision to move on, and do so when they occur.

· How confident are the Design Team and Steering Committee in the design? If the design is solid, then it will carry itself. If it is weak, and there is wavering confidence in it, then perhaps a pilot is the best approach.

Rollout

A rollout has the feel of a series of pilots, until the new People Systems program has been implemented throughout the designated facility. This is the most difficult and troublesome approach to take. The biggest problem is concurrently managing two different compensation systems. This can be an administrative and employee relations nightmare. One company began their implementation with this approach, rolling out the People Systems as they rolled out JIT pilots. They soon, however, encountered the complexity of trying to manage two different compensation systems and quickly moved to a flash-cut implementation.

Implementation Approaches

Type	When It's Used	Pros	Cons
Pilot	· Fear, skepticism. · Isolated area, products, facilities.	· Less initial development work. · Debugging opportunity. · Identify results early on.	· Differences in treatment. · Can impact overall People Systems success if not well implemented.
Rollout	· Coincide rollout of other initiatives · Event driven/ opportunities.	· Tailored response. · Easier assimilation, to a point.	· Concurrent pay systems difficult to manage.
Flash-cut	· Small to mid-sized organizations. · Strong management commitment and good employee relations.	· Minimizes differences. · Demonstrates commitment. · Timely support of other major initiatives.	· Major change. · Initial stress.

Flash-cut

The new People Systems are turned on overnight. This can be done after a single pilot, or initially for the entire facility. Although this approach may appear to be the most overwhelming, it is often the easiest to manage. It does require a solid design and excellent implementation planning. The advantages of a flash-cut implementation are: that the company is not trying to manage the same workforce with two different People Systems; that no groups of employees are receiving "special treatment"; and that the emotional responses accompanying these changes, although perhaps more intense initially, are generally shorter-lived.

When the implementations of other initiatives are being done by rollout, a flash-cut for the new People Systems may appear complex. It does work, however. An electronics firm converted all its employees to the new People Systems overnight. Literally, the next day they all had new JOB titles, grades, skill and performance requirements, etc. Two areas of the factory had not yet implemented JIT. Employees in those two areas were not required to participate in skills certification. Their performance factors were modified to fit their current circumstances. As they, too, became involved in JIT, the skills performance factor was put into effect.

6. Provide necessary training on design components.

Pre-implementation training is directed at the supervisors. They are the "point guards" of the implementation process—they must be out in front and take the lead in successfully executing the new People Systems. The Design Team and specialists active on the Project Task Teams can help out, but it's the supervisors who make it happen!

Supervisors are given a copy of the blueprint as reference, and training consisting of a two-part program that takes place over a number of sessions. First, the Design Team presents a thorough explanation of the logic behind the design, the details of each major component, and the expected impact of the High P·e·r·-f·o·r·m·a·n·c·e·s People Systems on the daily activities of the supervisors and the employees reporting to them. Then, the Design Team, assisted by technical specialists, provides focused training on:

- The skills development and certification program;
- The new P·e·r·f·o·r·m·a·n·c·e·s Feedback System;
- The Strategy-based Pay program;
- The Performance-based Rewards strategy, if applicable;
- New policies and procedures;
- The communication strategy;
- And the supervisors' role in the implementation process.

Though the Design Team takes a large share of the credit for putting the design together, at this point the focus shifts to the supervisors—they make or break the reality of reinventing the people side of your company.

7. *Develop or modify administrative support systems.*

Three administrative systems must be in place to support the new People Systems: a payroll or Human Resources Information System (HRIS); a training certification tracking system; and a system for change control or updating training and certification documentation as work processes change. The payroll and HRIS often require modifications to accommodate new JOB titles, grade or band structures, and performance ratings. Occasionally, an HRIS will include a module for skills training that can be modified to track certifications, and to flag recertifications. If such a module is not available, a simple PC-based program can be developed.

Companies generally have some form of documentation management or process change control system in place, in the form of standard operating procedures, engineering specifications, standards maintenance, etc. If a system already exists, it should be used to generate updates or modifications to skills training and certification documentation. If it does not exist, such a process must be developed.

8. Establish a continuous improvement committee.

When the implementation is complete, the People Systems project may be over, but the overall effort on your company's People Systems is not. A High P·e·r·f·o·r·m·a·n·c·e·s People Systems is designed, developed, and implemented within a continuous improvement mind-set. It is no longer acceptable for a new pay system or performance feedback system to be instituted and allowed to "stagnate" for years, eventually losing its alignment with the objectives of the business, and becoming disintegrated from other programs and initiatives. All, or portions, of the 10-Step Process should be reapplied periodically to ensure focus, alignment, integration, and system.

To manage and oversee the continuous improvement and renewal of the company's People Systems, a permanent Continuous Improvement Committee (CIC) is established. Membership on the committee may rotate, but the role and responsibilities remain constant. Membership should include employee or union representatives, supervisors, managers, and human resources specialists. It makes sense in the first iteration of the committee to include a few Design Team members to provide continuity with the design effort. Though the Continuous Improvement Committee is established during the planning and implementation stage, it seldom becomes active until the implementation is complete.

The role of the team is to ensure continuity with the original design intent, to maintain the integrity of the design, and to expose the People Systems to a habit of continuous improvement and renewal. The CIC's responsibilities may differ among companies, but in general should include the following:

- Monitor and evaluate the effectiveness of the new People Systems;

- Develop a system for collecting input and recommendations for improvements to the People Systems;

- Make final recommendations to and seek approval from an appropriate management group regarding changes to the system;

- Monitor personnel policies and practices relative to the new People Systems design; work with Human Resources to maintain consistent policies;

- Function as a certification appeals committee for those who perceive they have been unfairly denied a skills certification or recertification, or the opportunity to apply;

- Review proposed changes or modifications to the performance factors, subfactors, or weightings to ensure they are aligned with the objectives of the business;

- Present final recommendations to and seek approval from management for changes or modifications to the performance factors or weightings.

Reinventing the people side of the business is a breakthrough kind of activity—it's innovation. And sometime in the future, another reinvention may become necessary as the way work is done changes significantly. Meanwhile, incremental, continuous improvement will ensure that the new People Systems do not become victim to the entropy associated with the old traditional systems. When the next reinvention becomes necessary, it will take off from a higher plateau because of the habit of continuous improvement.

CASE FOR CHANGE—A REMINDER

If you are this close to the actual implementation, and the people of the company have not heard from management about the case for change since the early days of the People Systems project, your implementation will be in trouble. If you are this close to the actual implementation and people are going to be "surprised" at the impact of the soon-to-be-introduced People Systems, your implementation is going to be rocky. "If we made a mistake, it was that we treated this [new People Systems] as a stand-alone program and forgot about the links to the business strategy. People began asking at implementation, 'Why are we doing this?' " These are the words of one Design

Team project leader when asked what one thing would she do over again in the design process.

It was important for the Steering Committee and Design Team to have periodically communicated the case for change, and to educate the employees on the case for change, the resulting business strategy, and the need for a new high performance operating environment. This is the *work* of leadership. In the Brixco scenario, Jim, Judy, and Tom let the company down because they did not attend to this work. People did not receive ongoing education about Brixco's mediocre business performance, and their competitors' continuing success. Brixco's worsening business scenario should have been used to position BEAT as a new work covenant between Brixco and its employees, a new work covenant based on performance and empowerment. As a result, Brixco people had no logical "context" in which to fit the information they were receiving. The case for change had not been made.

A large company with facilities in the United States and Canada did an excellent job of carrying the case for change through all its communication opportunities. Five major "themes" were identified and frequently presented to employees. In putting together the communication strategy for the implementation of their new People Systems program, guess what? They built the communication around how the new People Systems program supported the five major "themes." This approach placed the new program in a familiar and compelling context.

People are seldom happy about major changes. If they understand the logic behind the changes, and have been involved in the change effort, or at least kept informed about the effort, change will take place more easily. People still may not want to change, but at least they have a compelling reason to do so.

IMPLEMENTATION

This is a remarkable time for the Steering Committee, Design Team, the Project Task Teams, and the management of the company. All the effort, the attention to detail, the involvement of employees from every level—it all comes down to this next-to-the-last step. It's implementation time! Whether you pilot, rollout, or flash-cut, this is an event. It requires the hoopla of an event, and remember that this event is primarily a communication event.

A multipart communication series works best to kick off the new People Systems. Keep the total elapsed time short, no more than several weeks. At the end of each communication session, employees should be told what will be communicated next, and when. This allows employees "soak time" between sessions; and they know that there are yet additional opportunities to get answers to their questions. A typical three-part series might follow this format:

1. A senior management kickoff. Before large groups of employees, the senior manager (or a cross-functional group of senior managers) reviews the case for change, business strategy, etc., and then establishes the relationship among the new People Systems, the business strategy, and the development of a high performance operating environment. There may or may not be an opportunity to ask questions; or perhaps a limited number taken. An effective technique is to incorporate at the end of the presentation the answering of a list of "most likely to be asked questions." Announce the next meeting.

2. Department meetings are conducted by department management, accompanied by Design Team members to provide an overview of the High P·e·r·f·o·r·m·a·n·c·e·s People Systems design. These are smaller group meetings and allow for questions and answers. Introduce the concept that the design is part of a continuous improvement strategy and will be modified accordingly over time. Announce the next meeting.

3. Small group meetings with supervisors and Design Team members are conducted to review the detail of the design. Examples and "What if?" scenarios are presented. The anticipated employee relations issues are addressed. Present the responsibilities and role of the Continuous Improvement Committee. Results of these meetings are provided to the Continuous Improvement Committee.

Sometimes at this point in the process, the implementation itself feels almost anticlimactic. But it takes a lot of work by a lot of people to get to this point. For the Steering Committee, the Design Team, and all the participants in the Project Task Teams, it's time to celebrate. It's time to feel good about a job well done!

**Synopsis: Process Step 9
Plan for Successful Implementation and Implement**

Objective: To prepare the organization for a smooth and successful implementation of the new People Systems.

Process: There are eight major planning activities to prepare for implementation:

1. Test the design.
2. Develop skills certification opportunities.
3. Anticipate employee relations issues.
4. Modify policies and procedures to support the design.
5. Establish cut-over guidelines for incumbents.
6. Provide necessary training on design components.
7. Develop or modify administrative support systems.
8. Establish a continuous improvement committee.

After these activities are completed, the implementation itself is primarily a series of communication sessions, and activities of the new People Systems themselves.

Results: A new People Systems that is successfully launched.

WRAP-UP

- The better the design, the easier the implementation. The more thorough the planning for implementation, the easier the implementation.

- Results at the end of Process Steps 8 and 9 are:

  - Detailed developmental work completed.
  - More employee involvement in the development of final details.

- A design document, or blueprint, that serves as a reference.
- A design that has been tested against the current pay system.
- Modified policies and practices to support the new People Systems.
- Administrative systems in place to support the implementation.
- A strategy for addressing people's specific concerns and issues.
- Guidelines for cutting-over to a new People Systems with an incumbent workforce.
- The outline to a multipart communication strategy to kick off the actual implementation.
- A continuous improvement committee in place to maintain the momentum and oversee design enhancements.

CHAPTER 15

The End?

Process Step 10: Monitor, Evaluate, and Continuously Improve

THE MUSIC SWELLS to a crescendo, the lovers kiss, and "The End" appears in the middle of the picture. That's the way movies used to end. All of them. With a note of finality—"The End"!

But no more. Many movies now leave you hanging. The music stills swells to a crescendo, the lovers still kiss, but it doesn't say "The End." You, and everyone else in the theater, *know* those two still have some issues to resolve . . . and sure, everything's all okay *now*, but wait until she finds out that his "part-time" job is selling fishing nets, south of the Fiji Islands.

There used to be a "The End" in business, too. Companies rolled out a new program, the music swelled to a crescendo, and—"The End"—everyone lived happily ever after.

But no more. There is no "The End" to *becoming* the High Performance Enterprise, or reinventing the people side of your business. The only "happy ending" available to the High Performance Enterprise is a lifetime of continuous improvement and renewal. Letting up, backing off, or forgetting to monitor, evaluate, and refresh programs, initiatives, and mind-sets are sure ways to subtly slip back into a new "traditional" operating environment.

How your company approaches the continuous improvement of its new People Systems will in part be determined how you approach continuous improvement in general. It cannot be haphazard, nor accomplished through desire alone. It cannot be left up to *only* the workers, or *only* management, or only technical specialists. *Everyone* in the organization must fully commit to the habit of continuous improvement as the only successful way to guarantee the growth and prosperity of the company—the only way of life for the High Performance Enterprise. To facilitate the involvement of employees in the continuous improvement effort of their People Systems, establish a formal continuous improvement process and designate a group responsible for managing that process.

In the 10-Step Process for this People Systems design, a Continuous Improvement Committee (CIC) was established by the Design Team as they planned for implementation. The CIC was couched in the following context:

"Reinventing the people side of the business is a breakthrough kind of activity—it's innovation. And sometime in the future, another reinvention may become necessary as the way work is done changes significantly. Meanwhile, incremental, continuous improvement will ensure that the new People Systems do not become victim to the entropy associated with the former traditional systems. When the next reinvention becomes necessary, it will take off from a higher plateau because of the habit of continuous improvement."

MONITOR

To begin its monitoring chores, the Continuous Improvement Committee will have the feedback from the small group meetings conducted during the communication phase of the implementation step. *After* the communication phase, it is important to keep employee reactions out in the open and "above ground" to stimulate ongoing dialogue. This is when the real work, the continuous work, of the committee will begin.

With the implementation complete, the CIC will regularly monitor the organization's adaptation to its new People Systems. Periodic focus groups are a practical tool for maintaining an open dialogue of employee concerns and perceptions. Focus groups give employees a chance to air concerns and issues, and to get their questions answered. Early focus groups might address issues still left hanging after the implementation. The Continuous Improvement Committee can then make recommendations to the Design Team and management on the need for further communications, or the clarification of current communications.

An occasional written survey can be a useful tool. One company, particularly concerned about employee response to the new People Systems, resorted early on to the use of a survey. The company had transitioned from a traditional operating environment with no formal feedback system and annual general increases to a new P·e·r·f·o·r·m·a·n·c·e·s Feedback System that included team and individual performance feedback tied to future pay increases. Surveys were distributed to their employees to be completed anonymously after each person had received their first pay increase under the new Strategy-based Pay program.

The survey technique was useful to the company for two reasons. First, when the results were "surprisingly" positive, it put the minds of managers and supervisors at ease. Second, feedback from the surveys was used to improve the design for the next iteration of p·e·r·f·o·r·m·a·n·c·e·s feedback.

A third tool for monitoring the People Systems is periodic supervisor focus groups. Supervisors can usually give an accurate description of employee morale, identify key issues, and make suggestions to resolve them. Though there may be a supervisor or two seated as members of the Continuous Improvement Committee, the CIC will benefit from meeting periodically with *all* supervisors. Not only will this help collect the supervisors' input on employee issues and perceptions, but it will also permit the CIC to monitor the progress supervisors are making in the transition to their new roles. Remember, some of the anxiety or problems being heard in the workforce may be a reflection of poor progress in transition by supervisors.

EVALUATE

An evaluation of the new People Systems involves determining if the system is meeting its objectives. Is it supporting the strategic success factors and targeted organizational profile? Are the results those that were expected? There is no easy or straightforward way to directly evaluate results of People Systems. You can use indicators to indirectly measure the results. For example, actual team and individual performance ratings are an indirect indicator of the success of the new People Systems. If the design accurately reflects the behaviors desired, the way work takes place, correctly identifies the skills necessary to succeed in the new broad JOBs, and the system is being applied, companies should expect a *positive* trend in overall performance.

Another way to indirectly evaluate the success of the program is to capture the perspective of the operating environment. An annual employee attitude survey can indicate changes in perceptions of the work environment. A test of progress toward the targeted organizational profile should be reflected in this survey. General statistics traditionally used by Human Resources—measures such as turnover and absenteeism—can also be indirect indices of success. Each one tends to improve with a new People Systems.

A properly completed design blueprint will include benchmarks that may be utilized for evaluating the effectiveness of the People Systems implementation. If a minimum number of training hours were established, it is easy to determine if this criterion was met. And did the workforce achieve the minimum requirement of additional skills spelled out in the blueprint?

ESTABLISH A CONTINUOUS IMPROVEMENT PROCESS

The Continuous Improvement Committee must develop a process for incorporating improvements into the new People Systems design. Without a formal process, with a predetermined time line, companies run the risk of never stabilizing their People Systems. A state of constant fluctuation can result from an ongoing stream of suggestions for improvement, and the expectation that all recommended improvements be incorporated.

Typically, the CIC works to manage these expectations. Some committees establish an annual improvement date that represents the cutoff point at which all approved improvements for that year are to be folded into the revised People Systems. Barring the correction of a major problem, changes will be incorporated once a year.

For an annual improvement date to be effective, the CIC should develop a process by which members of the company can bring their improvement ideas before the committee. Some companies use recommendation packets that provide instructions and forms to the individual or team on how to present and document their suggestions. The format of a recommendation packet is similar to that of a suggestion system in that it requests supporting documentation, estimates of costs and benefits, estimated time for implementation, etc. Employees submitting recommendations may be asked to present their ideas to the committee. It must be made clear in advance that all recommendations are subject to final management review and approval.

It has been our experience that the components of the design that tend to undergo the most improvement activities over time are the (1) skills training and certification program, and (2) the P·e·r·f·o·r·m·a·n·c·e·s Feedback System. These two People Systems components are the most sensitive to changes in work processes, and to changes in the objectives of the business. Changes in the work process require new skills, or a new way for skills to be organized. Business objectives are expected to change. Changes to objectives must be reflected in the P·e·r·f·o·r·m·a·n·c·e·s Feedback System.

Reviewing recommended changes or modifications to the performance factors and weightings is an important responsibility of the Continuous Improvement Committee. Every year, each work team or performance group will review and modify its performance subfactor data anchors (based on planned changes to their processes) to demonstrate continuous improvement—a raising of the bar for the year ahead.

Rather than have each team do this independently, the process is more effective when a central management group reviews and approves all proposed changes to the P·e·r·f·o·r·m·a·n·c·e·s Feedback System. In addition, the company may want to change the weights of the performance factors to communicate shifts in emphasis for the coming year. The CIC can take its final recommendations to the management group for approval. This approach helps maintain focus, alignment, and integration from an organizational perspective—a perspective that teams or departments sometimes lack. The process also minimizes the perception that one group or team has established easier goals for themselves than other teams.

If a Performance-based Rewards strategy has been implemented, the rewards performance factors will also need to go through a similar process. The Continuous Improvement Committee should work with the management group in recommending and establishing next year's actual performance goals for the organization.

These are a few ways for the CIC to monitor, evaluate, and continuously improve the company's new People Systems. The exact method chosen is less important than making sure it is done regularly. The High P·e·r·f·o·r·m·a·n·c·e·s People Systems Process is a way of reinventing the people side of your business. The "drawing board" it provides you comes equipped with lots of pencils and erasers, and plenty of clean paper. As people change, and companies change, and the world changes around us, going "back to the drawing board" must become a way of life for the High Performance Enterprise.

> ## Synopsis: Process Step 10
>
> *Objective:* To keep the new People Systems focused, aligned, and integrated with the business objectives.
>
> *Process:* · Ongoing monitoring is conducted by the CIC through focus groups and other means of two-way communication.
> · Techniques for evaluating the effectiveness of the People Systems are used. All employee surveys, trends in turnover and absenteeism, and actual performance trends are all ways to evaluate the new People Systems.
> · Continuous improvement of the new People Systems is maintained by the CIC. The CIC establishes formal procedures for making improvements to the design.
>
> *Results:* · A high performance operating environment.

GENERATING MOMENTUM

Unlike many business books, this book does not present a "romantic" view of how to address the *soft* people side of the business—there are no pom-poms and megaphones here. Instead, the blood, sweat, and "fears" of reinventing the people side of the business are evident on every page.

Some of you will have mixed feelings about what you have read. On the one hand, the processes described here make sense— companies are following them and succeeding. On the other hand, you might examine your current traditional operating environment and think not in a hundred years could we get our managers and employees to take on such a project. Yet, while reinventing the people side of your business may not seem attractive, what choices does your company really have?

It is more obvious every day that from a *competitive* viewpoint, the world is becoming increasingly a world of the "haves" and the "have-nots"! The few companies at the top of the heap, the "haves," have sound market share won as they produced products and services of the highest quality and lowest costs in defined, flexible processes manned by skilled and flexible workers. And the rest of the pack, the have-nots, fighting over the scraps of leftover market share with noncompetitive products flowing from traditional processes manned by workers shackled by an ineffective traditional operating environment.

Companies may not be able to choose the drivers of change that impact them, but they *can* choose how they respond. What choices does your company have? One of these days, perhaps a day already past, your company will have to make a choice between one of these two options: "To be a 'have' or a 'have-not' "—that will be the question.

The "have-nots" of Marxism were victims—they had little choice in their woebegone situation. However, becoming a competitive "have-not" is a clear matter of choice. Companies will choose, deliberately or by default, to take a second-class competitive role when they choose not to aggressively become High Performance Enterprises.

If you choose to be a competitive *"have,"* to become a High Performance Enterprise, then be prepared to take up the Strategic Process with its direction and context, and commit to reinventing the people side of your company through the 10-Step High P·e·r·f·o·r·m·a·n·c·e·s People Systems Process.

If you make the choice to become a High Performance Enterprise, what do you have to look forward to? What will it cost you, and what are the benefits?

What you *don't* have to look forward to is a magic potion, a silver bullet, or a quick fix! They do not exist. What you *do* have to look forward to is applying a defined process to your company—one that takes a lot of hard work, attention to detail, and an unrelenting commitment to high performance and empowerment!

THE COST OF CHANGE

What about costs? The picture in figure 15a shows exactly what will happen to costs if you decide to become a High Performance Enterprise. The process shown has been the same for every High Perfor-

Figure 15a
RESOURCES REQUIRED

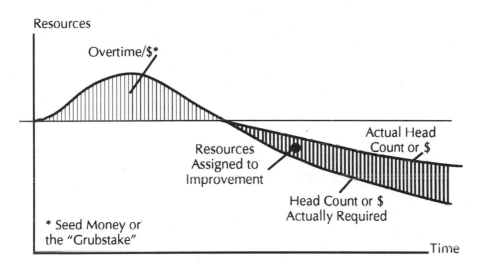

mance Enterprise, and has been accurate for every initiative they've undertaken

It shows that because there is no magic potion, you will need seed money—you'll need a grubstake. You will invest money up front in the form of time and education for the Steering Committee, Design Team, and Project Task Teams. And it will cost time and money to define and document your processes, to establish a change control process to ensure currency of documentation, to train employees on required skills, and likely you will need some outside help to ensure a successful and speedy design, development, and implementation. These costs are recouped by increased performance—not overnight, but in the near- and medium-term.

Figure 15a depicts a true-to-life scenario that will take place when you make the choice to become a High Performance Enterprise. Can you delay the choice until times are better? The fact is, "times" will never be "better" enough to make this an easy decision. By a perverse form of logic, if "times" will never really be "better," than this must be the best time.

The U.S. Congress described the situation well in a comment

about an unrelated but equally tough decision: "The 1980's have taught us that we are in a pay-now or pay-a-lot-more-later situation. While the cost of action is high, the price of inaction is staggering."[1] And, of course, your company can always make the other choice—to remain a traditional company, and become a competitive "have-not"!

Costs can be viewed from two perspectives: the costs from a resource and financial point of view and the costs as a result of maintaining a traditional operating environment (similar to the cost of poor quality concept). Both cost types should be considered in your analysis.

THE COSTS OF *NOT* CHANGING

Companies continue to downsize as a way to improve bottom line results. The obvious result is growing numbers of unemployed, especially in middle management ranks. A not-so-subtle fallout of downsizing is the heavier work load placed on those remaining behind. The heavier work load is not all bad. A survey of approximately 1,000 companies found that 86 percent of the employers had engaged in major restructuring. A surprising 66 percent of the people surveyed believed that their increased work load was reasonable.[2] Perhaps this is a testament to an underutilized workforce. Or it might be a collective sigh of relief from those who remain, that they still have any kind of job.

In situations of gross underutilization of labor, the action of downsizing leads to a fairly rapid and smooth adjustment of workers-to-work. People with increased work loads are in many cases energized because they see their efforts making a valuable contribution to the company.

However, when the downsizing pendulum swings too far, and companies maintain their traditional operating environment, they move toward the Japanese style of 12-hour work days, and an increased risk of *karoshi* ("death by overwork"), or the American phenomenon of "old-fashioned burnout." Many companies are seeing increased usage of mental health and employee assistance programs. And, for years, the best predictor of heart disease has not been smoking, cholesterol, or inactivity—it has been job dissatisfaction.[3]

Companies that must downsize for success's sake should move from a traditional operating environment to a high performance operating environment. Those companies who do not rethink how work is done, how jobs are structured, what skills are needed, and what p·e·r·f·o·r·m·a·n·c·e·s are required, will find that the survivors of downsizing will be able to withstand the long hours, increased stress, and crushing work load—until their health gives way. Such costs are ultimately too great for individual or company to bear.

Another cost of maintaining a traditional operating environment is pitiful improvement in people productivity—the increase in corporate productivity in the '80s was about 1 percent. With the increasing complexity of work, and an increasingly undertrained and underutilized workforce, many companies will not be prepared to compete in the global economy. While companies in the United States struggle to invest 1.5 percent of payroll in employee training, Germany invests 3 percent and Japan 4 percent, of their payroll expense. In the United States, 17 million workers need training in the basic skills of math and reading. The $30 billion spent on training in the United States was spent by less than 10 percent of the corporations, and most of this training goes to professionals.[4]

Quality is only part of the strategic weaponry for the 1990s—the "heavy weapon" is *time*. Companies who satisfy their customers faster, are winning—winning because to achieve this quickness-to-market, they have reduced their process times, made their processes more flexible, lowered their inventories, and as a result also lowered their costs. To accomplish all of this, however, a flexible workforce was required. Not to change—to remain a company with a traditional operating environment, with inflexible workers, without formalized skills training programs, and no real performance feedback—is surely a cost too great for any company.

Years ago, an advertisement for oil filters suggested strongly that regularly replacing an oil filter that cost only a few dollars was cheaper than replacing an expensive engine that burned up because of dirty oil. The cost "story" for becoming a High Performance Enterprise can be summed up in the punch line for that commercial: "Pay me now . . . or pay me later!"[5] Given the position of many companies today, "later" may be too late to *begin* the process of becoming a High Performance Enterprise.

THE PAYOFF

For most companies—yours, too—choosing to become a High Performance Enterprise means responding to the drivers of change with a world-class effort and, as part of that effort, reinventing the people side of the business. What are the benefits of following the Strategic Process and the High P·e·r·f·o·r·m·a·n·c·e·s People Systems Process? Here are a few ways your company will be different when you have successfully completed these processes:

· *A strategic direction, and a context of empowerment.* Strategic direction to provide a common purpose and vision for the company, and a context of empowerment in which to take action and achieve the dream of status as a High Performance Enterprise.

· *P·e·r·f·o·r·m·a·n·c·e·s to ensure performance.* In the High Performance Enterprise, the daily activities, transactions, and decisions of teams and individuals are aligned, focused, and integrated through the High P·e·r·f·o·r·m·a·n·c·e·s People Systems—it becomes the adhesive that enables the company to move the tens of thousands of p·e·r·f·o·r·m·a·n·c·e·s in unison as one *performance*.

· *The new work covenant.* A new two-way working relationship between the company and its people, the new work covenant is based on a shift from the entitlement mind-set to an expectation mind-set. Its two key elements are:

1. *Performance counts*—it is a performance-driven environment.

2. The context for performance is *empowerment*.

• *NewComp.* A powerful multi-step process that produces a reinforcement system that anchors the linkage from the case for change,
through the business strategy and objectives, to the p·e·r·f·o·r·-
m·a·n·c·e·s of the individual and team. Its two major components are
Strategy-based Pay, a method of reshaping base pay to ensure a
return on human assets; and Performance-based Rewards, which
reinforce shared business goals among *all* members of the organization. No longer a non-value-added element of an entitlement system, compensation becomes an integral component of the business
strategy.

• *Increased job satisfaction.* From the lowest level to the highest,
people are more satisfied with their work in a High Performance
Enterprise. People are more involved in their work, and their companies no longer ask them to check their brains at the door each
morning. The vast majority of managers and employees who work in
a high performance operating environment say they'd "never go
back to the old way."

• *Alternative job security.* In these insecure economic times,
many companies are unable or unwilling to make or keep the promise of traditional job security. Improving a person's employability by
increasing the breadth and depth of his or her skills portfolio *and*
flexibility is becoming an attractive form of alternative job security.

• *Continuous improvement and renewal.* Reinvention of the people side of the company is classic innovation. It is a process that
should take place only when dramatic change is required. In between innovations, the habit of continuous improvement and renewal provides a higher plateau upon which to base the next
innovation.

• *A realistic return on human assets.* No longer will an automatic,
annual increase in payroll costs be wasted on an entitlement environment. With an expectation mind-set, performance is expected of
managers and employees alike. Teams and individuals are accountable for p·e·r·f·o·r·m·a·n·c·e·s that contribute to the overall *performance* of the company, that contribute a return on the company's
human assets. The High Performance Enterprise pays for an employee's whole day, and gets the *whole* employee for the day.

THE BOTTOM LINE

We began with the promise of the '80s, a promise that many companies sought, but few fulfilled. Unfulfilled to a great extent because most companies continued with a traditional operating environment that swallowed up their improvement efforts and gave them little improvement in return. Why did companies cling to a traditional operating environment that no longer served them? For the most part, because they did not know *how* to do it, they did not have a process for changing it to something better.

Now, you have learned a process for the '90s—a process for establishing strategic direction and an empowered context for your company. And you have found a new "drawing board" for reinventing the people side of your business.

Thank you for the opportunity to "work" with you through the High Performance Enterprise. We wish you Godspeed! And we wish for you strength in persistence, faith in the people of your company, and the passion and openheartedness you will need to succeed!

References:

1. *Business Week* (special edition), "Reinventing America," 1992.
2. *Fortune*, November 30, 1992.
3. *Fortune*, November 30, 1992.
4. *Business Week* (special edition), "Reinventing America," 1992.
5. Fram Oil Filter tag line.

Glossary

Action Step(s). The distinct "substeps" within each of the 10 major Process Steps of the High P·c·r·f·o·r·m·a·n·c·e·s People Systems Process.

Ad hoc teams (problem-solving teams). Teams formed for a specific case, generally to solve a specific problem or address a specific issue.

Alternative job security (employability). Enhanced employability resulting from training in multiple skills is a form of "job" security because it makes employees more attractive to their own and other companies.

Apparent driver of change. Not the "real" or core or actual compelling reason to change, but rather an ostensible or surface and sometimes false force that drives companies to change in inappropriate ways.

BARS. Behaviorally anchored rating scales: a method for establishing an odd-numbered progressive series of ratings, with each end of the series anchored by a group of observable behaviors.

Baseline organizational profile. An outline of major characteristics of the current organization, with each characteristic, contrasted to the targeted profile, depicted in detail by a series of descriptive statements.

Blueprint. Detailed documentation of the People Systems design and development; includes an overview of the key factors upon which the design is based, the process followed for the design, a glossary of terms, and the details of each Process Step's design and development documentation.

Boundary(ies). (1) The limits or confines placed on the free movement of skilled workers; (2) the limit or confines placed on decision making, the degree of self-direction, or other operational activities for teams and individuals.

Case for change. A full statement of the facts and circumstances surrounding the compelling reasons for change, supported by convincing arguments and a strategic-level response; should create a sense of urgency and an environment that supports changes in mind-set.

Certification model. An outline in matrix form that organizes the operational skills for a new broad JOB and identifies for each skill, factors such as the required prerequisites, practice time, recertification period, recertification practice, and skills weightings.

Certification opportunities. The chance to apply for training and ultimately for certification for a skill or block of skills; a chance that may be limited by the company's need for particular skills, and available opportunities.

Certification process. A multistep method of formally training and then validating skills; generally includes verification of prerequisites, instruction, practice time, evaluation of competency, demonstration of the ability to instruct others, and, later, recertification.

Coach(ing). A form of team leadership characterized by facilitation, teaching, and providing opportunities for team members to encourage growth in skills and confidence; a form of leadership in the empowered high performance operating environment.

Compensation crunch. The situation faced by traditional compensation systems, i.e., squeezed between "how to compensate individuals" and "how to compensate teams."

Continuous improvement. An approach to achieving a higher degree of performance that relies on gradual, incremental, ongoing betterment rather than grandly innovative or breakthrough betterment.

Continuous Improvement Committee. A team formed during the implementation stage of the High P·e·r·f·o·r·m·a·n·c·e·s People Systems Process to monitor, evaluate, and continuously improve the People Systems design.

Continuous improvement stage. The final stage of the High P·e·r·f·o·r·m·a·n·c·e·s People Systems Process, during which a habit of continuous improvement and renewal is incorporated into the People Systems design.

DARS. Data anchored rating scales are a method for establishing an odd-numbered progressive series of ratings with each end of the series anchored by a quantitative data point.

Design stage. The first stage of the 10-Step High P·e·r·f·o·r·m·a·n·c·e·s People Systems Process, during which the company's new People Systems are planned and outlined for further development and then implementation.

Design Team. The cross-functional multilevel team of managers, employees, HR staff, and other technical representatives responsible for the design, development, and implementation of the company's new People Systems.

Development stage. The second stage of the 10-Step High P·e·r·f·o·r·m·a·n·c·e·s People Systems Process, during which the design of the company's new People Systems is expanded by adding specificity and detail to a series of design "frameworks."

Drivers of change. Compelling reasons for companies to change from the traditional operating environment; generally consists of either an impending threat to their survival or their continued growth and prosperity.

Employability. The state of being fit for work; enhanced by multiple skills, and experiences in multiple work situations.

Empowered context. A company mind-set or attitude that establishes a framework for activity based on the empowerment of all people at every level of the company.

Empowerment. That state in which the company's people have been enabled and permitted to share in the control and responsibility for the p·e·r·f·o·r·m·a·n·c·e·s that make up the *performance* of the company.

Entitlement mind-set. The state in which a company's employees believe that they do not have to really "earn" their pay, but rather are "owed" it because they put in time at work; produces an environment in which there is little relationship between performance and payoff.

Expectation mind-set. The state in which a company and its employees expect that performance counts—that pay and reward are directly linked to individual and team performance; produces an environment in which there is a direct relationship between performance and payoff.

Factor weighting. The relative importance or consequence attached to specific team and individual major performance factors.

Feedback. A process in which the factors that produce a result are themselves modified, corrected, strengthened, etc., by that result.[1]

Flash-cut. The brief, complete implementation of an initiative or program across an entire operation or organization.

Flexibility. In the sense of people and processes, the ability to respond to changing requirements by free movement of skilled workers within bounded areas of the process or alteration of the process to accommodate the required changes; *or* the ability to respond to business requirements with professional and management employees who have increased depth and breadth of knowledge and experience in technologies, processes, and products.

Flexibility mapping. The process of first defining the process, and then drawing boundaries around those areas of the process in which it benefits the company to have the movement of skilled workers without barriers.

Gap analysis. Specifically, in the 10-Step Process, the determination of "What's missing?" between the targeted and baseline organizational profiles, and what is the "action" required to close the gap; the process results in action items to be incorporated in the Migration Strategy for the company's new People Systems.

"Hard" process. A process approach characterized by focus, alignment, integration, and system (process).

High Performance Enterprise. An enterprise completely in touch with its customers, delivering high-quality products and services exactly on time, bringing new offerings to market in half the time; an enterprise that manages p·e·r·f·o·r·m·a·n·c·e·s in a way to produce outstanding performance, which guarantees a profitable bottom line.

High performance operating environment. An operating environment built on the *new work covenant*; an operating environment characterized by the fact that performance counts and that the context for performance is empowerment.

High P·e·r·f·o·r·m·a·n·c·e·s People Systems®. "Reinvented" People Systems that acknowledge, enable, and support the business objectives of the company because such People Systems provide the focus, alignment, integration, and system of a "hard" but "open" process for continuous improvement and renewal.

Implementation stage. The third stage of the 10-Step High P·e·r·f·o·r·m·a·n·c·e·s People Systems Process, during which the implementation of the design blueprint is planned and then actually implemented.

Initiatives. Action plans, a framework for action, selected to carry out the strategic success factors and business objectives of the company.

Job(s). The traditional definition of "job" as a narrow "collection of tasks, duties and responsibilities assigned to one or more individuals whose work has the same nature and level."[2]

JOB(s). A new, world-class definition of JOB as a broad collection of tasks, duties, and responsibilities, of perhaps differing natures and levels, shared by more than one individual or team.

Major performance factors. Important components of team and individual performance selected through a translation process from the company's strategic success factors and operational business objectives.

Migration Strategy. A project plan to move the company toward its targeted organizational profile; includes defined objectives, scope, schedule, and resources required to accomplish the effort, and a commitment to the 10-Step Process as the methodology for changing the company's People Systems.

Network of linkages. Not just *a* linkage, but a network or matrix of linkages: people systems *integrated* with the company's initiatives and its business objectives; *integrated* among themselves; and re*integrated* as a responsibility for all of management, not just for Human Resources.

NewComp®. *NewComp* represents a nontraditional approach to compensation. A powerful multi-Step process, *NewComp* produces a reinforcement system that anchors the linkage from the case for change, through the business strategy and objectives, to the p·e·r·f·o·r·m·a·n·c·e·s of the individual and team. Its two major components are Strategy-based Pay, a method for reshaping base pay to ensure a return on human assets; and Performance-based Rewards, which reinforce shared business goals among *all* members of the organization.

New work covenant. A new relationship between the company and *all its people* required by a shift to an *expectation mind-set*; a relationship defined by the high performance operating environment.

OJT. On-the-job training.

Operating environment. The conditions under which work takes place in a company; in the highest sense, the operating environment is the "process" in which all "work" takes place and from which all "results" flow; it includes all of the influences, circumstances, and prevailing atmosphere that directly and indirectly impact the way work is done.

Operating principles (world-class). Fundamental "truths" and driving concepts employed by companies to achieve world-class status as High Performance Enterprises.

Operational business objectives. The measurable, operationally oriented business goals that constitute the annual expression of the three- to five-year strategic drive to accomplish the company's strategic success factors.

Oral history. The gathering and preservation of historical data consisting of personal recollection;[3] in many companies, the gathering, preservation, and transmission of skills and knowledge by word of mouth from one employee to another, frequently with no supporting written documentation.

Organizational context. The prevailing mind-set of a company; it is the *de facto* "mental" attitude and disposition of the company; it underlies the company's operating environment.

Organizational profile(s). An outline of characteristics of the organization with each characteristic depicted in detail by a series of descriptive statements.

Paradigm. An overall concept (a model) accepted by most people in an intellectual community because of its effectiveness in explaining a complex process, idea, or set of data.

Pay. Base pay, the *fixed* pay rate that a person makes per hour, week, biweekly, semimonthly or monthly; the rate used as the basis to calculate pay premiums such as overtime and shift differentials.

"Pay at risk." Compensation linked to performance in a manner that a portion of the compensation may be "lost" if required performance levels are not achieved; most often the "risk" is against *future* pay increases; may also include the "upside" potential for more pay based on superior performance.

Pay Task Force. A Project Task Team chartered by the Design Team to follow the Strategy-based Pay Process in the design and development of new base pay systems to focus, align, and integrate pay with the company's business objectives and to support the desired high performance operating environment.

"People side of the company." In its *broadest* sense, the people side of the business is any part of the business where people impact or are impacted by the activities, decisions, and transactions of the company. In a *narrower* sense, it is (1) people, (2) the work they do, and (3) the environment in which they operate. In its *most* narrow sense, it is a company's human resources programs, policies, and practices. For this book, it is the work people do and selected HR programs, policies, and practices.

Performance-based Rewards. A form of variable compensation focused on reinforcing improvement of shared and common goals among members of an organizational unit.

Performance subfactors. A group of specific, measurable performance elements that represent how a major performance factor appears in a specific area or organizational entity (JOB team, section, department, etc.).

P·e·r·f·o·r·m·a·n·c·e·s. The daily tens of thousands of individual activities, decisions, and transactions taking place at every level and in every process across the company that make up the *performance* of the company.

Pilot. A trial or test of a program or initiative that takes place in a small segment of the entire operation under controlled conditions to determine the impact on specifically identified performance.

Process Steps. The 10 major steps of the High P·e·r·f·o·r·m·a·n·c·e·s People Systems Process.

Project Task Teams. Teams chartered by the Design Team to help with specific design issues or detailed development and documentation of selected design components; also teams chartered by the Design Team to help with implementation planning and implementation.

Project teams. Generically, teams convened to perform the work involved in a specific project; also called "task force teams."

Promotion mind-set. An organizational attitude that holds that recognition comes in the form of pay and promotion; an attitude frequently accompanied by an "entitlement" mentality of nearly automatic time-in-grade upward movement.

Readiness assessment. An evaluation to determine the state of preparedness of a company to begin a People Systems redesign project; includes an evaluation of the state of the case for change, the mission/vision package, observations of inconsistencies and conflict of the planned People Systems with the current programs, etc.

Real driver of change. An actual compelling reason to change, not an apparent or surface driver of change; generally, a fundamentally different way of doing business.

Renewal. The replacement of what no longer serves the company well with that which is new and more appropriately aligned and integrated with the current needs of the company.

Resource teams (support teams). Generally, a cross-functional team of technical and functional specialists formed to support one or more work teams.

Rewards. *Variable* pay distributed apart from base pay. Generally, rewards programs that are designed specifically to reinforce selected business objectives. Gainsharing and team incentives are typical examples.

Rollout. A gradual, area-by-area implementation of programs or initiatives.

Skills:

- **Core skills.** A group of skills that constitute minimum knowledge or expertise required to perform work in *all* JOBs, represented by skills such as reading, basic math, an understanding of the company's initiatives, safety, and housekeeping.
- **Support skills.** Skills particular to the new broad JOB but not directly related to work performed in the process or on the product—generally, skills that do not add value; may include skills such as material handling, inspection, expediting, etc.
- **Operational skills.** Skills that represent the "meat" of the JOB—skills that constitute the work performed in the process or on the product—the primary skills that generally add value. In the new broad JOB, an operational skill may represent what used to be an entire discrete, narrow job.
- **Technical skills.** Skills that represent an advanced level of basic operational skills, or an incremental level of expertise (e.g., not only operate and set up the machine, but also repair the machine).

Skills portfolio. An accumulation of skills in which a person possesses hands-on experience, and in which the person can demonstrate proficiency.

Soft-issues mind-set. A pervasive attitude toward people issues and programs. The four aspects of a soft-issue mind-set are: (1) lip service to importance of people; (2) a fear of the complexity of the people side of the business; (3) conflict avoidance; and (4) the "squishy" factor, i.e., the feeling that dealing with people and people issues is hopelessly qualitative, indeterminate, subjective, and without definition.

Steering Committee. The team responsible for establishing the charter for the People Systems Design Team, for establishing and documenting the context for the project, and for reviewing the work of the Design Team.

Strategic direction. A long-term path or course for the company that consists of a definition of the company's purpose and a definition of the organization of the future.

Strategic Process. A step-by-step process for use in defining the high performance operating environment and becoming a High Performance Enterprise.

Strategic success factors. Major themes or areas of change and improvement; or broad, general goals that identify the major achievements that over time will enable the company to complete its mission and fulfill its vision.

Strategy-based Pay®. A method for reshaping *base pay* to ensure a return on human assets by aligning and integrating the company's pay systems with its business objectives and high performance operating environment.

Targeted organizational profile. An outline of major characteristics of the desired future organization with each characteristic depicted in detail by a series of descriptive statements.

Team(s). Generically, a group of people working together in a coordinated effort;[4] in the high performance operating environment a variety of teams from ad hoc problem-solving teams to work teams function together in an empowered environment.

10-Step Process. The High P·e·r·f·o·r·m·a·n·c·e·s People Systems Process.

Traditional compensation. The pay and reward systems of the traditional operating environment, focused on control and consistency and not linked to the business objectives of the company.

Vision into action. A process for translating the strategic direction of the company into a framework for action.

Work teams. In the high performance operating environment, groups of people organized around performing work according to defined processes, and to continuously improving those work processes.

Working to rules. A concept in which workers do exactly what they are told, but exhibit no initiative to do more; a concept supported by old-fashioned labor union leadership and by old-fashioned company management.

References:

1. *Webster's New World Dictionary*, 3d College Edition, 1988.
2. American Compensation Association, Certification Course 2, 1991.
3. *Webster's New World Dictionary*, 3d College Edition, 1988.
4. *Webster's New World Dictionary*, 3d College Edition, 1988.

Index